PLAY AND INTERVENTION

SUNY Series,
Children's Play in Society

Anthony D. Pellegrini, Editor

PLAY AND INTERVENTION

Edited by
**Joop Hellendoorn,
Rimmert van der Kooij
and
Brian Sutton-Smith**

STATE UNIVERSITY OF NEW YORK PRESS

Production by Ruth Fisher
Marketing by Fran Keneston

Published by
State University of New York Press, Albany

For information, address the State University of New York Press,
State University Plaza, Albany, NY 12246

Library of Congress Cataloging-in-Publication Data

Play and intervention / edited by Joop Hellendoorn, Rimmert van der
  Kooij, and Brian Sutton-Smith.
      p.   cm. — (SUNY series, children's play in society)
   "Second Amsterdam Play Symposium, held in the Netherlands in 1991
. . . This book contains most of the main presentations from this
symposium"—Introd.
    Includes bibliographical references.
    ISBN 0-7914-1933-9 (alk. paper). — ISBN 0-7914-1934-7 (pbk. :
alk. paper)
    1. Play—Psychological aspects—Congresses. 2. Play therapy—
Congresses. 3. Play—Research—Congresses. I. Hellendoorn, Joop.
II. Kooij, Rimmert van der. III. Sutton-Smith, Brian.
IV. Amsterdam Play Symposium (2nd : 1991) V. Series.
BF717.P576 1994
155.4'18—dc20   93-28930
                                                               CIP

10 9 8 7 6 5 4 3 2 1

CONTENTS

PART 2: PLAY FOR CHILDREN WITH SPECIAL NEEDS

**PART 3: THEORY AND RESEARCH ON SCHOOL
             PLAY INTERVENTION**

GENERAL INTRODUCTION

During the last decades, play has sometimes been presented as the ideal way of intervention for almost every conceivable kind of problem: emotional problems, attention disorders, learning difficulties, social isolation and so on. Furthermore, the pace of this concern to use play for solving practical problems seems to be increasing, with politicians now even taking over the torch from the child care professionals. Almost inevitably this will lead to the recognition that play is not always really suitable for all of these usages. Play may have its own disorderly functions to serve which do not always lend themselves to those who would use them for the more orderly purposes of civilized society. We must ask critically, therefore, how much of this novel attention is based on wishful thinking and how much on research.

During the Second Amsterdam Play Symposium,[1] held in the Netherlands in 1991, play theorists, researchers and practitioners from many countries gathered to share new developments in this field. Children were not present, but their influence was felt in many ways. This book contains most of the main presentations from this symposium, grouped around three themes: (1) Play therapy, (2) play for children with special needs, and (3) theory and research in school play intervention.

Play therapy nowadays knows many applications for children with emotional and behavior problems. Play in this context is viewed as a pleasurable and nonthreatening means for a child to confront conflicting ideas and feelings, to work them through and to find new ways of coping with everyday life. Different methods of play therapy are in use, corresponding to the major theoretical schools of therapy. Traditionally, therapists are influenced more by their (often sound) theoretical foundations than by research results. Process and effect research in this field are still in rather poor shape, in contrast to the study of play in general. However, since practice is flourishing, a more systematic approach (as exemplified in this volume) to play behavior and therapeutic interaction of child and therapist may already help practitioners to become more effective. Moreover, it may lead the way to more substantial research.

For children with special needs, play has long been a closed book. For professional workers as well as caregivers in this field, the emphasis has been on helping the children compensate for and cope with their disabilities. The trend was to make them function "as normal as possible." Much less attention has been paid to what was already there, and to make the most of the "normal" aspects of special children's lives. In the last decades, however, there is a growing concern for these children's own identities and their own ways of playing. Research is still scarce but preliminary results suggest that in many handicapped children play develops along the same pattern as in children without handicaps. However, handicaps can interfere in many ways with play development, for example, by restricting mobility (as in children with visual or motor handicaps) and thus impeding exploration. In this section, different kinds of programs for different kinds of special children are discussed.

In the 1980s, school play interventions have become everyday (if perhaps somewhat trendy) occurrences in many schools in the Western world. Their rationale sounds almost ideal: learning better by playing, by doing something nice and pleasurable. What could be better in our hedonistic world? Idealization and wishful thinking apart, many play scientists are concerned with the real value of these play programs.

The contributions to this volume vary in theme and content. Some discuss the theoretical foundations of play interventions, others highlight their application in educational or therapeutic practice. There are also some critical notes against badly designed research. The leading question remains: is play really such a powerful means for change as some practitioners think? Or are the many play interventions offered by various agencies the effects of a giant idealization campaign or just the newest trend in pleasure seeking? Or is play the thing which eases the King's conscience, whatever his therapeutic or didactic aim?

PARADIGMS OF INTERVENTION

Brian Sutton-Smith

The Dilemma of Intervention

This introductory chapter is about the multiple ways in which we as parents or as professionals have intervened in children's play these past 200 years, as well as about the multiple rationales we have used for such interventions. Throughout this paper I wish to speak occasionally in the first person about my own feelings and reactions to the different kinds of research in which I have participated. I have reached that point in life when the scholarly pretense of impersonality is no longer a convincing disguise for myself. It is my belief, furthermore, that a central issue in social science at this time is to understand the way in which the narrative of the investigator's personal life interacts with his or her scholarship (Sutton-Smith in press-a).

I had my first experience of play "intervention" in children's lives in 1952, when I arrived in the United States as a Fulbright research scholar. I was for a time a member of a research team headed by child psychiatrist Fritz Redl, famous for his work with aggressive children. We spent our time making observational samples of extremely disturbed children in a variety of settings provided for them in a therapeutically oriented outdoor camp in Michigan. We watched them in their games, at crafts, boating, swimming, indoor and outdoor meals, and sought to discover what interaction of ecological and clinical variables could account for any therapeutic or untherapeutic experiences they might have in these programs (Avedon & Sutton-Smith 1971, 408-418). It was our assumption that any such knowledge we discovered could be used in future programming for these children.

At the time I found myself somewhat culturally disoriented by the extremity of the children's symptoms, both violent and regressive: some of them attacked each other with oars while in boats on the lake, in my presence as I took notes; and at least one stored up his feces in a suitcase under his bed in the log cabin. More importantly for the present focus, I was disturbed by the very idea that children's play should be programmed. Unwittingly, in my prior years in New Zealand I had come to assume that children's own folkplay was traditional and valuable and that games organized for children were, on the contrary, an unfortunate invasion of their playlife. This attitude was probably derived from the historical movement called romanticism which English speakers associate particularly with Rousseau, Wordsworth and Coleridge, and which continues to permeate the disciplines of folklore, children's literature, children's art, and progressive education. In particular, much of my dissertation work on the history and psychology of the unorganized games of New Zealand primary school children (Sutton-Smith 1954, 1981) was directly influenced by correspondence with various world folklorists amongst whom the view prevailed that in the modern world children's traditional games were being constantly encroached upon by adults and should be preserved if at all possible. To them, to organize children's play was an anathema.

Paradoxically, in my reaction at that time I did not remember that in my own personal game history I had derived excitement from organized sports equal to that from any unorganized folkplay. Nor could I have predicted that 40 years later I would spend much of my time in a Headstart-funded project on how to enlist the support of highly skilled four-year-old players to teach less skilled players how to play. This being done in order to decrease the latter's probability of a life history of peer rejection and school dropout (Fantuzzo 1990).

I resurrect my memory of this earlier attitude against intervention in children's play not to justify it, although in many circumstances it may be justifiable, but to bring into the foreground that there are many different attitudes towards the nature of childhood and the nature of play. Therefore, it seems imperative to me to try to approach this question of intervention, of the use and misuse of children's play, by some analysis of the sources that underlay our different ideas about this issue. I will call these *paradigms* of intervention in order to suggest that I am talking about deepseated and systemic patterns of thought, most of which have existed in Western Culture for between one hundred and two hundred years.

Paradigmatic Childhoods

If modern childhood has been invented, as Aries says (1962; Luke 1989), and if child psychology has also invented its own childhood, as William Kessen says (1981), then we need to attend to the presuppositions thus engendered to see how they are fundamentally affecting our notions of intervention. The position to be taken here is that Western society has constructed (as in Berger & Luckmann 1966) a number of very general paradigms to define "childhood"; and that the starting points for their evolution are the well-known historical events and ideologies, i.e., the Reformation and the rise of Capitalism, the Enlightenment, romanticism, the theory of Evolution, and, more recently, Feminism and the child-oriented Market Place. The paradigmatic childhood that may be derived from each of these historical occasions can be labelled as follows:

> The Child of God
> The Child as Future
> The Predictable Child
> The Imaginary Child (and the Disorderly Child)
> The Child as Consumer
> The Gender Androgynous Child

The opinion advanced here will be that the paradigmatic childhoods we have come to construct have been substantially selected from one or other of these packs of historical and ideological playing cards and that each pack predisposes different views about intervention. What they have in common is the advocacy of intervention itself. Leaving children alone has apparently not been much of an alternative since Rousseau stage-managed the discipline of natural consequences for Emile, and John Locke created his alphabet blocks to get children off the streets.

Once again, to begin personally, let me tell you first of my life experience of being in turn and in various combinations a Professor of Education, of Psychology and of Folklore. It is only quite recently that I have been able to acknowledge to myself that in each of these roles I was working with a different paradigm of childhood. I always thought of myself vaguely as an interdisciplinary person using the premises of one discipline to critique the products of another. I began my work life as an adolescent in Teachers College and from the very beginning was enshrouded in idealization. In order to pass the entrance interview it was doxological to answer the question: "Why do you want to teach?" with the response, "Because I like children."

After passing that entry point about liking children, most subsequent ideology about children in Schools of Education focused, not surprisingly, on the pursuit of multiple methodological promises for the possible ascension of children and youths into some successful future. "Children could learn. Teachers could have enduring effects. Children are the future", it was said. On two occasions, as a Professor of Education at different Universities, it was my experience that in Colleges of Education, particularly as one passes through the job interview, there is some pressure to demonstrate that your own research and practical activity has or could make a meaningful contribution to the future of children and their schooling. In consequence, I believe there is a fundamental missionary quality to education. If you are not in some sense in the business of saving literate or mathematical souls or of aspiring to educational progress, Schools of Education will make you uncomfortable.

Obviously the historical pack of cards from which such a phenomenology is derived must include the Reformation and its promise of a personal future with God, if one follows the appropriate prescribed behaviors. There are many religious countries and religious schools where the child that has been constructed is the Child of God. Usually in those places a maximum amount of intervention in the lives of children is warranted by the desire for the preservation of their innocence and for their salvation. For example, in Protestantism there could hardly be enough intervention, because every moment in the day (not just the ritual moments) was in His Presence. Prior to today this often meant the exclusion of play from the child's school life. My own experience in New Zealand was that in those private religious schools where there was some comprehensive control over free play, the children's own illicit play was incredibly more rebellious. Gross intervention almost guaranteed grossness of response. I have mentioned this issue of religiously instigated intervention because it is obviously so fundamental to all that follows in Western society, and because it begins that permanent uneasiness with playfulness which I believe still exists almost universally in our secular world, and which continues to make it difficult to think on the matter without ambivalence. How otherwise to explain that play, the major interest of children, is nevertheless the major form of social scientific neglect in research on childhood?

As a footnote, let me indicate that this generalization does not in any way cover the heterogeneity of religious practice. In a New Jersey Quaker school where one of my students carried out intensive observations, the playground was notable for the extent of positive intervention by teachers to help newcomers be integrated into play, to participate occasionally on demonstrating new games, to prevent any signs of aggression either of the playful or hostile kind, but surprisingly enough not to intrude on signs of boy-girl play, even when it was of the rough-and-tumble implicitly sexual kind. These Quakers apparently took seriously, "make love not war." They intruded against war foreplay but not against love foreplay.

The eighteenth century Enlightenment picked up this religious belief in the City of God, or the millenarian future, and promulgated the notion that the rationality that had been achieved in the physical sciences could be achieved in the social sciences. The secular republic could ensure rational and inevitable progress. Various programs of utopian historical inevitability were heralded and, as we know, our twentieth century has been in part succored and in part cursed by that historicist inheritance. About mid-nineteenth century, in the United States in particular, children increasingly were located as the medium by which such future progress could be ensured. At that time the noted American educationist Horace Mann contended that the schools alone could ensure that equality of opportunity would prevail and inequities be removed from the economic landscape. By this century Historicism, the view that progress is irrevocable and its course predictable, has in general ceased to appeal to historians. Megill (1985), in his *Prophets of Extremity*, holds that the failure of the Socialist International in World War I was the final blow. The paradox is that, even so, childhood has subsequently continued as Historicism's residual legatee. Children are still thought of as "the future." Our progress inevitably lies in their hands, so we constantly tell them.

One could argue that such certainty about children's role in the future is itself a major burden for them and leads to all sorts of justifications for sacrificing their playing pleasure for society's long term benefit. The hothousing of early childhood is the most potent example. David Elkind's polemic *The Hurried Child* (1981) suggests, at least, that some percentage of the American population proceeds with such intemperance.

The Child as the Future then can be associated with some combination of religious enlightenment and educational history. It is a construction that we cannot do without (after all: who doesn't want children to make some progress?) and yet it can lead to quite profound future oriented interventions in their everyday lives. Apparently, although we have long conceded cross-cultural relativity (as in the United Nations), we have not yet conceded cross-age relativity to children of different ages. It is after all possible to think that, say, two-year-olds (or four, six, eight, etc.) have something special to contribute to us ludically and aesthetically, and to celebrate that fact.

Although I began as a schoolteacher, the bulk of my professional academic life has been as a child psychologist examining children's play, their impulsivity, their aggression, their masculinity and femininity, sibling position differences, children's narratives, their film making, their drama, their toys, and their games both within and across cultures. Throughout all of this work I was concerned with being a scientist, not a teacher or a missionary. It is not that I ever said to myself, "it is my concern to be a scientist," it is just that within psychology one becomes immersed in the conventions of methodological reliability and validity. There is a self-justification in the feeling that one is working on the discovery of permanent systems of behavior and relationship. It is assumed that one is deriving laws which will have some inevitable usefulness simply because they are empirically based. In subsequent years I have come to realize that this notion of psychology has more to do with the promise of the medical sciences than the possible achievements of psychology. Psychology deals largely with what I like now to call local science. That is: with regularities of behavior and attitude which are customary but seldom permanent in the groups studied. Still, whatever the aspiration about science, one is dealing therein with what might be termed The Predictable Child. Within this framework it is not one's major function to bother much with the practical consequences of a moral or idealistic kind. One presumes in a general way that all this empirical activity will be of some use to mankind, but maintains a rather skeptical attitude towards those who try to make practical applications from one's findings. In fast, one's academic promotion is likely to be withheld by one's colleagues if too much attention is given to such idealistic or practical motivations. Science is meant to be hard, not only in methodology but also in ontology. Science is primarily the pursuit of knowledge, not the pursuit of intervention.

Imagine my surprise, therefore, to discover in recent years the point of view of Michel Foucault, who says quite contrarily that from the very beginning the biosciences (psychology, sociology, medicine, etc.) have been about experts intervening and gaining control over other people (1973). Children, the insane, the poor, and the criminal, were irrational elements in the developing seventeenth-century national states. The children were confined increasingly in schools where they would ultimately be divided into different age groups and defined by their status in a variety of physical and mental exams, which is how we know them today. As they were examined they became predictable, whether those exams were carried out by physicians, school psychologists, clinical psychologists, pediatricians, or others. The examinations categorized them according to developed norms, and they were treated by the experts in terms of those norms which this very science had created.

Bioscientific knowledge as conceptualized by Foucault, therefore, is intervention, not just objective science. It creates the categories of the language by which we confine and help both others and ourselves, because we convert these forms of knowledge into the evaluations which we manage. Think, for example, of the enormous practical effects of the social construction of such terms as: stage of development, mental retardation, IQ, schizophrenia, self-concept, achievement motivation, prosocial behavior, sex typing, hyperactivity, and so on. In Foucault's view we become the victim or victims of the language we create in our science. Either we are put in expert control of the category or we are controlled by the experts of the category, but in both cases the category controls the thinking.

Now it is possible to be somewhat less pessimistic about all of this than Foucault, because life is not quite that predictable and because there is a heterogeneity of response regardless of categorizations. Furthermore, in diminution of human pain and suffering it is not clear that these socializations have caused more pain than they have alleviated. Nevertheless, such retort cannot gainsay that we have developed a notion of childhood development in our society as something which is predictable; and for which we can find the remedies sanctioned by science whatever the problem may be. In the United States this does seem so self-evident to much of the population that columns of psychological advice appear everywhere (every Thursday even in the New York Times) on the guidance of childhood, family, sex life, etc. One reads these essays written in what is often only desperate or mundane common sense with the realization that they have very little to do with science as methodology and much to do with science as a myth. In sum, if we see the Enlightenment and Religion as playing a strong role in our belief of the Child as the Future and as often justifying our stringent control of them to ensure that future; we can see science, particularly evolutionarily influenced developmental psychology, as justifying the view that we know and can predict how children will develop, and that therefore we are justified to be the ones in control of the information and interventions in that process.

My own saving grace in much of this is that I have also always believed the Imaginary Child is found in children's folklore, although it was only with my appointment to a Professorship in Children's Folklore at the University of Pennsylvania in Philadelphia that I began to assume some responsibility for that institution. I was by then, in 1977, so much of a developmental psychologist that at first I had some difficulty in even hearing what those folklore students were saying to me. I proceeded as I had for some years at Teachers College, Columbia University, where most of my students were either in psychology or education, in presenting material about children's games, story making, film making, etc. in developmental order, illustrating that my major interest was in such things as how seven-year-olds differed from eleven-year-olds who differed from adolescents, and so on. Developmental psychological information is largely about age sequences and as a discipline it still carries on the nineteenth-century ideology of species and personal evolution as its central concern.

My folklore students were not interested. They were interested in the quality and character of the play performances in the contexts in which they took place. They were not interested in abstractions about the individual players (their aggression, their need for arousal, their intrinsic motivation, their flow). They were interested instead in groups and their communications, their customs and traditions and their aesthetic face. All of a sudden I was face to face with the very Romanticism that had first brought me into the study of childhood. This was what had first affected me when, like Wordsworth, I began to use my own memories of childhood to inform the several books I wrote for children and published in the 1940-1950s. What we have to discuss now is, therefore, the Imaginary Childhood (not the Child of God, the Child as a Future or the Predictable Child).

These folklore students were very antagonistic to most of the controlling mechanisms which Foucault had in mind. Their intuitions were to support and foster and investigate those folk (including child folk) who were left over from another industrial era, or to find ways in which people within our contemporary era continued their quirky collective life despite the surrounding industrial, bureaucratic and informational oppressions. They studied play as graffiti, as riddles, as obscene rhymes, as jump rope, as superstition, as playground festival, as kissing games, camp songs, parody, swapping, garbage, collections, levitation, etc. This was classic romanticism insofar as it was concerned with what is imaginative, what is outside the conventional expectations, what has a moral and aesthetic heart that defies those conventions, and what is often also quite irrational and typically a fringe behavior. In fact, one is inclined to think that the twin of the Imaginary Child is the Disorderly Child, or perhaps even the Trickster Child.

Romanticism is a large household and also provides the historical frame for much of the work in children's literature, child art, and progressive education, which sees the child's future very much as a product of the child's imagination and the collective imagination of the group. The Imaginary Child is clearly a child who should not be much intervened with and one senses that attitude in most of those who defend the freedoms of child play, child art and child centered education. Nevertheless, the actual history of child care, of child education and of child play is, I believe, a history of relative defeat of these aspirations. Foucault wins and Rousseau and Wordsworth go down to relative defeat. Even most of the literature on the imagination indeed is a literature that rationalizes the imagination as a handmaiden to reason. This is as true of the philosopher Kant, who is the first to accept the imagination as a revered faculty, as it is of Piaget in our own time. In general, such rationalists of the imagination deal with the issues of the imagination as an irrational force, simply by excluding them from view or by saying, for example, that they are not play at all, but are rowdiness or obscene or unmanageable. Only children's folklore holds on with this leftover irrational detritus of older culture. The very triviality of children's folklore as an academic discipline is itself symbolic of our loss. Children's folklore is to child psychology as a drugged mouse is to a caged elephant.

The message of the Imaginary Child then is to discover descriptively what is there and to celebrate it as well as to understand it in terms of its aesthetic face; the latter being a way to be inquiring without controlling. Much of my current play research is focused on this aspiration and has lead to intricate studies of the way in which children's play can be considered as dramatized performance involving its own distinct nonverbal gestural semiotics (Sutton-Smith 1989). The moment this is said, however, most adults will think of the excesses to which that might lead rather than think of what it might yield in its own right. I imagine the reader is no exception. And what that tells us, I think, is that the Imaginary Child is pretty much a fugitive in our society, and that almost anything we do about childhood is a Foucault-like form of intervention, usually hiding under the name of socialization. The only "imaginary" we really enjoy with respect to childhood is, as with Wordsworth, the imagination of our own childhood. The reason that we have declared childhood as "innocent" is perhaps that it is necessary for us to hold ourselves innocent of the kinds of irrationalities that childhood actually engenders. Or perhaps to hold children innocent of the kind of irrationalities that characterize our own adulthood and that, therefore, implicitly deny the validity of our worthiness for the future towards which they are supposed to work.

What these speculations promote is that there is a dialectical aspect to the Imaginary Child. A great deal of our canceling out of the promise of romanticism comes from our fear of the Disorderly Child. We want our romanticism but only in civil terms. We do not wish the freedom we ask for to be used to countenance children's disorderliness, rowdiness, nonsense or destructiveness.

There is another rather awkward childhood to be considered, derived from developments in The Market Place, which we might call the Child as Consumer. The historical antecedent here is that of the child exploited as a work unit throughout most of history; The child as a piece of property. It is towards the end of the eighteenth century that many European children begin to receive children's books, toys and clothing, and become established as a category in their own right by the very property they possess. The subsequent story in Zelizer's words in *Pricing the Priceless Child* (1985) is that as children have become more useless as workers, they have become more valuable as consumers; symbolized by all the gifts we give them and by their own conspicuous consumption of multiple posses-sions. That heyday for children has arrived only quite recently, how-ever, with the vast expansion of the toy industry and of television's influence. We may predict a future of increasing intervention by the market place in children's own solitary play. As enraged parents sometimes say of each new media or toy that appears: "It leaves no room for the imagination"; "It is an invasion of the family space"; "It interferes with the parent-child relationship." But then parents have been saying this since the more traditional and violent fairy tales were marketed for children in the early nineteenth century. So this kind of commercial and media intervention has long been a source of parental irritation.

It seems that the child's world is becoming, like the adolescent world has been for sometime, a special marketplace for the market-ing of recurrent fashions in media, clothing, food and travel. Children now control enormous amounts of money and have in consequence entered the market economy as consumers. We have moved to what we might term the commodification of childhood.

Finally, another childhood which has emerged on the scene from the Feminism of these past two decades is the Gender Child or perhaps the Androgynous Gender Child. There is increasing pressure from some feminists for both girls and boys to get more prosocial training; and they urge that boys in particular must be socialized to be more cooperative and be prepared to participate in child and home care and not indulge in playfighting nor play with war toys. Alternatively, the girl of the future is one who should have the equality to participate in the practice of male sports or male politics. Both suggestions are androgynous, implying cross-sex participation in traditional opposite-sex characteristics.

Converting Paradigms to Rhetorics of Intervention

Most current examples of intervention make it possible to see the impact of the tacitly presupposed paradigmatic childhoods, sometimes operating alone, sometimes in concert.

(1) First, there is the presupposition that has recently become a hot issue in the United States, i.e., whether playtime or recess for children during school hours should be abolished or very much curtailed. Traditionally it has occupied fifteen minutes mid-morning and sometimes an additional thirty minutes after lunch. Most typically, this traditional practice of providing children with a lightly supervised free play time is being curtailed because of greater legislative and educational pressure on the schools to improve their standards of achievement. But there are ancillary reasons given for intruding on the playground which have to do with pressure on schools from ambitious working parents, from liability suits following frequent playground accidents, from costs of playground supervision after the unionization of teachers, from playgrounds being endangered by criminal behavior (drugs, molestation, violence), and from physical educationists or teachers who wish to substitute what they see as their own more adequately designed forms of play exercise. Most recently, it is being argued that because of legal liability children must have as much supervision in the playground as they have in the classroom (one teacher for every twenty-five children), a requirement which would make recess time prohibitively expensive. Clearly you can see this intervention as a wanton deprivation of children's rights to traditional social play, or you can see it as a wise administrative measure to decrease accidents, unhealthy associations and legal liabilities for the schools. The Child as the Future seems most implicated, but the Disorderly Child who falls off the jungle gym, has accidents and molests other children is also a phantom presence.

(2) A second example is the increasing advocacy at the Nursery School level that playfighting (also called rough-and-tumble, pretense aggression, etc.) be stopped in the playground as it is usually stopped within the school itself, because it is noisy and it is believed

to be associated with real fighting. There are those who associate it with violence, war and sexism, and feel it should be abolished altogether, a movement given vote in the recent book *The War Play Dilemma*, by psychologists Carlsson-Paige and Levin (1987). On the other hand there are those whose research demonstrates that playfighting is not the preserve of violent children but rather, at these earlier age levels, is the practice of nonviolent boys whose ability to pretend to fight rather than to actually fight is the mark of their general maturity and social acceptability (Pellegrini 1988). Seeing that most of the Paige and Levin data are taken from interviews with nursery school teachers, we might assume that the new feminist conceptions of what is now more suitable androgynous behavior for boys is an underlying influence. As one goes back historically, the statement would be made that "boys will be boys"; and after some corporal punishment administered to those who had acted most outrageously, the playfighting would continue (Turner 1948).

(3) Along the same lines but of greater political significance is the widespread attempt to ban war toys. There is little satisfactory evidence that playing with war toys makes children more violent in general (see the review in Sutton-Smith 1988a). What my student Kathleen Connor (1991) found in her research was that when shown films of war toy play, males and females differed radically on whether they thought they were looking at merely playful aggression or at real aggression. Presented with fourteen video examples of playful toy aggression, the four-year-old subjects of the study found only two of them to be true aggression. The male students were very much like the children, seeing few events as real aggression. The female college students saw over half of them as aggression, and the nursery school teachers saw practically all of them as aggression. It is very clear from this data that playfighting or war toy behavior is gender-coded. However, experience is also important: women who had played with war toys when young voted more like adult males, and men who had not played with war toys when young voted more like adult females. Females are apparently more likely to see such playful aggression with toys as "nasty"; they point in defense to the children's words such as "I'll shoot you" or "I'll kill you." Males by contrast are more likely to see it as good rough-and-tumble fun, pointing to the fact that no one is actually hurt. What is play violence is clearly in the eye of the beholder. So is the intervention which follows. While there is much that is new in this intervention deriving from modern feminist views about childhood, as well as in their greater worries about a patriarchal engendered violent world, there is also much that is quite old. Female nursery teachers and school

teachers have been active in suppressing the excess of male play-fighting and male aggression throughout the twentieth century.

(4) A fourth example is the attempt to have sexist differences in games or play objects removed from school playgrounds. Usually this takes the form of changing the toys that are available at the preschool level (Liss 1983), but it can include proscriptions about any games being allowed in the playground that are not open to both sexes. This usually means requiring the girls to be allowed participation in ball and bat games. Given the finding that children's play seems to be the major cultural agency for the development of sexist attitudes, we can expect much greater pressure of this kind. Eleanor Maccoby (1990), famous for her work on sex differences, has recently talked about children's play as "Gender School," and as the critical setting where sex differences are more marked than anywhere else.

(5) Then there is the issue of play in schools in general. In their book on *School Play*, Block and King (1987) and their collaborators record multiple examples of teachers using play and games as positive and negative reinforcers in ways that might be regarded as injudicious. The opportunity to play is used manipulatively as a reinforcement for work and sometimes is likely to be captiously withdrawn. Much of school play is carried on surreptitiously by the children and seems to be a form of self-preservation in hard circumstances. King calls this "illicit play." On the other hand, there is the outstanding group of studies beginning with the work of Sara Smilansky (1968), in which teachers train children in fantasy, for example, to act out stories that were read to them. This appears to improve the children's performance in a variety of cognitive and verbal curriculum skills. The section, later in this volume, on Theory and Research on School Play Intervention shows that here, too, there is debate about the validity of the claims and the reality of the playfulness involved. In general, it seems that the use of play in the classroom greatly contributes to children's motivation for classroom studies and is quite justified for that reason. It is benign intervention in a situation otherwise made boring by overly serious pressure on the very young, which in the long run makes them more likely to drop out of the educational process. Classroom play can palliate an excessive concern with intervening on behalf of a time-frozen conception of the child's future. Although by way of codicil it must be added that if this kind of curriculum play is used as an argument for the dismissal of playground play, as has happened in the disputes over the worth of the latter in the United States, then obviously the curriculum play can be part of a larger and more pernicious form of

intervention. For an example of this larger usage, in a battle between parents and administrative authorities over whether playground play should be restored, see my account of the Loudon County case in which after seventeen years of no recess it was finally restored in 1988 (Sutton-Smith 1988b).

(6) This is the century of solitary play. Up to this point, we have been largely discussing interventions in social or public play. Most controversy over play is about what children do with each other in public settings. Little attention is usually focused on the important distinction between public and private play. This is the century in which more time than ever before has been spent by children in playing alone. Family size and the shift from a collective and manual way of life to an individual and symbolic way of life appear to be the underlying causes. Not incidentally most of the major work in play theory in child psychology is predominantly concerned with the reactions of solitary children to objects of play: Piaget's cognitive processes of assimilation (1951), Erikson's hallucinated masteries (1950), Berlyne's novel stimuli (1960) or the Singers' individual imaginative children (1990). Although the 1990 United Nations Children's Right Charter does not make the distinction between public and private play, the latter is implicit in its 16th article which quotes the child's right to the protection of privacy (Wilcox & Naimark 1991). What children do most with their privacy is play. The protection of private play is what is at stake here. And this brings us back to interventions deriving from the market place and having to do with the child as a consumer of toys or of television. It is often said that these interventions leave nothing to the imagination, suggesting negative consequences for the future of childhood.

Talking about private play, consider again the issue of toys which was discussed earlier with respect to whether or not they increase aggression. This is the century of the development of a mass toy market for children's private play, unprecedented in history (Sutton-Smith 1986). Much of the recent public discussion has to do with whether war toys should be banned. In Sweden the government has succeeded in getting the local toymakers not to produce such toys anymore. The International Playground Movement (IPA, the association for the Child's Right to play) succeeded in getting a UNESCO resolution against such toys (Nilsson 1990). Apparently this is not much of a problem for most schools which do not allow toys to be brought in anyway. In extensive observations in nine Philadelphia preschools we found no war toys present although the children often used other school-provided toys quite ingeniously for the same end

(Sutton-Smith, Gerstmyer & Mechley 1988). Ironically, in Sweden the toy retailers import such toys from overseas and the Swedish armament trade is as healthy as ever. The question arises: if one could deny war toys in the market place, would this be an unfair intervention in children's free choice? In the United States with its archaic if constitutional gun laws this is a highly controversial issue.

It would seem characteristic of toys that the best of them (blocks, clay, houses, dolls and toy characters) are engineered to allow a child to play with them privately, even though parents may also hope that they will play with them persistently and gain valuable information. What the children see as toys, to be used for their imaginative purposes, the adults often seem to envisage as tools for learning about reality. Children watch television for fantasy excitement, when their parents and many communication theorists see only a tabula rasa interaction in which the child must copy everything he or she sees (Postman 1982). The children, it seems, take the caricatural toys (they are never very real) and transform them to their own empowerment. The children perceive ontology when the adults conceptualize epistemology. The children feel the enjoyments of present play while the adults cognize future consequences.

Unfortunately, the adult cognitive and futuristic premises appear supported in a general way by the function-oriented cognitive theories of Berlyne, Piaget and Vygotsky. Although these theories have seldom been examined by specific research for their applicability to the case of toys, they have nevertheless become the public relations argument of toy companies who find profit in sharing with the psychologists and the general public the same desperate concern with the children's future. The dilemma here is the conflict between the adult aspiration for functional outcomes and the children's desire for enjoyment and autonomy. Most probably, intervention occurs at the moment of choice of toys, by eliminating those that the child might prefer. Given that children are, decade by decade, becoming increasingly influential in making their own consumer choices, parents may become more desperate about this "invasion" of their own powers.

Private play presumably includes the right to play with television-advertised toys, and to play in the presence of television, as children often do, and even to play imaginatively in one's head with the images of people seen on the screen. In a current study, we found that in our sample of twenty-four, blue collar nine-year-olds, who on first interview named us (on the average) fourteen persons with whom they played in their minds, only a quarter of these personages were derived from television and most of them were songsters. Three-quarters were real persons, family, friends, or teachers. Apparently, television is not quite as powerful an influence on mind play as has often been opined. Consider, for example, the vein of thought which suggests that the commercial development of television's character toys (G.I. Joe, etc.) is taking away the individuality of children's play (Kline 1991). Our data and that of some others suggest that this invasion of private play may not be as complete as has often been asserted (Snow 1974; James & McCain 1982). Still, the issue is whether television is an upsetting intrusion into play life or whether it is not. It is conventional middle-class opinion that it is such an intrusion (Zuckerman 1976). But then it has always been conventional middle class opinion that novel media for children are unfortunate interventions into family life, beginning with fairy tales in the early nineteenth century and currently focusing on video games and cartoon programs. Here we have a clash between those who are concerned with the child as consumer. As the commodification of childhood becomes increasingly extensive, this clash of interventions should increase in intensity.

A third intervention in children's private play, oddly enough, comes from the recent advocacy that parent-child play should be greatly increased. It was the central theme for the biennial meeting of the International Council for Children's Play (ICCP) in Andreasberg, Germany, in 1990 (Sutton-Smith, in press-b). It was said that with increased alienation within families and between generations because of television, single families, divorce etc., there was a need to reach out for new unifying forces for the family. Examples were given by the scholars present at the conference of parents playing sports with their children, reading fairy tales to them, playing with computers with them, and playing games with them. Interestingly, almost no one gave examples of fantasy play with children (something advocated both by the Singers (1985) and the Sutton-Smiths (1974)). One study presented by Otto & Rieman (1990) of Germany showed that fantasy play with parents was what most children preferred, while sports play with children was what most adults preferred. In short, most adults thought about playing with children primarily as a form of skill training, teaching or moralizing and used it as a form of socialization (the Child as Future). Most children, however, wished for more participation in their imaginative play (the Imaginary Child), although whether that would guarantee them against further intrusion must be held doubtful. When Kelly-Byrne (1989) played with a child for a year in the child's chosen fantasy play, she found the child to be a complete despot for about three months, after which there was a gradual relaxation and granting of more equal rights to the investigator. Perhaps parents know intuitively that there would be such an invasion of power (the Disorderly Child) if they actually played along with their children's fantasies. Clearly, the kind of intervention represented by parent-child play is a tricky phenomenon requiring much more play knowledge than most parents currently possess.

A recent example of direct television intervention in parent-child play is provided by a program on the children's cable television station called Nickelodeon in the United States. This program, called Family Double Dare, has families competing against each other as teams going through obstacle courses, in which family members share in common a great deal of amusing unpleasantness such as getting pies in the face, falling in pools of water and being covered with green if antiseptic slime. The network also specializes in comedies in which the power roles of parents and children are reversed; sometimes the scene is a school (Welcome Freshmen, Pete and Pete); sometimes a ranch (Hey Dude); and sometimes a court (Kid's Court). The latter is the most serious because the child juries recruited from children visiting Universal Studios in Orlando, Florida, have to decide who is guilty, child or parent, child or child, according to the reputed crime. Guilt or non-guilt is finally determined by the amount of noise registering on the noise meter as parties in the jury shout their choice. These child juries very often find parental laws and attitude are the guilty party. Across this network there is a heavy attempt to suggest in these play forms that children should have more power. In effect, in its own eyes the network is intervening on behalf of the children, and incidentally also on behalf of their play rights. Their sanctioning of the Disorderly Child is perhaps the harbinger of a time when our culture will permit children to live in their own present rather than in our future, although one suspects that that time is a long way off yet. A recently formed adult society in the township of Loveland, Cincinnati, Ohio, has named itself "Citizens against Mind Pollutants," and they have chosen the Nickelodeon channel as one of their targets.

A final issue concerning private play has to be the way in which the therapist does or does not play actively with the child. Traditionally, the therapist purportedly did not much intervene, but now participation is said to be increasing. Whatever its special benefits (also documented in the section on Play Therapy in this volume), this is a much more intrusive sort of play therapy. The paradox of therapeutic intervention is that the Disorderly Child is allowed expression, but in the long run on behalf of the Child of the Future. Therapists, more than any other adult of this generation, understand the children's need for the expression of irrationality. But unfortunately they do not balance this with an understanding of the needs of everyone for such sublimation. The end of their therapy should not only be a child who is reasonably well oriented to reality and to the future, but one who has also learned how to continue playing with his or her irrationalities. As this paper shows I do not hold that play is much about growth, it is more about compensation. So the function of play in my mind is to pretend that we exist in a life worth living, which is something required by both children and adults at all times in their lives. The Imaginary or Disorderly Children do not exist so that they can become the adults of the future, but so that they can become the Imaginary and Disorderly adults of the future, in ways that are sufficiently theatric to be consonant with civilization.

Conclusion

One may sum up by saying that the variety and extent of intervention in children's play has been greatly increasing over this century. In public play we have proceeded from the institution of organized sports and playground provisions to the abolition of recess, the abolition of playfighting, the control of sexist play and the control of play in school by teachers (Cavallo 1981; Mangan 1986). In private play, we have intervened with toys, with television and with the advocacy of parent-child play. While there is much controversy over the particulars, intervention of one kind or another, by one authority or by another, appears to be the typical answer to the conflicts involved around contemporary children's play.

The implicit message of this paper is that if our interventions are themselves genuinely playful, or allow children their own genuine playfulness, we will be further ahead than we were with our present array of rhetorics about the paradigms of childhood. It is more probable that by allowing there to be a generation of child players as well as being ourselves a generation of adult players, we will treat children and ourselves more fortunately. As it stands we are typically hypocrites who pretend that children play and that we adults do not. In this way children remain the residual legatees of historicism and as such assure us of their innocence and our righteousness; of their prospects and our good faith in the future we have provided for them. In fact we have provided them with an increasingly stressful childhood and an increasingly undesirable future. We are well overdue in substituting for all these paradigms of childhood one that will put both adult and child on the same existential footing, that would be the paradigm of the Playful Person.

PART 1

Play Therapy

Play therapy is perhaps the best known kind of play intervention. Although the term is often misused for all kinds of supposedly helpful educational measures, we would like to reserve it for interventions directed towards helping children resolve inner conflicts. Play has often been described as particularly helpful in this area, because of the freedom it provides to express thought and feeling in a childlike way, and to share these with a helpful adult (the therapist) on a cognitive-emotional level the child can grasp.

Research in this field has been scarce, although the situation is not quite as bad as Anglo-American authors sometimes state (Smith-Acuna, Durlak & Kasper 1991). In some European languages extensive studies on process and effect of play therapy have been published (Schmidtchen 1978, 1986, in German; Harinck & Hellendoorn 1983, 1987, in Dutch). However, the emphasis in the literature is clearly on theory. This general trend is reflected in this section of *Play and Intervention*.

In his introductory chapter, *Jerome Singer* brings together many different points of view on the use of play as therapy. Interestingly, most of the empirical foundations come from neighboring fields: play in general, play development, expression of emotions, information processing; areas where much more research has been done than on play therapy itself. Singer views play as a powerful medium for therapy because it enables the child to work out, on its own cognitive level, the dialectical tension between different and sometimes opposite needs. In play, with the help of the therapist, the child is better able to elaborate and finally integrate his or her private "scripts". This helps the child to gain cognitive control, and to

23

achieve a more realistic sense of uniqueness and of self.

Still, this introduction leaves us with a lot of questions about the therapeutic value of play and about the role of play throughout the therapeutic process. Some of these points are taken further in the next chapters.

In her impressive paper on the problems of interpretation in play therapy, *Bertha Mook* approaches the phenomena of play and of interpretation from a phenomenological and hermeneutic point of view. Inspired by Gadamer and Ricoeur, she argues that play is a primary and autonomous phenomenon, a text with multiple levels of meaning, from which new meanings may emerge. In the circular structure of the therapeutic play dialogue, child and therapist both contribute to the creation and unfolding of a play narrative. This play experience may in itself already be therapeutic. But if the therapist understands the play narrative as sense as well as reference, timely interpretation may enhance its therapeutic value.

Stefan Schmidtchen writes from a client-centered background, constantly seeking to reformulate its theoretical assumptions in accordance with his research. His contribution tries to clarify how play therapy could achieve important effects, notably the reduction of behavioral symptoms and the improvement of personal competence. He contends that play implies a spontaneous learning process, which may be guided and stimulated by the therapist. To optimally accomplish this, therapists should be client-centered in the sense that they constantly concentrate on what might be relevant learning steps for each particular child. In addition, the child needs empathic attention and positive emotional support to sustain the learning activity. The process described is supported by empirical data from a quantitative case study.

Starting from a more purely Rogerian (person-centered) framework, *Herbert Goetze* tries to delineate four different stages in the therapy process, which reflect a changing relationship between child and therapist. The first stage is "non-personal," the second "non-directive," followed by the "client-centered," and lastly the "person-centered" stage. This process concept is illustrated by a case description. By means of a qualitative and quantitative analysis of the child's play behavior in this case, the existence of at least two different stages (non-directive and client-centered), characterized by definite differences in play behavior, becomes plausible.

Gerd Schäfer, an exponent of psychoanalytic play therapy, also tries to clarify the special place of play in therapy. In Winnicott's terms, play can be seen as an "intermediate area", an area in which things are still uncertain, not fully defined by objective form, but open to subjectivity and inner experience. In an external reality which constantly asks a child to react in more or less established ways, it is difficult for a child to form its own structures, in accordance with its own inner feeling. Play provides an opportunity to temporarily shelve that reality and thus find one's inner self again.

The last two chapters in this part are more directly concerned with therapeutic practice. *Dorothy Singer* outlines the many possibilities of imagery techniques in play therapy. The great advantage of imagery, provided the specific technique is well geared to the emotional and cognitive abilities of the child, is that it often permits communication and interaction with the therapist on topics a child might resist in verbal exchanges. The many case illustrations provide abundant evidence of what children can do with imagery.

In some of the papers in this part on Play Therapy research questions were posed and (preliminarily) answered. In *Berendien Van Zanten*'s contribution, attention is drawn to the relations between the results of play therapy and its indication, in particular the presence or absence of basic working conditions. In her evaluation study on twelve cases, it appears that the absence of one or more basic conditions, and especially a lack of changeability in the parents are useful predictors of therapeutic failure. The message is clear: before starting therapy, therapists would do well to more carefully consider all indications and contra-indications.

/1

The Scientific Foundations
of Play Therapy

Jerome L. Singer

The object of this paper is to set natural-occurring children's play and also the use of play as psychotherapy into the broader context of current developments in scientific psychology. We have witnessed great progress in the past thirty years with the so-called cognitive revolution that has provided not only vigorous research but also yielded intriguing building blocks for new theory linking information-processing to emotion on the one hand, and to motivated action on the other. While the various "schools" of psychotherapy may still persist primarily for professional, political, and sociological reasons, I propose that we can identify a fundamental integrative thrust if we examine the current scientific literature. There may be, for example, remnants of practitioners who call themselves "classical Freudians" or "Kleinians" and who continue to reduce complex behavior to the sexual and aggressive energies associated with oral, anal, and sexual body orifices. Psychoanalysis on the whole, however, has moved to the domain of "object relations" and in so doing has placed its emphasis much more upon the ways in which the developing individual organizes the complexity of experience and seeks, on the one hand, to establish a sense of individual identity while, on the other, striving to sustain feelings of attachment and intimacy with others (Singer 1988). This movement of psychoanalysis has brought it much more in line with theory and findings emerging from psychological research in personality, exemplified most recently in the contributions of

27

Tomkins (1962, 1963, 1991), McAdams (1985, 1989) and Epstein (1990), the cognitive studies of Kreitler and Kreitler (1976, 1990), G. Mandler (1984), and the so-called social cognition literature (Cantor & Kihlstrom 1987; Singer 1985; Singer & Salovey 1991). Needless to say the writings of Lewin (1935), of Piaget (1962) and Vygotsky (1962) were formative influences on this emergent perspective.

Two Forms of Thought

It is becoming increasingly clear to those of us who study both adult and children's imagination that the make-believe or pretending of early childhood is fundamental for the development of all competent adult cognition and emotional functioning. Piaget (1962) emphasized the role of symbolic play as a precursor for those eventually emerging processes of logic and orderly thought sequence whose epistemology was his main concern. Increasingly, we can also recognize that mature human thought and information processing is not limited only to scientific or mathematical sequences that are sequential in nature and characterized strongly by verbal expression and grammatical structure. The seminal analyses of Jerome Bruner (1986) have made it evident that effective thought takes on a narrative or subjunctive form as well. In our processing of information we must not only organize it into logical structures but also examine the alternative and future possibilities or even consider the darker alternatives that appear in any new human experience. Indeed, we store information, as is increasingly clear in memory research, by organized verbal schemas, on the one hand, and through narrative episodes or possibilities in the form of fantasies and daydreams, on the other (Singer 1985; Singer & Salovey 1991). Narrative thought and subjunctive structure reflect the human capacity for what the great neurologist Kurt Goldstein (1940) called "taking an attitude toward the possible." He believed this capacity reflected the optimal functioning of both a healthy and intact brain. Through this orientation to the possible, one becomes capable of exploring a range of potential futures or, in effect, traveling through time and space to a different or better childhood or maturity (Singer & Singer 1990). Sigmund Freud (1962) also used the term *trial* or *experimental action* to characterize thought and the emergence of his concept of the ego.

This capacity for reconstructing one's past or for planning for one's daily activities through mental rehearsal or simply daydreaming about future vacations, sexual opportunities, or fantastic space adventures also serves a broader function. Our imagination liberates us from the tyranny of *this* place, of *these* particular duties and obligations, of *these* particular people in our social milieu. We accomplish this restructuring not only through the abstraction of high-level logical or mathematical processes. We also draw on our capacity for creating narrative and for using our skills at imagery to provide us with alternative temporary environments that we can manipulate for self-help and ultimately put into the service of orderly living or simply for sustaining hope and effort (Singer 1974; Singer & Bonanno 1990; Taylor 1989). As Bruner has proposed, the object of narrative thought is not "truth" but verisimilitude or "life-likeness." He writes: "Efforts to reduce one mode [the narrative] to the other [the paradigmatic or logical] or to ignore one at the expense of the other inevitably fail to capture the rich diversity of thought" (Bruner 1986, 11).

Viewed from this perspective, the simple make-believe play of the child (pretending early on that a stick is an airplane, that a soft toy can talk or respond to nurturance or admonition, that a few blocks or dolls can become the basis of an imagined city in which a relatively lengthy story unfolds) can be regarded as a fundamental precursor of the full-blown adult imagination. Without an adequate development of this narrative, subjunctive, or imaginative dimension the child is subsequently handicapped both in cognitive and emotional development (Leslie 1987). Indeed, without sufficient practice in the skill of generating fantasy for self-regulation, the child not only will experience difficulties in school adjustment but also, if psychotherapy is required at some point, may not move ahead effectively into the process.

Information Processing and Emotion

In the so-called cognitive revolution that has dominated psychology since about 1960, we perceive a new model of the human being. We now look on babies and children as information-seeking organisms striving to organize and to integrate novelty and complexity; they are curious and exploratory but also more likely to feel comfortable and to smile (as the research by Papousek on infants has shown) once they can experience control over novelty and assimilate new information into prior concepts and scripts about the sequence of events. The "smile of predictive pleasure" in babies, described by Papousek (1987) and his collaborators, and other signs of positive emotion, (smiling and laughter associated with familiarity in adults) suggest that while cognition and emotion may be different systems in terms of bodily structure, they are closely related in actual human response (Izard 1977; Kreitler & Kreitler 1976; G. Mandler 1984; Tomkins 1962, 1963).

Theoretical analyses initiated by Tomkins (1962, 1963) have contributed greatly to the paradigm shift toward the cognitive-affective view of the human organism. Tomkins' work has succeeded in putting emotions back at the center of active research in personality and in social psychology. He led the way in demonstrating that a cognitive perspective that involved an emphasis on the fact that human beings are continuously assigning meanings and organizing their experience in schemas and scripts does not preclude a significant motivational role for affect or emotion. With the support of increasing empirical research, carried out on both children and adults by investigators such as Izard (1977), Ekman (1973; Ekman et al. 1982) and many others, we can now regard human beings as showing differentiated emotional response patterns that are closely intertwined with responses to the novelty, complexity, and other structural properties of the information that is confronted from moment to moment.

This cognitive-affective perspective broadens our conception of human motivation considerably. Rather than reducing all human motivation to some symbolic reflection of infantile sexuality or aggression, one can propose that the basic emotions that have now been shown to exist across human species in the research of Ekman and of Izard are motivating human beings in dozens of different situations independent of presumed drive pressures. Situations that permit experience and expression of positive emotions or that allow for appropriate control of negative emotions are intrinsically positively reinforcing. Those situations that are more likely to evoke the negative emotions of fear, anger, distress, or shame, or that have blocked the expression of socially adaptive control of emotions may be experienced as inherently punishing or negatively reinforcing (Singer 1974, 1984; Tomkins 1962).

Memory and anticipation become central features related to emotional experience. This is accomplished by identifying, labeling, and gradually organizing new information into mental representations that are technically labeled as schemas. These structures include schemas about persons or physical objects, schemas about self and others, and also scripts about action sequences or prototypes that become means for encapsulating a variety of common features of situations and persons into one fuzzy concept (J. Mandler 1983, 1984; Singer & Kolligian 1987; Singer & Salovey 1991).

The Child's Task in Information Processing

The problem for the child becomes, in effect, one of making sense of a complex world through the gradual formation of schemas and scripts and through the assimilation of new situations into established organized mental structures or, as language increases, into lexical categories as well. Confronted with extreme novelty that cannot at once be easily assimilated into established structures, a child may respond with fear or terror. Once a match can be made between new information and some well-known schema, and the novelty or ambiguity of the environmental situation can be assimilated, the child may respond with a smile of pleasure. When the new situation is only moderately complex and some overriding schema is still available, the child may move to explore the moderate amount of novelty in the situation, and this evokes the positive affects of interest and excitement.

Children and adults live in a situation of a perennially delicate balance between the potential for fear or anxiety evoked by new situations and the excitement of exploring such situations. By such exploration one can assimilate incongruity into established schemas, enrich such schemas, or start to form new ones. The persistence over time of large amounts of unexpected or ambiguous information evokes the negative affects of anger or of distress and sadness (Singer & Singer 1990; Tomkins 1962). We all learn to bring to each new situation sets of expectations of what may occur. We practice such expectations through brief anticipatory fantasies, some more realistic than others depending on our maturity, the complexity of our schema structure, and our social development. Our task in each new situation is then to examine new information and determine whether it confirms or disconfirms some of our anticipations. George Mandler (1984) has particularly developed the implications of interrupted sequences of action and thought and of confirmations and disconfirmations of anticipations as the basis for emotional response.

If identifying and organizing new information becomes the fundamental, overarching demand placed on the child, then we can begin to understand the evolutionary function of imaginative play and the thought processes that seem to grow out of such play. As Piaget has shown, children strive to accommodate themselves to the environment and also to the speech, gestures, and other physical actions of adults or older children. In these efforts children succeed through some form of successive approximation, but at the same time they need to be able to assimilate such new actions into organized mental structures. This assimilation process is at first expressed by children through repetitive actions and talking aloud. What seems like the intrinsic unmotivated character of play to an adult represents the child's continuing effort to create new meaning structures and to provide itself with a sense of control and power by reducing large-scale settings, persons, or social interactions to meaningful structures that can be assimilated into the as yet limited number of schemas the child has at its command.

The startle responses or terror evoked in a toddler by the size and noise of a huge passing truck may be gradually transformed into curiosity and interest as the child attempts to reproduce the noises and movements of the truck through creating its own sound effects and through manipulating blocks or toy trucks. Imaginative play may thus be understood as a means by which the uncontrollable qualities and complexity of one's physical and social environment can be gradually miniaturized and manipulated. In effect, a great deal of adult thought also involves a similar effort to create, at least temporarily, a world one can control through replaying memories or experiences through anticipation and fantasy. Indeed, it can be argued that the very act of rehearsal and anticipation, or even of elaborating possible future events into somewhat more bizarre fantasies, may gradually approximate possible situations we *may* ultimately encounter. Such mental rehearsal may leave us better prepared to handle these or, at least, to be less frightened by them when they do occur (Singer & Singer 1990).

Attachment and Individuation: A Persistent Human Dilemma

Beyond the cognitive demand for meaning assignment and organization and its link to the arousal of emotion, human beings also must confront a persisting dialectic tension in their general motivation throughout their life span. This tension becomes evident in some of the very earliest months of childhood. On the one hand there is the need to feel close to others, to be attached to or encompassed by parents, older siblings, or other caregivers and, later, by friends, or by a group by means of some symbolic group participation (e.g., a religious, ethnic, or nationalistic association). On the other hand, we all experience to varying degrees the need to preserve some areas of personal autonomy, some sense of privacy, personal competence, and individualized skill development. We must move through life in effect struggling to preserve a balance between affiliation with others or with groups, thereby gaining a sense of community, while we also strive to maintain a sense of individuality and personal power (Angyal 1965; Bakan 1966; Rank 1945; Schachtel 1959).

More recently in the framework of an object relations oriented psychoanalytic analysis, Blatt (1990) has thought to show how the early childhood struggle between attachment and individuation may, if one pole or the other is overemphasized, become a focal area of conflict and eventuate in particular forms of psychopathology. Bonanno and Singer (1990) have further extended this polarity to identify a series of personality dimensions that recur in the literature along with particular affective tendencies, defensive patterns, variations in physical illness proneness, and the emotional disorders that had already been identified along such dimensions by Blatt. This conceptualization, while still largely speculative, is built around some available research evidence that suggests that optimal personality functioning and a hardy physical health status necessitate a reasonable balance between one's needs or strivings for affiliation and one's abilities to experience autonomy or individuation (Bonanno & Singer 1990).

Within this conceptual framework the child's make-believe world is one that represents a continuous working out of the dialectical tension between the need for closeness and affiliation and the need for privacy with its concomitant experience of personal power and individuality. Indeed, the very act of beginning to form individualized images, memories, and anticipatory fantasies becomes, in our crowded and sensory-bombarded world, the last refuge for an experience of individuality and personal privacy. For the developing child, seeking to sustain relationships with parents and others and to feel the warmth of what Schachtel (1959) called embeddedness-affect, and the ability to create private games and to engage in floor play or to sustain a relationship with a personally possessed stuffed animal or invisible playmate provides the experience of individuation that also seems so necessary in our human condition.

In view of this persistent human attachment-individuation tension, the emergence of an increasingly complex imaginative dimension subject to reasonable control (a kind of cognitive skill in itself) sustains the need for self-definition, for a sense of uniqueness and private power.

Of course this very dilemma of attachment versus individuation is not only reflected structurally in the degree of priorities assigned by children to social interaction or to imaginative experience. It is also the basis for the content of the play behavior. The themes of play in the child often reflect the continuing tension between the desire for closeness and the desire for assertions of personal power, importance, or the need for privacy. Such manifestations are readily identifiable in play therapy observations.

Piaget has been criticized by other researchers such as Bretherton (1984) and Sutton-Smith (1966) because they feel he tended to devalue the importance of play as a source of mature adult imagery and as the foundation for the playfulness that characterizes all human thought. Bretherton also pointed out that Piaget tended to think of imaginative play as declining after the age four or five rather than recognizing the importance of play as a forerunner for Bruner's narrative thought. The research of the author and his colleagues with large numbers of children from diverse backgrounds who were observed during spontaneous play has made it clear that pretend play goes on well into the early school years and continues either "underground" in private thought or in the more sanctioned group forms of make-believe that are observable through the life cycle (Singer & Singer 1990).

Even games with rules, which are certainly an important step in the child's development of orderly and regulatory processing and self-control, often include elements of pretending or evoke private or shared fantasies well into adult life. If one watches adults and children playing relatively structured games like Monopoly, one can frequently observe the tendency for the players to introduce make-believe components, sometimes even taking on particular make-believe roles for themselves as they participate in this otherwise rule-organized game. The reordering of the "given" realities is just as much a fundamental feature of human thought as is the attempt at faithful accommodation to the environment through coherent schemas, which Piaget emphasized in his epistemology. Indeed it was only on his late, posthumously published work that he finally addressed the question of the origins of possibility (Piaget 1980).

To assert that imaginative play has a variety of short- and long-term benefits may reflect some cultural bias, as Sutton-Smith has argued in some of his papers (Sutton-Smith & Kelley-Byrne 1984). But even the subversive quality of *Mad Magazine* cartoon humor, of cards such as the Garbage Pail Kids, or of the punning and teasing of adults by children may serve an important balancing function for the child in a world in which children are powerless. In the face of life tragedies, parental neglect or abuse, parental poverty or humiliation, abandonment, illness, or death, the ability to step back from the situation and to create playful narrative offers at least some solace if not a complete way out of the distress. Those children who do not experience encouragement that fosters the development of a symbolic dimension through storytelling, pretending, or through repetitive sensory or physical play or games with rules, may find themselves condemned either to impetuous instrumental activity or to a sense of isolation or extreme dependence on conventional rituals.

Of special importance is the conception of transformation, or the emergence through play of what Leslie (1987) has called a metarepresentational mode of thought. He has proposed the challenging question:

> If a representational system is developing, how can its semantic relations tolerate distortion in these more or less arbitrary ways? . . . [How] is it possible that young children can disregard or distort reality (as in using a banana as a telephone). . . . Why does pretending not undermine their representational system and bring it crashing down? (412)

Leslie's argument is that a major step in development involves the "decoupling" of the direct representations that we sustain of objects, persons, or situations from their perceptual images into a new set of metarepresentations that are symbolic or mental representations of the same original set of objects but now treated as part of an entire system of thought that one can modify, manipulate, analogize, or transform to metaphor. With some help of adults but also on the basis of an inherent capacity in the child, the ability emerges to create a frame in which otherwise very stable objects can be transformed into representations that bear only a tenuous link with their original shapes. If we walk into a room and perhaps unexpectedly see an elongated object on the floor, we may jump because we think it is a snake until we recognize with relief that it is a telephone extension cord. This is an "error" because we had no reason initially to treat the objects of the room as other than percepts. When on another occasion we say to a child playing "Explorer" with us in the same room, "Look! There's a dangerous snake!" the telephone cord is already being treated in this metarepresentational mode, as cued by our remark. Its only casual resemblance to a snake suffices to permit an abuse of what ordinarily might be a fixed representational and semantic structure.

Leslie's conception of the theory of mind implies that human beings have available a domain of metarepresentations that they can manipulate to make inferences about causes, predictions about future events, recognize the consequences of ignorance, distinguish reality from fantasy, acquire a language of words and phrases depicting mental experiences or states, and infer motivations. Such a development begins perhaps in the middle of the second year but does not really reach its peak until the third and fourth years, although some children may use words like *know, remember, pretend* and *dream* by the end of the second year. As Leslie puts it:

> Pretend play is thus one of the earliest manifestations of the ability to characterize and manipulate one's own and others' cognitive relations to information. This ability which is central to a common sense theory of knowledge, will eventually include characterizing relations such as believing, expecting and hoping and manipulating these relations in others, for example, getting someone to expect something will happen by promising. (1987, 422)

The compensatory or psychologically adaptive role of imaginative play and the adoption of a metarepresentational schema system is exemplified by an example provided by Piaget (1962). His daughter, just a little less than four years old, was told that she could not go into the kitchen because pails of hot water were being prepared for her bath. The little girl then said, "I'll go into the pretend kitchen then. I once saw a little boy who went into the kitchen, and when Odette went past with the hot water, he got out of the way."

There is good evidence that play between parents and children is a universal experience that has a mutually reinforcing impact (Singer & Singer 1990). In a study by Van Hoorn (1987), observations of a diverse mixture of Chinese, Filipino, Mexican, and North American mothers of European descent were made during play interactions with their infants. Despite some cultural variations in games played, there was considerable evidence of mutual enjoyment. Games were characterized by the range of interactive behaviors that promoted cooperation and successive attainments. The positive emotions of joy, surprise and laughter were consistently in evidence.

Imaginative Play, Psychopathology, and Psychotherapy

A fuller exploration of the implications of children's make-believe play for psychopathology and psychotherapy would take us far beyond the scope of this paper. The general thrust of the previous paragraphs suggests that pretend play, the capacity to create miniature, possible worlds, is a critical feature of the healthy development of a child. The available evidence as reviewed by Dorothy Singer and myself elsewhere has suggested that emotional disturbance and cognitive and affective difficulties are often associated with an inability to sustain imaginative play in middle and early childhood. Some classic cases in which children's play revealed elaborate, unrealistic fantasies reflecting their troubled life experiences demonstrate that those children who could sustain such play had better prognoses once play therapy was initiated (Singer 1973; Singer & Singer 1976, 1990).

A critical role for the psychotherapist with children is to help them to find ways of miniaturizing their private fears, brutal experiences of abuse, exposure to parental quarrels or neglect into manageable chunks. The therapist's encouragement of play by the provision of an appropriate setting of toys or (for middle childhood) of games conducive to symbolic representations of children's troubles casts the therapist in the role of the needed mediating parental figure. Delineating in play form key life issues or conflicts and significant adults or siblings, helps the child to develop new schemas and scripts and new knowledge structures that can later reduce the ambiguity, confusion, or affects of fear and terror that new situations may present.

I believe that a key feature of the play therapist's role is to provide a model for the child of a zestful, curious, lively approach to one's experience. While the therapist must often avoid moralizing about the child's hatred or about presumed parental or sibling cruelties or neglects reflected in play, this does not preclude an emotional response. The therapist's own professional curiosity and willingness to share thoughts and play possibilities, conveyed in a spirit of liveliness and humor, can open the troubled child to the joys of the world of introspection and fantasy. By such an approach one can change the fearful, despairing, or angry child, trapped in a mental world of limited constructs, schemas, or scripts, into one who can savor the excitement of reshaping what had seemed like the "given" world of recent experiences into a domain of innumerable possibilities. By replacing and thus reshaping schemas, the child can gain at least some sense of control and power within a small region of a vast, seemingly impenetrable universe. The skilled play therapist, whether psychoanalytic or cognitive-behavioral in orientation, not only provides the child an opportunity to identify and work through specific problems but also enhances the child's development of the capacity for play, a powerful cognitive tool for further enhancement of a sense of self and individuation as well as a continuing private theater for developing new scripts of affiliation and attachment. The medium of make-believe in childhood, internalized by middle childhood into a richly elaborated fantasy capacity, becomes eventually a major functional system through which all of us can entertain opportunities and possibilities for warmth, closeness, and communion with others while still sustaining our sense of individuality and privacy.

/2

Therapeutic Play: From Interpretation to Intervention

Bertha Mook

Early child psychotherapists were quick to realize that the child's inner world is revealed through play, and that it should therefore be incorporated as part of the child's language in psychotherapy. Play thus became a central avenue for therapeutic communication with children in the traditional psychoanalytic as well as in the humanistic and existential approaches. In this paper, I will present my viewpoint that these traditional approaches underestimate the potential significance and the transformative power of play. Besides, they created a rift between interpretation and understanding which has led to a divisive impoverishment and may have hampered further developments in the field.

In recent times, we witness an increasing and expanding clinical and research interest in the phenomenon of play and play therapy which has enlivened this relatively dormant field and has strengthened its empirical basis. This can be seen in the development of new directions and innovations in the use of play techniques across multiple modes of therapeutic intervention including behavioral and family therapy (e.g., Schaefer & O'Connor 1983; Schaefer 1988).

Despite such promising new developments, the position of the traditional approaches to play interpretation have not changed in any significant way. The phenomenon of play itself remains elusive and escapes our attempt at definition (Schaefer & O'Connor 1983;

Mook 1989). Also, the phenomenon of interpretation is difficult to grasp, and the task of interpreting play in the therapeutic context remains obscure. In the face of these problems, I believe that the field of interpreting therapeutic play is in need of a renewed foundational understanding of the phenomena of play and of interpretation.

Inspired by the phenomenological hermeneutics of H-G. Gadamer and Paul Ricoeur, I aim to make an initial contribution to this task by turning to Gadamer's ontological concept of play and to Ricoeur's theory of interpretation. In this chapter, I will first reflect on the role of play and interpretation in psychoanalysis, and of play and understanding in humanistic and existential child therapies. In the next section, I will turn to a phenomenological and hermeneutic approach to the phenomena of play and interpretation respectively. Finally, I will attempt to apply this perspective to the interpretation of therapeutic play.

Interpretation and Play in Psychoanalysis

The concept of interpretation in psychotherapy is associated with psychoanalysis to such an extent that it tends to be identified with it. In traditional psychoanalysis, interpretation is seen as the major technique of therapeutic intervention and indeed as the foundation of analytic practice. Within psychoanalysis, interpretation is subordinated to a body of analytic theory concerning personality, psychopathology and principles of practice. In analytic practice, the gradual manifestation of unconscious symbolic material has to be interpreted in terms of a definite set of key signifiers and their derivatives. In traditional psychoanalysis, the analyst tended to make only single interpretative statements. Freud (1937) wrote: "Interpretation applies to something one does to some *single element* in the material such as an association or a parapraxis" (261).

In early child psychoanalysis, interpretation remained the basic technique of intervention and *play* was substituted for free association. Freud formulated children's play as a symbolic expression of their unconscious conflicts, their anxieties and their traumatic experiences. In her pioneering work with children, Anna Freud (1928) found that nonverbal material like play and painting reveal unconscious conflicts more directly then words, and are as such direct vehicles for interpretation. However, she did not value play in its own right but saw it only as serving an intermediary means of expression when the child could not yet verbalize his or her thoughts and feelings. In fact, Anna Freud was of the opinion that the significance of play in analysis has been greatly overstated although she did admit that imaginative play could reveal important material. For her, what was *said* between the analyst and the child remained of paramount importance. With Melanie Klein (1932), the child patient's play was accepted as a communicative mode in its own right. She interpreted play strictly in terms of Freud's theory of unconscious symbolism in the context of her own very concrete conception of the child's inner world. She held that even very young children understand and benefit from interpretations. Meltzer (1978) comments that Klein in her interpretations seldom linked themes together but tended "simply to delineate the separate fantasies and the particular anxieties connected with them without much sorting out" (93). She believed that the elaboration of these fantasies into consciousness diminish the child's anxieties. Most of child analysis today is still based upon the traditional approaches of Anna Freud or Melanie Klein with little modification.

In D. W. Winnicott (1974) we find the first psychoanalyst who genuinely sought to understand the meaning of play for children. He saw play as unfolding in its own space in between the child's inner world and outer reality, and recognized it as a creative experience which is vitally important and therapeutic in its own right. Winnicott critiqued child analysts for their exclusive focus on play content and symbolic meanings, and for disregarding the meaning of play as a creative and intensely real experience for the child. He was also the first to emphasize the importance of the therapist's involvement and participation in the child's play. In his words (1974, 38): "Psychotherapy takes place in the overlap of two areas of playing, that of the patient and that of the therapist. Psychotherapy has to do with two people playing together."

Although Winnicott adhered to the basic principles of psychoanalysis, he cautioned against the frequent and untimely use of interpretation. He saw interpretation outside the ripeness of the material and the readiness of the child as indoctrination and an attempt to produce compliance with the analyst. He was convinced that only timely interpretation within a mutual playing context could move the analysis forward. He even held that the child and not the analyst has the final answers. In striking terms he wrote: ". . . the significant moment is that at which the child surprises himself or herself. It is not the moment of my clever interpretation" (1974, 54).

In recent developments in child and adult psychoanalysis, there is a limited but growing awareness that the concept of interpretation calls for modification and expansion, and that it is not always the chosen mode of therapeutic intervention. The most striking examples come from advances in psychoanalytic self-theory and clinical experience with borderline patients. According to Ornstein & Ornstein (1980), the movement is away from single interpretative statements towards more comprehensive reconstructions, and away from an exclusive inferential mode of interpretation towards the inclusion of an empathic mode of listening and communication. Such developments are promising and point towards a tentative rapprochement between major therapeutic schools of thought.

Humanistic and Existential Psychotherapy

As we know, the blueprints of humanistic and existential psychotherapies developed partially in reaction against psychoanalysis. They are based on a radically different view of personality and a consequently different model of therapeutic intervention. Inspired by humanistic ideals, and by the philosophy of phenomenology and existentialism, these approaches reject the Freudian concept of the unconscious as well as the primary psychoanalytic technique of interpretation. Instead, they focus on the importance of *understanding* the client's ongoing experiencing and on a facilitative therapeutic relationship.

In the application of humanistic and existential therapies to children, play is incorporated and seen as one of the possible means of self-expression. However, the interpretation of play is rejected. Therapeutic play in itself is not particularly encouraged nor is the therapist's participation in play. The most important principle is the *freedom* given to child clients to express themselves in whatever way they want to (Guerney 1983). These approaches, like psychoanalysis, have their roots in adult psychotherapy and remain predominantly verbal in character (Mook 1988).

A valuable exception is the phenomenologically-based Dutch approach referred to as imagery-communication (or "imagery interaction") which was specifically developed for children by a group of colleagues at the University of Utrecht (e.g., Langeveld 1955; Vermeer 1955; Lubbers 1971). Imagery-communication stresses the central role and value of play and other creative expressions as powerful means of therapeutic communication and change. Therapists are expected to facilitate the child's play and to become active participants in the child's play world (Hellendoorn 1988). Congruent with a phenomenological approach, the understanding of lived experience is emphasized but interpretation is avoided, or at least, minimized.

When we reflect on the status of play and the role of interpretation versus understanding within the mainstream psychoanalytic versus humanistic and existential approaches, we are struck by the mutual exclusiveness of the two positions. In psychoanalysis, play is basically seen as a symbolic expression of unconscious conflicts which need to be interpreted in terms of psychoanalytic theory. In humanistic and existential therapies, on the other hand, play is seen as an expression of self and current experiencing which call for therapeutic understanding. The psychoanalytic positions on both play and interpretation are clear but constrained by their particular theoretical frame of reference. This constitutes their strength and their limitation. The humanistic and existential therapies, in comparison, have barely articulated their concept of play which leads to vagueness and an undervaluation of its potential role and meaning.

In my view, the traditional therapeutic approaches have left us with polarized positions on the meaning of play and the role of interpretation versus understanding as if these basic modes of intelligibility are mutually exclusive. This state of affairs has led to an underestimation of the potential value of play, and to unnecessary restricted formulations of understanding and interpretation. This brings us to my thesis, that is, that we are in need of a renewed foundational understanding of the phenomena of play and of interpretation. By turning to the phenomenological hermeneutics of H-G. Gadamer and Paul Ricoeur, I aim to contribute to this task.

In the next section, I will first focus on the phenomenon of play, and subsequently, on the phenomenon of interpretation, before returning to the interpretation of therapeutic play.

The Phenomenon of Play

The quest for a deeper understanding of play extends beyond psychology to other human science disciplines like education, anthropology and sociology which all approach play from their own perspective. The scientific investigation of play in psychology and related disciplines have in common that they offer only partial explanations of an essential universal and foundational phenomenon. In his review of the history of play theories, Scheuerl (1975) came to the same conclusion and laments the resulting fragmented status of the field. Part of the problem lies in the experimental research approach which is analytical and explanatory in nature. In our study of play, we also need complementary research approaches like phenomenology and hermeneutics which are attuned to the unity and the whole-ness of the phenomenon and seek to understand the nature of play itself.

Already in 1938, Huizinga posited that play is a primary and irreducible category of human life and that it underlies and per-vades all expressions of human culture. In a highly insightful and convincing fashion, he revealed how play is part and parcel of our language, art, poetry, myths, and even our religion. For Huizinga, the function of play is exhibiting, showing, imagining something else—something that is often more beautiful, or higher, or more dan-gerous. For example, children like to play that they are a prince, or a father, or a bad witch or a tiger. In their play, they are transposed, which brings them very close to believing that they *are* what they are playing, without totally losing their sense of reality.

Systematic phenomenological studies of play have sought to explicate its essential structure as lived and experienced. In sum-marizing some general phenomenological aspects of play, Scheuerl (1986) concluded that play creates its own world and is free from external constraints. In its effortless to-and-fro movements, it is exciting and attractive in itself because of its own inner tensions, sur-prises and excitements, variations and configurations, all of which absorb the player who is immersed in it. In contrast to the purpose-fulness of daily life, play fulfills itself on a separate figurative or symbolic level. Scheuerl poses a polarity between play and reality within which play has to find its own balance—a formulation which still remains unclear.

From an existential-phenomenological point of view, play is seen as a mode of being-in-the-world which is essential to human life and to childhood in particular. For Buytendijk (1932), the essence of play is revealed in the playful mutual relatedness between the player and his/her play objects. He pointed out: "Play is not only someone playing with something, but also something playing with the player" (90). In adopting Buytendijk's concept of image, Vermeer (1955) sees the playing child as being lured away by the sensopathic appeal of the playthings and by his/her own play images. From her own exten-sive study, she concluded that in the child's play world, a double-meaning structure unfolds between the created play images and reality. For example, a table may be given the imaginary meaning of a house, wooden blocks may serve as a bridge and part of the play-room as a forest in preparation for the unfolding of imaginative play events. The double-meaning relationship leads to an adaptive exchange of expectations and surprise and lends play its magical and exciting character. Although Vermeer's contribution has proven its fruitfulness in the practice of play therapy, the phenomenon of play remains caught in between the player and reality. With both Scheuerl and Vermeer, play has not yet become an autonomous phenomenon in its own right.

With Gadamer's (1982) ontological quest into the mode of being of play, this fascinating and elusive phenomenon is newly illuminated. In *Truth and method*, he sets out to free the concept of play from its overly subjective meaning which it derived initially from Kant and Schiller, and which still pervades the psychological theories of play. Without losing sight of the player, Gadamer emphasizes that the true subject of play is not the subjectivity of the player but play itself. He asserts that play has its own essence and its own thematic horizon. Where phenomenologists emphasized the reciprocal relationship between the player and his play object, Gadamer goes a step further in asserting the *primacy of play* over the player. He writes: "All playing is a being played. The attraction of a game, the fascination it exerts consists precisely in the fact that the game tends to master the players" (95). Play itself draws the players into its spell and keeps them there. This absorption of the players into the play frees them from the burden of reality. The playing and being played involves a sense of freedom and risk. In the medial movements between the player and his/her play object, ever new configurations are created which order the play and lend it its particular structure. Gadamer stresses that the function and the sole purpose of play is to *represent itself*. The players play themselves out and fulfill in it their own heightened self-representation. He further writes that play, like art, is an experience that changes the person experiencing it. Herein he points to the transformative power of play.

Gadamer's work reveals that the phenomena of play and art are closely interwoven and mutually constitutive. He shows that play is the proper artistic event, and that the reality of play is the play of art. Play finds its perfection when it is transformed into the structure of a work of art. For Gadamer, a child's imaginative play also presents us with a transformed structure. Despite its dependence on being played, it is a meaningful whole which rises above the identity of the player and the real world in which the player lives. As a structure, it reveals its own significance and its own truth. Gadamer (1982) writes: "In the representation of play, what *is* emerges. In it is produced and brought to light what otherwise is constantly hidden and withdrawn" (101). The representation in play is therefore revelatory and its essence is recognized as truth.

In my reading, Gadamer's ontological concept of play succeeds in restoring play as an original phenomenon by freeing it from previous subjectivistic and dualistic subject-object conceptions. In Howard's (1982) words, Gadamer has shown that our experience of play "responds to a different synthesis of the role of subject and object, one that does not fracture the givenness of truth as at the same time poetic, normative and productive" (143).

Gadamer's ontological understanding of play throws a new light on its possible role and meaning in play therapy. It poses a direct challenge to the psychoanalytic conception of play as a symbolic expression of the child's unconscious as well as to the humanistic conception of play as self-expression. Gadamer's message is that we lose the essence of play and fail to understand it if we reduce it to subjectivistic explanations. Play as a primary and autonomous phenomenon transcends the subject. As a meaningful whole with its own structure, play is directly representational and revelatory in its own right.

It is further important to note that play from a hermeneutic perspective is seen as a text, and imaginative child play as a text includes a play story. In a therapeutic context, the unfolding play themes are gradually configured into a play narrative which may be developed and extended over a series of sessions till the story has been fully told. Such a play narrative can be shown to resemble the structure of a narrative as conceived by Ricoeur (1984) in that it is a configurational act which is prefigured in reality and refigured by the listener. In this sense, a play narrative can be regarded as a means of discourse.

In brief, we could say that play is an autonomous phenomenon and an imaginative exploration of the child's relationships to him or herself, to others, and to his/her world. Imaginative child play constitutes a novel text that opens up a new perspective on reality.

The key question of the meaning and the interpretation of therapeutic play achieves a new focus and a new horizon in the light of Gadamer's work. In his hermeneutic approach, play and art expressions are seen as texts and subject to the same general guidelines for interpretation. Unfortunately, Gadamer does not provide us with a systematic methodology nor with a practical illustration of his hermeneutic interpretation of play or art. However, in referring to works of art, he stresses that interpretation depends on the possibilities that the work itself possesses and on the compelling quality of its representation. The interpretation should do justice to the binding quality of the work which imposes itself on the interpreter in a special and immediate way. In principle, the same holds true for the interpretation of imaginative play.

Before returning to the problem of the interpretation of play in psychotherapy, we will first look at Gadamer's and Ricoeur's hermeneutic approach to interpretation.

The Phenomenon of Interpretation

In hermeneutics, the concepts of understanding and interpretation are closely related in that interpretation is always based on understanding. In general terms, the hermeneuticist aims to understand and interpret the meaning of written texts. However, Gadamer has extended the object of hermeneutic understanding to the broader field of human communication including verbal dialogue, play and art, and Ricoeur applies his hermeneutic theory to all forms of discourse. This makes their approach particularly relevant to psychotherapists who seek to understand and interpret their client's verbal and non-verbal expressions. Further, a hermeneutic approach to the concepts of understanding and interpretation leads us back to their foundation and helps us to undercut the divisive conceptions that prevail in humanistic versus psychoanalytic therapies.

For Gadamer (1982), understanding and interpretation have a dialogical character and a circular structure. To understand means to grasp and be grasped by the meaning of what the other communicates. Understanding is based upon pre-understanding and rooted in history and tradition. In verbal communication, it takes the form of a conversation in which both partners offer their perspective on a topic or a theme. It is born at the moment that an agreement between the partners is reached through a fusion of their mutual horizons in which the perspectives of the individual partners are transcended. Understanding therefore is not reproductive but productive as it leads to a broader and new perspective. Gadamer sees interpretation as a concrete application of understanding to the specific circumstances of the individual case.

The work of Ricoeur (1976, 1974) leads us to a detailed and comprehensive grasp of the concept of interpretation and the nature of the interpretive process. In his phenomenological hermeneutics, he used to be primarily concerned with the interpretation of words and texts which are characterized by what he calls a surplus of meaning, or multiple levels of meaning, such as symbolic and metaphorical expressions. In this context, he sees interpretation as a work of deciphering the intended hidden meanings, or unfolding levels of meaning implied in the literal meaning of a text, and appropriating this understanding to self-understanding in applying the hermeneutic circle.

In exploring the problem of hidden meanings, Ricoeur (1974) enters into a dialectic with Freud and with Hegel. He points out that Freud's interpretation of the unconscious is regressive towards the subject's past history, and that Hegel's interpretation is progressive in becoming aware of future possibilities. Ricoeur first demythologizes the realism of the Freudian unconscious as well as the idealism of the absolute idea in Hegel. He then concludes that hidden meanings reside in both the unconscious and in the configuration of future possibilities, and that a hermeneutic approach allows them to emerge.

Ricoeur's (1976) general theory of interpretation is based upon his theory of discourse which forms an integral part of it. His theory of discourse includes a set of dialectical polarities of which the dialectic of event and meaning, and of sense and reference are the most important. Discourse is actualized as event and understood as meaning. As an event, it is an act realized temporally and in the present moment. As meaning, it endures and opens up what is said to others. The meaning pole of the dialectic can further be broken down into the dialectic of the utterer's meaning and the utterance meaning. The utterer's meaning is the subjective side and points to what the speaker intends to say. The utterance meaning is the objective side and refers to what he in fact says, or to what the sentence means. The sentence in turn includes the dialectic of sense and reference, or the "what" and the "about what." The sense indicates the ideal meaning of the sentence, and reference points to the relationship of language to the world. Ricoeur sees this dialectic of sense and reference as basic. After all, it is only because we are in the world that we have experiences to express in verbal or nonverbal ways.

In his theory of interpretation, Ricoeur integrates not only the concept of understanding but also that of explanation. He reminds us that in Romanticist hermeneutics, the concepts of understanding and explanation were seen as a dichotomy, a contrasting duality both from an ontological and epistemological point of view. As such, understanding and explanation were regarded as two irreducible modes of intelligibility, which led in turn to two opposing methodologies with explanation applied to the natural sciences and understanding to the human sciences. Interpretation was seen as a derivative of understanding.

Ricoeur points out that a dialectic between understanding and explanation is already present in the dialogical situation. We explain something to someone so that he can understand. Understanding is more directed to the intentional unity of discourse and explanation more to the analytical structure of the text. Ricoeur (1976) writes: ". . . in explanation we ex-plicate or unfold the range of propositions and meanings, whereas in understanding we comprehend or grasp as a whole the chain of partial meanings in one act of synthesis" (72). The term *interpretation* applies to the whole dialectical process that encompasses both understanding and explanation as two different stages in a unique hermeneutic circle. Ricoeur describes this interpretive process as occurring in two phases: first as a move from understanding to explanation, and second as a move from explanation to comprehension. In the first phase, understanding is a guess, a naive grasp of the text as a whole. In the second phase, comprehension is a sophisticated mode of understanding supported by explanatory procedures. Explanation is thus seen as mediating between two stages of understanding.

In the actual interpretation of texts, the dialectic of understanding as guessing and explanation as validation is applied to the meaning of a text as an individualized whole. This guessing is necessary because a text has a plurivocity of meanings as well as potential horizons of meaning that can be actualized in various ways. Next to the meaning of a text in a general way, there may also be multiple meanings expressed in metaphorical and symbolic expressions. Methods for validating guesses in the process of understanding have been worked out by Hirsch (1967). Ricoeur agrees with Hirsch that this type of validation is based on a logic of probability rather then on a logic of empirical verification. It aims to show that one interpretation is more probable than another in the light of what we know, rather than claiming that it is true. The dialectic of guess and validation are circularly related as subjective and objective approaches to a text. It is roughly the counterpart of the dialectic between event and meaning.

In the second phase, the move from explanation to comprehension can be compared to the dialectic of sense and reference. In written texts, the referential function to reality is suspended, and as readers we can imaginatively actualize the potential reference of the text in a new situation. Ricoeur suggests that in this phase, the reading of a written text as an autonomous whole could be subjected to a structural analysis. As such, the text is abstracted from the intention of its author as well as from its world and enclosed in its own interior. Examples would be the structural analysis of myths by Levi-Strauss or of narratives by French structuralists like Barth. A structural analysis could serve as a stage between a naive and a critical interpretation, or a surface and a depth interpretation in the hermeneutic arc between explanation and understanding. In Ricoeur's view, the kind of world opened up by the depth semantics of a text points to its referential function. This implies that the sense of a text is not something hidden but something disclosed. To understand a text is to follow its movement from sense to reference.

The process of interpretation always involves the dialectic of distanciation and appropriation. To appropriate and make one's own what was previously foreign remains the aim of all hermeneutics. The process of distanciation is related to explanation. It enlarges the horizon of the text and its appropriation in turn enlarges the horizon of the reader. Ricoeur compares this process to Gadamer's concept of the fusion of horizons which leads to a new understanding. In Ricoeur's (1976) words: ". . . interpretation is the process by which disclosure of new ways of being—or new forms of life—gives to the subject a new capacity of knowing himself" (94).

The Interpretation of Therapeutic Play

In the light of Gadamer and Ricoeur's concepts of understanding and interpretation, let us return to our subject of the interpretation of therapeutic play. In doing so, we have to remind ourselves that Ricoeur never addressed the interpretation of play as such. However, his hermeneutic approach to the interpretation of symbols, metaphors, narratives and discourse in general is illuminating and relevant for our topic.

In imaginative play, like in symbols and metaphors, we are faced with a surplus of meaning or with multiple levels of meaning which call for deciphering. In play, we find simultaneously literal and play meanings, or real and imagined meanings. Out of the tension inherent in this double-meaning structure, new meanings spring forth and a new play text emerges. For example, for seven-year-old Emily, a blanket draped from a table becomes a slide in a playground where she as mother with her two little girls are going to spend the day. For little Sara, her beloved marble family including mothers with multiple children, become exploding bombs when her own mother leaves their family. In the spirit of Ricoeur, we might say that it is exactly the eclipse of the real world and the reduction of its literal sense that allow new configurations and new meanings to emerge. In play therapy, these new configurations project not only the child's conflicts and difficulties but also his innermost possibilities of new ways of being in the world.

In the practice of play therapy, the therapist can be seen as a participant observer in the child's play. Within the circular structure of the therapeutic dialogue, the therapist and the child play together and both contribute in a unique way to the creation of a play narrative, as well as to its understanding and interpretation. Before any deliberate attempt at interpretation, we should first of all remind ourselves of the transformative power of play in that the play experience itself changes the player who experiences it. The facilitation of imaginative play is already a therapeutic intervention that implies change. Within a hermeneutic perspective, the therapist who aims to understand and interpret the child's play needs to be open, receptive and attentive to its possible horizons of meaning. S/he attempts to grasp and be grasped by the play as a whole to let the play reveal its own representation and its own truth. Interpretation of the child's play expressions in Gadamer's sense are never abstract or generalized statements but always a concretization and application of understanding to the specific circumstances of the individual child and itself subject to the hermeneutic circle. This implies in practice that therapists in their understanding and interpretation of play be open to let their perspective be shaped and modified by the perspective of the child. The fusion of their horizons will lead to an increase in play—and in self-understanding, and consequently, to a forward movement in therapy.

We can delve deeper into the nature of play interpretation by submitting the structure of play to several dialectical polarities analogous to Ricoeur's theory of discourse. Play is clearly actualized as an event and understood as meaning. As an event it is temporal and transitory but as meaning it preserves its identity. Within the play meaning, we find the dialectic of the player's meaning and the play's meaning. The player's meaning represent the subjective side and points to what the child intends to say. The play's meaning represents the objective side of what the play actually says and means. Gadamer's concept of play confirms the importance of this distinction. In traditional psychoanalytic play interpretation, this dialectic is overlooked as only the player's meaning is taken into account which leads to an overly subjective interpretation.

In Ricoeur's first phase of the interpretive process, we recognize the play dialectic of event and meaning. Here we aim to understand the play text as a whole in grasping and synthesizing all its partial meanings. As Ricoeur points out, this kind of understanding involves a guessing because of the multiple meanings involved in specific as well as in general play expressions. Understanding as guessing is counteracted by explanation as validation in which we aim to argue that one interpretation is more probable then another in the light of what the text reveals and what we know of the child's world. In the practice of play interpretation, this phase of the interpretive process emphasizes the importance of listening and openness to grasp and be grasped by the play itself and by the possible implied meanings. This understanding in turn calls for a critical validation.

In the second phase of interpretation, we encounter the important dialectic of sense and reference. How does the play's meaning refer to reality? We might answer this question by applying the understanding arrived at in the first phase of interpretation to the concrete circumstances of the child's real world. However, when it is necessary to open up some depth dimensions of the play text, we can turn to a more sophisticated mode of interpretation by making use of other explanatory models as an intermediary step in the hermeneutic arc between explanation and comprehension. For example, we might apply a psychoanalytic explanatory model to therapeutic play, with the reservation that such explanations will be subjected to the critical questioning involved in the hermeneutic circle of explanation and understanding. We know that in psychoanalysis, the player's meanings are seen as symbolic expressions of unconscious conflicts and interpreted in terms of a fixed set of key signifiers in which all other signifiers are anchored. In his hermeneutic reading of Freud, Ricoeur has shown that the strength and the limitation of psychoanalytic explanation lies in this regressive and reductive interpretation. With this in mind, psychoanalytic explanations could serve as hypotheses that are submitted to a critical circular questioning in view of the therapist's understanding of the meaning of the play text as a whole. Alternatively, the play text could be subjected to a thematic structural analysis. In either case, the deeper meanings revealed by the use of an explanatory model have to be critically appropriated to the overall process of interpretation. The world propositions then opened up by the depth dimension of the play text enables us to move from its sense to its reference.

The foundational dialectic of sense and reference warns us against a premature interpretation of play in terms of reality. We have seen that play is an imaginative and autonomous phenomenon and as such dependent on the suspension of the referential function to reality in order to bring forth a new text. This understanding of play calls first of all for an interpretation of the play world itself in terms of the actions, thoughts and feelings of the play figures, the unfolding themes and the configuration of the play text as a whole. Timely interpretations within the play world will help the child to explore and work through her/his personal and relational problems in an imaginative way. Once the child's play story has been told and understood at this level, its reference to reality can be explored. Play interpretations can then be linked to the child's specific life circumstances which may foster their understanding, acceptance and integration.

/3

Stimulating and Guiding Children's Spontaneous Learning in Play Therapy

Stefan Schmidtchen

In a recent outcome study, my colleagues and I were able to demonstrate that play therapy is effective in reducing behavior disorders and improving personal competence. Particularly so in the areas of psychological and physical fitness, interactional and achievement skills, as well as emotional expressiveness and flexibility (Schmidtchen, Hennies & Acke 1993). Unfortunately, as a result of the generally poor state of play therapy theory, there is a lack of explanatory theory about the origin of these effects within children's play activities. Despite the existence of a certain amount of empirical research on the outcomes and processes of play therapy (Schmidtchen 1986), it seems that the general theoretical assumptions in this area (Schmidtchen 1991) do not adequately fit the various empirical data.

In the following reflections some light will be cast upon this issue. I will try to demonstrate that the mentioned outcome effects are the product of learning processes, especially structured learning processes. With reference to Piagetian structural learning theory, it will be shown that within spontaneous and therapeutically guided play activities children try to assimilate and accommodate their internal structural behavior programs or schemata to the demands of developmental and environmental impacts.

Theoretical Assumptions About Learning Processes
Within Spontaneous Play Activities

In an empirical study (Schmidtchen, Wörmann & Hobrücker 1977) we found that during ninety-five percent of time in play therapy contacts, children are involved in play activities. As shown in the case studies of Buck, Dinter and Vogiatzi (1989), these activities are goal-directed and internally motivated, primarily by the following motives:

- seeking and regulating social contacts and interactions;

- engaging in self-controlled behavior and experiencing being the originator of one's own behavior;

- producing social problems and practicing problem solving behaviors;

- carrying out creative acts in various areas;

- training and experiencing sensory and motor skills.

We found that about eighty percent of children's play activities are energized and directed by these motives. Furthermore, we found that the content of these play activities was *not* determined by specific episodic events from the children's personal life but by general themes such as managing contacts, mastering problems, and experiencing and training one's own abilities. Structurally speaking, the children were engaged in producing, training and improving general programs for autonomously mastering the demands of their internal and external world. They were not primarily engaged in solving specific problems of everyday life.

In explaining these empirical data, we found that they best fit Piaget's theory of schema reproduction and his equilibrium concept of schema modification (Piaget 1969). In this concept, which is perhaps better named a *dis-equilibrium* concept, Piaget formulates theoretical assumptions about the activating process of modification of schema components. He claims that the structural components (or elements) of the basic programs for self and environmental mastery develop themselves to higher forms of adaptation and fit, and that special play activities promote these developmental processes.

In this sense, the learning activities of the child within play therapy can be understood as an internally energized and goal-directed attempt to modify significant components of behavior schemata. These are related to self-development, social competence, solving one's behavior disorders, etc.

Piaget (1969) further proposes in his equilibrium concept that the modifications of the structural elements of schemata are activated through processes of *dissonance* among different schema components. These dissonance processes (called "incongruence" by Rogers 1959) can be activated by modifications of the play goal. For example: children can decide for the first time to play a motor game like "Pedalo," in which they must regulate their equilibrium by means of feet only and thereby alter their former goal of avoiding Pedalo because of supposed motor incompetence.

Other dissonances can be activated through perceptual differences between well-known internal representations of the world and newly perceived aspects. Further, there can be dissonances between the children's personal standards of cognitive and emotional evaluation of behavior components and discrepant standards of the therapist or co-players.

In the theory of structural learning one must distinguish between a semantic and an energetic point of view. In the semantic view one looks for dissonances and their different meanings; in the energetic view one looks for different states of activation. Heckhausen (1969) described these changes between the states with his concept of the *activation circuit*. The enhancement of these different states can be explained by the Piagetian equilibrium versus dis-equilibrium concept. States of equilibrium are states of nonactivation, producing informational redundancy, emotional calmness or boredom. States of disequilibrium are states of activation, producing uncertainty, emotional curiosity or anxiety, frustration, etc. These states are relevant for leaning processes and must be enhanced and guided in therapy. They are the activating force for cognitive and emotional dissonance solving.

Before discussing the implications of these assumptions for therapeutic strategies, let me give a short summary of the major statements of the structural learning theory within play activities:

a. Learning is not seen as a conditioning process in the sense of operant or classical conditioning, but as *structural information processing*, with cognitive and emotional components.

b. The structural components which can be modified by learning are parts of a behavior program called *schema*.

c. The schema is organized in several components, comprising: energizing activities, goal seeking activities, attempts to regulate one's perception, information processing, emotional evaluation, self-supporting and planning activities (Schmidtchen 1991).

d. The activating forces of learning are highly energized states of dis-equilibrium characterized by cognitive and emotional dissonances (or incongruences). The emotional dissonances can manifest themselves as feelings of uncertainty, frustration, anxiety, fear or anger; the cognitive parts of the dissonances can manifest themselves as cognitive problems.

e. It is assumed that people produce states of dis-equilibrium when the emotions of boredom or curiosity are so great that they can no longer endure the state of equilibrium. In this way children also actively construct situations of dissonance, primarily within play activities.

f. The chosen states of dis-equilibrium can be reduced by procedures aimed at overcoming the dissonances. These are called problem solving activities and are the significant learning acts.

g. However, no learning occurs if the reduction of the state of dissonance is a result of regression to earlier behavior programs.

h. To alter this nonlearning behavior it is helpful (1) to understand and reflect the feelings of anxiety which produce the perceptual distortion mechanisms, (2) to encourage a realistic view of dissonances, and (3) to enhance problem solving activities.

Strategies of Therapeutic Guidance in Play Therapy

The strategies of therapeutic guidance are closely related to the assumptions of structural learning theory. However, not only the strategies of modifying inhibition processes in the form of perceptual distortions of dissonant cues are relevant. At least as important are strategies to protect children's spontaneous play against outside disturbance, as well as those which encourage interesting play sequences by using new play ideas or by producing dissonances between old and new schema components. Every activity involving the creation of new schema components or testing the limits of old programs should be encouraged. Thus, therapists should stimulate and reinforce all cognitive and emotional states of dis-equilibrium and make use of their relevance for learning.

As the states of dis-equilibrium are charged with feelings of restlessness, uncertainty or frustration, it is helpful to give the children a feeling of understanding, to share with them the unpleasant sensations by means of empathic partnership and emotional support. Thus, the clients obtain energetic support (some therapists like Orlinsky & Howard 1978, speak of positive power) for their efforts to produce problem solving behavior. This form of empathic partnership for dissonant cognitions and feelings is typical for the client-centered approach. It also occupies a prominent position in the theory of structural learning and the successive guidance of learning activities by therapists.

However, the states of dis-equilibrium and problem production are not the only relevant agents in schema modification. Also relevant are the client's endeavors to gain a new state of equilibrium. In the practice of play therapy, these endeavors are play activities which the client produces to solve problems. These may take the form of (1) concentrating on the dissonant elements of the problem barrier, (2) analyzing the barrier conditions, and (3) defining subgoals to overcome the barrier. Next, the child needs to search for ways and means to overcome the barrier and attain the subgoals. This last search is the most important learning activity in the process of problem solving. It requires cognitive and emotional heuristic abilities involving creativity, reasoning, originality, practical intelligence, endurance and help seeking behavior. It also requires enduring positive self-support.

An Empirical Study of the Structural Learning Process in Play Therapy

In this paragraph, some empirical evidence will be outlined from a recent case study to demonstrate the processes of structural learning and therapeutic guidance within different play sequences. Figures 3.1 and 3.2 introduce the category systems for the analysis of the problem solving behavior of the children and the guidance strategies of the therapists.

Transcripts of all (videotaped) play scenes during therapy contacts formed the basic material for a micro-analysis of play sequences. These transcripts are organized in the following way (as exemplified in figure 3.3). On the left side of the transcript, a precise description is given of the relevant elements of play behaviors and therapeutic guidance behaviors. These behaviors are divided in action sequences defined as semantic relevant elements of the play process. For the child, the sequences reflect definitive aspects of relevant components of the structural learning process (the categories of problem solving

C 1:	non goal-defined behavior
C 2:	definition of a behavior goal and acting out a goal-defined behavior
C 3:	analysis of environmental conditions
C 4:	analysis and selection of means for goal attainment
C 5:	behavior blocking through a barrier
C 6:	search for means to overcome the barrier
C 7.1:	overcoming the barrier in the direction of the desired goal
C 7.2:	failure to overcome the barrier; unsuccessful ending of goal attainment behavior
C 8:	short disruption of goal attainment behavior
C 9:	evaluation of one's own behaviors
C 10:	successful ending of goal attainment behavior
C s+:	positive emotional self-support
C s-:	negative emotional self-support
C 0:	not classifiable

Figure 3.1 Categories of Children's Problem Solving Behavior Within Play Activities

T 1:	marking and specifying relevant conditions for learning
T 2:	interrupting specific activities to support client's perception of learning activities
T 3:	verbally reflecting external behavior
T 4:	empathically reflecting internal behaviors
T 5:	stimulating specific learning activities
T 6:	demonstrating model behaviors
T 7:	giving empathic attention to learning acts
T 8:	encouraging endeavors for self-activity and self-help
T 9:	confronting of external behavior norms
T s+:	giving positive emotional support
T s-:	giving negative emotional support
T u:	not classifiable

Figure 3.2 Categories of Therapeutic Guidance Strategies in Play Therapy

behavior in figure 3.1). In the same way, therapist actions with regard to co-playing and guidance behavior are described and categorized in terms of guidance strategies (figure 3.2).

The right side of the transcript in figure 3.3 is reserved for the classifications (corresponding to those given in figures 3.1 and 3.2) yielded by the structural analysis of play and guidance sequences.

Description of client's (C) and therapist's (T) interactions and behaviors during play	Classification of C and T behavior
1. _____ 2. _____ 3. _____	
10. Client: C tries to pedal without holding on, does not succeed, says "I can't do it" 10. Therapist: says: "sorry," sighs deeply	C 7.1 C 5, C 9 T 7, T s+
11. Client: He tries once again to pedal. Once again he fails. He laughs. 11. Therapist: She laughs too, and says "my god"	C 7.1 C 5, C s+ T 7, T s+

Figure 3.3 Transcript Specifications for Analyzing Play Sequences (Game "Pedalo")

This analysis was carried out by a rater who videotaped and transcribed the child and therapist activities for all play scenes of this therapy. Tables 3.1 and 3.2 show the first results of the structural analysis.

In a first trial, two play scenes were analyzed. These involved the motor game "pedalo" and the building of "a fort." In table 3.1 the frequencies of client's problem solving categories are listed. The most frequent categories were "Recognition of a barrier," "Search for means to overcome the barrier," "Overcoming the barrier," "Evaluation of own behaviors" and "Positive self-support of own behaviors."

Despite the tentative nature of this first analysis, it is evident that the model fits the data and that a sufficient number of typical problem solving categories can be identified. Accordingly, it seems probable that the analysis of other play scenes will yield further support for the theory of structural learning.

Finally, let us have a brief look at the results of the structural analysis of therapeutic guidance behavior (table 3.2). The prominent strategies for supporting the child's learning process are: "Marking and specifying relevant behavior acts," "Stimulating learning activities," "Giving empathic attention," "Confronting external behavior norms," and "Giving positive emotional support" of the child's problem solving endeavors.

In these few examples, it can be seen that the structural analysis of therapeutic guidance behavior yields interesting information concerning the most important strategies for guiding the child's learning abilities within play. The structural analysis of therapist strategies shows that the therapist should concentrate on the relevant learning steps of the child and should give help in the form of specific stimulation of learning endeavors, as well as empathic attention and positive emotional support. All these strategies strengthen the child's spontaneous self-learning activities and are consistent with the Piagetian (1972) and Rogerian (1974) concept of nondirective guidance.

Table 3.1   Results of the Structural Analysis of Client's Problem Solving Behavior (Frequency of Categories in Play Scenes)

CATEGORIES		SCENE 1 PEDALO	SCENE 2 "FORT"
C 1	No goal behavior	1	4
C 2	Definition behavior goal	5	4
C 3	Analysis conditions	1	—
C 4	Selecting means for goal attainment (GA)	7	8
C 5	Recognizes barrier	23 (20%)	15 (17%)
C 6	Searches means to overcome barrier	6	14 (16%)
C 7.1	Overcoming barrier	33 (29%)	18 (20%)
C 7.2	Failure to overcome	2	—
C 8	Disruption of GA behavior	7	4
C 9	Evaluating own behavior	7	11
C 10	Successful end GAB	1	1
C s+	Positive self-support	16 (15%)	1
C s−	Negative self-support	3	7
C 0	Not classifiable	—	2
All categories		112	88

Table 3.2 Results of the Structural Analysis of Therapist Guidance Behavior (Frequency of Categories in Play)

CATEGORIES		SCENE 1 PEDALO	SCENE 2 "FORT"
T 1	Marks/specifies learning conditions	21 (28%)	59 (50%)
T 2	Interrupts to support cl.'s learning activity (LA)	1	1
T 3	Reflects external behavior	7	6
T 4	Reflects internal behavior	5	4
T 5	Stimulates specific LA	4	14 (12%)
T 6	Models behavior	3	1
T 7	Empathic attention to LA	7	15 (13%)
T 8	Encourages self-help	—	3
T 9	Confronting norms	14 (19%)	4
T s+	Gives positive support	11 (15%)	7
T s-	Gives negative support	—	5
T 0	Not classifiable	1	—
All categories		79	119

/4

Processes in Person-Centered Play Therapy

Herbert Goetze

Play therapy has been used for treating maladjusted children for decades. Numerous approaches to play therapy have emerged, like gestalt therapy with children (Oaklander 1978), existential child therapy (Moustakas 1953), non directive play therapy (Axline 1947), etc. One approach of major importance derives from the Rogerian framework and is called "Person-Centered Play Therapy" (PCPT).

PCPT is a preventive, curative and after-curative approach in the tradition and lineage of Carl Rogers and Virginia Axline to promote self-adjustment and self-actualization of the child by using verbal and activating means. PCPT is characterized by certain activities and attitudes of the therapist, by certain child activities and by specific process characteristics (Goetze 1981).

The play therapist in PCPT shows unconditional positive regard and acceptance towards the child, emotional warmth, self-congruence, and a professional helping attitude. Given these conditions the child will explore the environment (play therapy room), play materials (toys), personal resources (therapist, other children) and limits (as introduced by the therapist). The children learn to express their needs by using verbal and nonverbal cues. They will talk about unresolved personal conflicts, using materials to express deeper emotions in a more symbolic form.

The Process in PCPT

PCPT is supposed to be dynamic, thus making it difficult to describe different process characteristics typical for any child. Processes in PCPT, like any learning experience, are never linear. The question arises how these processes can be described, sequenced and structured. Nevertheless, there have been some attempts at classification of the process sequences in PCPT:

- exploration / aggression / constructivity (M. B. Rogers 1972)

- exploration / aggression / creativity and feeling good / anger and conflict with the therapist (Whitee 1975)

- dealing with anxiety / dealing with social conflicts / dealing with reality (Ehlers 1981).

These attempts to describe the process sequences focus on behavioral and emotional changes during therapy. They are descriptive in nature, because they are based upon authors' observations and experiences in therapies of long duration.

Our own approach in sequencing the process is more concept-based. We categorize the process by using terms like *nondirective, client-centered* etc., which are derived from the person-centered psychology framework. In this sense, processes in PCPT are believed to reflect a changing relationship between child and therapist, and it is this changing relationship which makes it necessary to define new tasks, goals and methods for each separate phase. Our proposed sequence model is simultaneously descriptive and normative. It is descriptive insofar as it describes the normal, natural process of PCPT. It is also normative because it prescribes different actions to be taken by the therapist during different therapy stages.

Basically, any relationship during therapy moves from alienation to closeness. We hypothesize a continuous development from distance to closeness which can be conceptualized in a four-stage process. It starts on a *non-personal* level; this leads next to *nondirectivity*; the main part of therapy is *client-centered*; PCPT is finished during the *person-centered stage*.

The stages are delineated and characterized as follows:

- *Non-personal stage.* Child and therapist are not yet well acquainted and do not know much about each other. Consequently, there is still little emotional warmth, empathy, and congruence to be communicated by the therapist. The situation is characterized by personal distance, facade, coolness, unpleasant feelings, use of stereotypes and labels. But at the same time there is a strong wish to leave this unpersonal stage.

- *Non-directive stage.* This new phase is characterized by the well known eight basic therapy principles of Axline (1947): establishing rapport, accepting the child completely, establishing a feeling of permissiveness, recognition and reflection of feelings, maintaining respect for the child, the child leads the way, therapy cannot be hurried, and the value of limitations. It is the therapist's task to establish and nurture a warm climate and a positive relationship as a basis for those experiences the client is going to have at a later stage. The main goals in this stage are: to get to know each other by direct experiences (not relying on diagnostic data), to learn to accept the child unconditionally; and to develop a sense of how to fill out this space of freedom for the expression of personal needs.

- *Client-centered stage.* This stage is "client-centered" in the sense of integrating information and techniques to resolve problems. By now, a firm relationship has been established. Therapist and child know each other well by having interacted and communicated for a longer period of time during the therapy sessions. More is known about the unfulfilled needs and unsolved problems of the client. Thus, the therapeutic tasks become clearer. This implies a growing importance of information from outside (such as can be found, for example, in Individual Educational Plans (IEPs) and other diagnostic information from other sources). At this stage, the danger that these data will overshadow direct experiences in the play room has diminished; rather, by now they may be helpful to enlighten parts of client's personality that are not actualized in therapy. Therapy itself also changes: Axline's principles are still practiced, but it becomes possible to verbalize "beyond" what is articulated by client and to focus more on specific unresolved problems. For this purpose the therapist may find it helpful to use or to "borrow" techniques from other humanistically-oriented approaches for children, such as nonverbal exercises, role play, psychodramatic techniques, gestalt exercises, dreams, drawing, sand play or puppets. The therapist can also use classical or cognitive behavior techniques or relaxation approaches such as progressive muscle relaxation, meditative exercises, guided imagery or autogenic training.

- *Person-centered stage*. The therapist's role in this stage becomes more that of a partner. The reflection of feelings becomes less essential because by now the child has learned how to deal with them. The therapeutic task is to integrate the therapy experiences in "real life" and (eventually) to finish therapy. Because "the world outside" often remains difficult and one has to prepare the child for a confusing world, with little change in the client's home, school and cultural conditions (risky neighborhood, environmental, societal or even global crises), generalization of therapy experiences is essential. To accomplish this, the therapist can use many different means: e.g., trying to "inoculate" the child against discouraging messages, strengthening self-esteem, enabling the child to deal with distress by relaxation exercises to practice at home; using value-approaches, talking-over strategies, exercising self-nurturing strategies. All with the main goal that the clients learn to listen to their "inner voice," to be self-directive, to act independently, and to take care of themselves.

This sequence model has descriptive and normative functions, and reflects the main approaches within the Rogerian person-centered psychology framework. Although this model may seem consistent, logical and socially valid, empirical data to support its notions are still missing.

The case study to be described below may help to demonstrate the existence of the hypothesized phases in PCPT by using qualitative and quantitative analysis. For economical reasons a short-term therapy will be used for the analyses (with a length of fifteen sessions). In such a brief therapy, only the non-directive and the client-centered phase of our model can be expected to emerge, leaving out the last stage of person-centeredness, which can be arrived at only after a longer period of therapy.

It is hypothesized, that after a careful implementation of observational means the predicted time structure (two separate time factors) will emerge, representing the "non-directive" and "client-centered" stages of PCPT.

Method

Sönke was the play therapy child who underwent PCPT with a student therapist under my supervision (Wessels 1982). He was a nine-year-old learning disabled third-grader attending a special school. Important stages in his short life were:

- his parents' divorce shortly after his birth;
- at eight months: delivery into a full care institution;
- at four years: return to his mother's and her boy friend's home; with Stefanie, their new child, just born;
- at six years: referral to a special school for mentally handicapped children;
- at eight years: rescheduled to a special school for learning disabled children.

Both parents were alcoholics, who had many problems in taking care of their children. For instance, they often failed to wake them up early enough to get ready for school. Sönke normally did not talk about his parents, supposedly because they told him not do so. However, he seemed to have a warm and tender relationship with his mother.

In school he showed changing moods. Often he entered the school day somewhat nervous. Usually he was rather withdrawn from his peers and seemed isolated. This, in turn, led to rejection by others which made him suffer even more. From time to time he had outbursts of rage and tantrums without any apparent reason. However, he then was able to get the attention of others, which was not the case when he was behaving "normally."

Sönke felt inferior in terms of body and mental skills, had low self-esteem and seemed easily hurt by others. He had not developed any kind of frustration tolerance. Given these characteristics he did not seem an ideal client for PCPT: he showed socialization and social skill deficits which could not be compensated easily within PCPT, in view of the non-directive basis of this approach. On the other hand, he was a client who might profit quite a bit from PCPT because of his feelings of inadequacy, failure, loneliness and shyness. What we expected from a PCPT with Sönke was that he would become aware of his negative feelings and would work on them, and that he would build a more positive self-esteem in our environment of unconditional positive regard. If he should learn to overcome his intellectual blocks which could be explained partly by a vicious circle, it was even envisaged that after a while his cognitive achievement would improve.

The Therapy

Fifteen sessions were held with Sönke at a special school for slow learners located in a low income area of Hamburg. The therapist was a special teacher, a thirty-two-year-old female, who participated in a training program at the University of Hamburg for treating emotionally handicapped children. She also took part in a supervision group. The therapy room was located in a quiet area of the school building and was equipped with play therapy room essentials: dolls, blocks, doll's house, sand tray, musical instruments, etc.

Data Sampling and Analysis

All sessions were videotaped. Through unstructured and structured behavior observation and ratings qualitative and quantitative data were gathered which allowed description of Sönke's PCPT. A system of play observation categories was used which previously had proven its relevance for play therapy settings (see table 4.1 below). The categories covered different kinds of play activity, interactional activities as well as verbal behavior. For characteristics not accessible to observation (such as emotions like fear, anger, joy, sadness) rating scales were used, to be rated by experts.

The first data analysis was qualitative-descriptive to clarify what problems were met by Sönke in PCPT, and what happened during the PCPT process. The second part of our analysis was quantitative: data from each session were used in a factor analysis. It is hoped that a structure of two separate time factors will emerge, representing the first (non-directive) and second (client-centered) part of therapy. Next, separate categories were examined to uncover significant differences in Sönke's behavior over the two phases of therapy.

Results

Sönke's play therapy proved to be of great benefit for him, at home as well as in school. After therapy, his teachers rated him significantly lower (i.e., more positive) on important dimensions like emotional lability, social anxiety, low task behavior, negative social behavior. On the MVL (a test instrument sensitive for behavior changes through play therapy) his score after therapy was significantly better. Overall, Sönke's PCPT was rated as very successful. The positive outcome make this therapy a perfect subject for the process analysis we had in mind.

Qualitative Analysis

In this paragraph Sönke's activities during fifteen sessions are summarized. Comments will be added with regard to background influences from outside therapy.

Session 1.   Sönke explores the environment, enjoys the materials, likes to drink the juice we offer him.

Session 2.   Sönke wants to open the room with the key by himself. He explores further what he can do here. He decides to play with the toy cars: he plays accidents: the cars fall down and crash.

Sessions 3-4. Continues to play with cars (again many accidents)

Session 5.   This time cars are buried into the sand. For the first time he tells us something, still very cautious, about his parents: "Papa and Mama sometimes quarrel a lot—sometimes twice for us."

Session 6.   Again Sönke plays car accident games. He talks briefly about his school problems. He molds plasticine and throws the plasticine through the room and into the water. He shows anger while doing that. He jumps on it and cries: "Now you get it! Now you see what you get for doing this. You get killed, at once." He does not say whom he is talking about. But he appears to be relaxed after that game. At the end of the sessions Sönke says: "Next time you tell what we are going to play."

After this session the supervision group in which the therapist takes part discussed his case. They proposed to use a metaphor: to read to Sönke a German fairy tale about a man as big as a thumb.

Session 7.   The fairy tale is read to him. For fifteen minutes Sönke listens extremely attentive. However, he does not talk about what he just heard but continues with his car accident game, this time a little more cautious.

Next, there was a four-week break because of illness.

Session 8.   Sönke starts quite distantly, does not touch the therapist, does not really greet her. He seems to be nervous about what may be reflected back to him about his play. When the therapist reflects his feelings, he says: "Shut up, if you don't want to get smacked." Or: "Of course, what did *you* think?" He repeats again the accident game, this time more violently.

Incidentally, one toy car breaks down. He is horrified and tries to repair it. He then goes on to play with Play Mobile figures: a war is going on between two parties and lasts until everybody is dead.

An interim session with Sönke's teacher revealed that keys had been stolen in class, with Sönke as the main suspect. He often seemed to take away keys. The supervision group discussed how this problem could be met in therapy since Sönke did not openly talk about it or admit his guilt. It was recognized that keys fascinated him: he often opened the therapist's car with the key, he liked to open the play room with the keys. So the question was: how to meet this key need in a way that would be really satisfactory to him? A flooding procedure was proposed and put into action: the whole room was filled up with old keys.

Session 9. Sönke is clearly embarrassed to see all those keys. Then he gets more and more excited, jumps around, and tries the keys on the doors. He washes them, counts and arranges them in a neat order. Unexpectedly, he starts talking: that he usually takes away keys from the bags of other kids during break time. The therapists listens attentively. Next, he talks about his natural father: "I want to call him. I'm going to blame him. I'm going to tell him that my name is different from his now. He does not know that yet . . . I am glad to have a different name from his. . . . You know what he did? He took away all our money, drove away and drank." At the end of this session he mentions that soon it will be his birthday and that he wants a birthday surprise the next time.

Session 10. This time Sönke does not want to open the room with the key. The small surprise box the therapist brought him, with a castle to fold, does not interest him much. Apparently he is thinking about his school problems. He is suspected to have stolen the purse with keys and money of a schoolmate, and he is very depressed about this. After a while he seems to be more relaxed, and he begins to enjoy the folding task. While working, he talks about his parents, how they blame him and that they drink a lot. He and his sister are never going to marry, they will look for their own apartment instead and live there, so they will be rid of their parents.

Session 11. Sönke loves to do the folding of the castle. While learning how to do it, he gets more self-confident and shows positive self-talk like: "I do it this way" or "Good, I did it." He also briefly comments on his parents: "If they continue to behave like this, my sister and I will run away and call our aunt to take us away. Sometimes they drink so much that they don't know where they had put the keys." Therapist: "And this happens quite often that they drink too much?" "Yes, too much." After this comment Sönke jumps on the therapist's lap and kisses her.

Session 12. Colors his castle and says: "If you look at my mother, you know, she has quite a pretty face. But, I don't like to mention it, she was so drunk again, when we were invited last week." He then remembers the time at the beginning of therapy when the therapist visited his house: "When you entered our apartment, things looked pretty badly, didn't they? My home sometimes looks like a jungle. Our neighbors, they have a nicer apartment." At the end of this session he accidentally sees the keys and says: "Those keys, you can take them to the wreckers."

Session 13. His castle is fixed, and he jumps though the room with joy. He asks if he can bring his sister.

Session 14. He makes a play around the castle, a war with play mobile figures.

Session 15. This is the last session. Sönke brings his sister; they play together, while he is explaining everything in the playroom to her. Then they play hide-and-seek. At the end he is allowed to take the castle home. He is so much excited about this that it is easy to say goodbye to the therapist.

To summarize. During sessions 1-6, the car accident games were most important. In session 7, the fairy tale was told to him, and in the next session he showed his aggression more openly. During sessions 9-15, the keys were introduced, and his problems with his parents were worked through.

Quantitative Analysis

A quantitative analysis was carried out to find out whether two different therapy stages could be distinguished more objectively, without the bias that may have crept into the subjective judgments of the qualitative analysis. One method to find out about different time dimensions is a factor analysis across a continuum of time samples. Factor analysis was also useful in this case because we dealt with a large amount of descriptive variables, while we would like to reduce that amount. In our case, observational and rating data from sessions 1-15 (the total sample) were intercorrelated.

With the data from Sönke's PCPT across sessions, a factor analysis was executed. The variables were the fifteen sessions as time points of measurement; the behavior categories served as "subjects" in the usual sense of factor analysis.

As mentioned above, the data used for our factor analysis were derived from different sources:

- Rating scales used after each session (emotions, play behavior, other activities, relationship with therapist, verbal behavior),

- The Borke observation categories (Borke 1947),

- Ratings of therapist's behavior,

- Self ratings of child and therapist.

The unrotated solution produced two factors with eigen-values over 1, which together explain 81.4 percent of variance. The rotated solution is shown in table 4.1, and graphically in figure 4.1. It can be seen that sessions 10-14 define one factor: factor 1 loadings are quite high, and factor 2 loadings are low. Factor 2 is defined by variables (sessions) 1, 2, 3, 5 and 6. The sessions 4, 7, 8, 9 and 15 are not well identified by either factor. The graph demonstrates clearly that sessions 10-14 have a great deal in common and build a time cluster. Sessions 1-6 vary considerably more, but form also a cluster.

So it can be argued that Sönke's therapy consisted of two different therapy stages: Sessions 1-6 (with the exception of 4) and ses-

Table 4.1 Factor Loadings on the Two Factors

SESSION	FACTOR 1	FACTOR 2	COMMUNALITY
01	0,291	<u>0,807</u>	0,73547
02	0,362	<u>0,819</u>	0,80193
03	0,356	<u>0,874</u>	0,89070
04	<u>0,681</u>	0,554	0,77024
05	0,535	<u>0,746</u>	0,84253
06	0,538	<u>0,678</u>	0,86549
07	0,627	0,606	0,75937
08	0,549	0,549	0,60313
09	0,542	0,579	0,62843
10	<u>0,748</u>	0,462	0,77337
11	<u>0,820</u>	0,437	0,84608
12	<u>0,891</u>	0,263	0,86293
13	<u>0,851</u>	0,368	0,85998
14	<u>0,731</u>	0,459	0,74473
15	0,613	0,682	0,84014

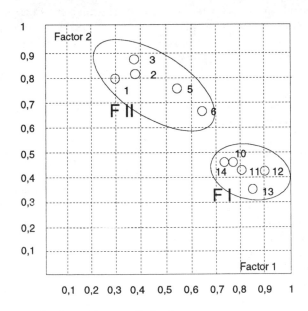

Figure 4.1 The Two-Factor Solution

sions 10-14. The middle part of therapy (sessions 7-9) does not fit into this structure and may perhaps be interpreted as a transition stage preparing Sönke for new experiences still to be made. Session 15 was different since it was the last therapy hour, and had a quite different structure since he played with his sister.

With the data from our qualitative analysis, this formal structure can be filled by therapy contents: during sessions 1-6 Sönke played car accident games, while in sessions 9-14 Sönke's problems with keys and with his parents were worked through.

There is still the question about the internal validity of the stage concept: if two different stages exist on an abstract level, behavior variables on a concrete level should differ significantly between these time phases. To investigate these differences, behavioral data from the first 6 sessions and the last 6 sessions were compared. Table 4.2 reveals that significant differences were found between the two stages on many behavior variables, on play behavior, on the variety of interaction with the therapist, and on verbalizations. Sönke was also rated more self-congruent, warmer and much better able to express emotions.

Discussion

Our research question was whether in the presented case the existence of two hypothesized phases of PCPT could be demonstrated. Cautiously, from our qualitative descriptions and quantitative analysis of behavior observations and ratings, we may conclude that this is indeed the case. By applying factor-analysis, two different clusters of sessions could be shown to exist in this example of play therapy. The t-tests revealed many differences on important variables between these two clusters. These could also be filled qualitatively by the content analysis of Sönke's therapy sessions.

While the first stage fitted in pretty well with Axline's nondirective principles, the second stage was initiated by Sönke's wish that the therapist should introduce something new. This second part differed from the first because of additional therapist stimulation directed towards the client's problems. While the first part of therapy was characterized by listening and accompanying Sönke's games ("car hitting"), the last part revealed a different quality. Sönke's command to the therapist to direct play activities meant a turning point in his therapy, allowing the therapist to stimulate more specifically by introducing materials and suggestions which seemed relevant to Sönke's problems.

Table 4.2 Differences on Behavioral Scores Between Therapy Stages (t-test)

	SCORE STAGE 1	SCORE STAGE 2	T	P
Functional games	15.3	8.6	3.77	.01
Games of "Gestaltung"	6.0	15	2.73	.025
Simple role play	5.61	3.3	2.73	.025
Complex role play				n.s.
Rule games				n.s.
Passivity	5.8	9.5	3.64	.01
Exploratory behavior	3.5	2	1.54	.10
Free movements	0.8	0.5	1.45	.10
Non-intended use of materials	2.5	0	1.74	.10
Testing out the limits				n.s.
Provocative behavior				n.s.
No contact with therapist	11.2	6.8	1.89	.10
Reactions to therapist's comments	4.2	7.7	2.85	.025
Eye contact with therapist	4.3	7.3	1.79	.10
Asking for information; comments	9.7	11.7	2.47	.05
Asking for directions				n.s.
Giving directions	2.2	1.4	2.78	.025
Asking questions about himself	0	2.2	1.56	.10
Asking questions about therapist				n.s.
Letting therapist join the game				n.s.
Body contact with therapist	1	1.5	3.39	.01
Grasps therapist's stimulation				n.s.
Comments on therapist's activities				n.s.
Comments on therapist's verbalizations				n.s.
Comments on therapist's person				n.s.
No comments	11.3	7.5	2.18	.05
Verbalizations about things	2.3	15	4.34	.025
Verbalizations about own person	2.7	7.2	3.19	.025
Verbalization about self				n.s.
Verbalization about therapy setting	6.2	3.3	2.75	.025
Comments on own activities	17.7	6.3	3.6	.01

(continued on next page)

Table 4.2 *(continued)*

	SCORE STAGE 1	SCORE STAGE 2	T	P
Being with-it	5.4	6.7	3.3	.01
Verbalization—general	4.4	6	5.86	.005
Non-directive behavior	5.8	3.6	4.29	.005
Stimulation	1	2.5	4.83	.005
Warmth	4.9	5.2	5.38	.005
Self-congruence	5.4	6.5	4.92	.005
Self-exploration	1.3	1.2	1.45	.10
Play behavior	2.4	6	6.16	.005
"Session was positive"				n.s.
General rating of child's mood	16.2	18	2.84	.025
Change of play center				n.s.
Change of play activities	7.2	6.3	2.78	.025
General rating of child				n.s.
Emotions	5.5	6.4	10.23	.0005
Curiosity about play room	5.2	2.5	1.92	.10
Statements and comments about play	29.8	20.3	2.17	.05
Hints about aggressive content	8	6.5	2.97	.025
Talks about other issues while playing	0.5	2.2	2.14	.05

Referring to the proposed sequence model of PCPT we feel justified in attaching the labels "non-directive" and "client-centered" on the analyzed time clusters. Of course, results from this case study cannot be overgeneralized by stating that these phases always exist in PCPT reality. However, our procedure is open to further replication with other clients, therapists and settings.

5

Games of Complexity: Reflections on Play Structure and Play Intervention

Gerd E. Schäfer

Play is a complex phenomenon. The factors that contribute to play include cognitive thought, emotional processes, cultural rituals, social patterns, steps in the development of moral awareness, sense experiences, and aesthetic evaluation.

It is possible to approach the complex nature of play in either of two ways. First, one can attempt to isolate the specific factors in play and, once they have been identified, to re-assemble them. The second method is to try to identify a grammar within which the specific factors function. The first approach may well show complexity but fails to explain how this complexity functions. For this reason I concentrate on the second approach.

I contend that one can only achieve a satisfactory grammar of play when one is aware of the specific subjective processes involved in understanding play. Therefore, I attach great importance to a psychoanalytical approach, in which the grammar of play events can be understood against a background of ontogenetic development.

Play as a Healing Process in Psychoanalysis

If we summarize the work that has so far been done on the "healing forces in children's play" by Zulliger (1965, 1966, 1970), Bittner (1976), Schäfer (1979, 1980), Fatke (1980) or Datler (1985), one is struck first of all by the functionalism of the approach. Most of these authors treat play merely as an expression of internal psychological conflicts, thus placing it in the framework of ontogenetic paths of development. Traditionally, psychoanalytic play therapy uses play under two headings: (1) First, it may be employed as a substitute for free association, of which young children are still incapable. In this case it is a diagnostic technique for identifying the current state of the child's pathology. (2) Secondly, it can be used as a tool for intervening therapeutically in the child's psychological knots.

This traditional perspective considers therapeutic play as operating predominantly on three levels: the id level, the ego level, and the level of object relations. The therapeutic effects on the id level are due to the fact that, besides cognitive operations, there is a lot of room for primary process-like operations. Thus communication develops on an unconscious level without being suppressed. On the ego level, the healing process can be helped along because in play one can express and foster nonrational, sense-oriented and aesthetic sensitivity. In play all these may be incorporated in meaningful communication, conflicts may be encountered openly and solutions sought, with a minimum of repression. On the level of object relations, new corrective experiences can be gathered in the course of play, with the therapist as "new object" (Freud 1965).

To my mind, the healing function of play is not due to just one of those factors holding a secret cure. Rather, I would suggest that this healing function occurs by using the whole spectrum of ways in which experience can be gathered, by id, ego and object relations, but also by physical, sensual, aesthetic, imaginative and finally analytical thinking.

While traditional psychoanalysis has added several dimensions to our understanding of how complex play is, I feel it has not added much to our knowledge about how this complexity functions. In particular, it has largely failed to consider play as a feature of a healthy psyche. Engaging in play is characteristic of the child that has succeeded in finding a balance between itself and its surroundings, while very often a child whose psyche is not in a healthy state must first learn how to play. More psychoanalytic research is needed on this relationship between play and mental health. Here, Winnicott shows us a way.

Winnicott's Theory of the Intermediate Area

Winnicott's place in the psychoanalytic tradition of child therapy is (in his own words) that of a transitional figure, between those who think of play as a method of discovering unconscious processes (play as a substitute for free association), and those who consider play as therapeutic and educational in itself. Thus he is not only interested in whether play gives access to unconscious psychical phenomena, but rather in how play deals with the unconscious, the imagination and external reality all at the same time. To this problem he addresses his "theory of the intermediate area":

> Of every individual who has reached the stage of being a unit with a limiting membrane, an outside and an inside, it can be said that there is an *inner reality* to that individual, an inner world that can be rich or poor and can be at peace or in a state of war. This helps, but is it enough?
>
> My claim is that if there is a need for this double statement, there is also need for a triple one: the third part of the life of a human being, a part that we cannot ignore, is an *intermediate area of experiencing*, to which inner reality and external life both contribute. It is an area that is not challenged, because no claim is made on its behalf except that it shall exist as a resting place for the individual engaged in the perpetual human task of keeping inner and outer reality separated yet interrelated. (Winnicott 1971, 2)

While this is not the place to discuss in detail Winnicott's theory of what he calls the "intermediate area" or "potential space," I should like to point out two important features of this theory. First, the "intermediate area" forms a structure a person can employ at any time during the entire course of his/her life. Secondly, this area is the result of a successful separation process, completed in early childhood. In this process, the child learns to distinguish between itself and its nurturing or facilitating environment: its "good-enough mother." As the child develops, this area can differentiate further. It then changes from play to cultural experience.

Return to Ego-centeredness

Following on from Winnicott, considering play as a therapeutic and educational process makes it necessary to get away from a purely linear concept of child development. Successful cognitive development enables the individual to curb his/her egoistic needs in the face of demands made by reality, and to come to terms with the material and personal object world. This process of differentiation tries to achieve a clear distinction between the subject and the world around it. It also enables the cognitive equipment to perform its task of understanding and processing external reality with as little egoistic interference as possible. If, during adulthood, ego-centered considerations again start to play a part in these cognitive functions, this must be seen as a faulty method of processing reality, as a relapse into earlier and more childish forms of thinking.

In contrast to this, Winnicott's approach would see a necessity for retaining at least some aspects of what might be referred to as a "childlike" way of thinking. Winnicott holds the view that adults too have a need for an area in which subject and object need not be kept quite separate. It is in this intermediate area that play operates. This means that the preliminary steps in the developmental process are not simply deposited in the individual as a sort of residue that has been outgrown. Instead, they are retained, with their own function to fulfill, particularly in processes that resemble play, such as creativity and cultural activities.

A related view has been expressed by Noy (1969, 1973, 1978, 1979), who based his thinking on the concept of two levels of mental functioning. Psychoanalysis, as is well known, distinguishes primary and secondary process. The primary process, which is closely related to the unconscious, has a grammar which follows that of dreams. The secondary process is comparable to cognitive thinking. Noy saw it as the task of the secondary process to experience external reality, independent of the subject. The task of the primary process, on the other hand, is to register and process the personal meaning which this external reality has for the individual subject.

For this last task to be performed, however, an intermediate area is needed, where the internal and external worlds are not kept separate, but where they are free to interact. Play is one of the areas in which relations with this early ontogenetic heritage are maintained, enabling it to be constantly integrated in the developing person.

From this we derive a first principle to guide any intervention in play. Intervention should be structured in such a way that it is attuned to and interacts with the nonrational as well as the rational component in play. If one were to assess play purely according to criteria derived from the principle of reality, then the mediating structure of play would be infringed or even negated.

On the Dialectics of Intermediate Processes

There are two phenomena in a child's relations with its caregiver (mother) which enable it to establish the intermediate "play space."

On the one hand, the good-enough experiences the child had with its first caregiver (normally the mother) are incorporated in play and in everything to do with play. The transitional object, and later games and toys, represent this experience of the closely knit mother-child relationship. Because the child had a good experience of being held by mother, it is capable to re-experience this with an object, such as a toy. To that extent, a toy is a substitute for the good mother.

However, transitional objects and play also require a certain distance. The periodical absence of the mother is also important. And so is her return, or her delayed return. Only when a child experiences a "bearable lack" can it develop wishes or generate illusions. Where the child does not experience this lack, or where the mother is overprotective, illusion becomes hallucination and can no longer be distinguished from reality. A state of "as if" can only develop in this dialectic of the familiar within the unfamiliar on the one hand (the idealized good mother in a reality which supplies new surroundings) and a bearable distance, absence or even loss on the other hand (which enables the exploration of new worlds which are not the mother). This state of "as if" has often been described as characteristic of play.

If it is true, then, that the ontogenetic development of a transitional region as described serves as the basic pattern according to which play develops later on, play processes should occur in situations that obey the dialectic of familiarity and a bridgeable absence. Thus, play can only come into its own as part of the healing process when, either from an internal source (from within the child) or from an external source (the therapist), there is the assurance that illusion can govern part of the external world. On the other hand, empathy must not be too close, so as not to impede the experience of absence which is essential for the process of illusion to get under way.[1] Any intervention must be in accordance with this dialectic of basic familiarity and independent distance.

A Path Through Formlessness

In Winnicott's view the newborn infant cannot be considered independently of its caregiver (mother), but exists in a state of relative formlessness, out of which the subject must gradually find its form. The child needs an adequately nurturing and facilitating environment in order to maintain the state of formlessness (not to be confused with inactivity), until it can derive its subjective form through a process of demarcation, in interaction with its environment. If the child is exposed to frequent intervention and in this way kept under constant pressure to react, its inner experiences (which are still relatively unformed) cannot be easily synchronized with external reality. In the face of this constant pressure to react, it is even possible that a "false self" (Winnicott 1965a, 1965b) will form. Such a false self is not synchronized with the internal experience, but instead forms a protective screen, depriving the inner self of the chance to devise its own structures.

When an intermediate area has been established with reasonable success, in the process of separation between mother and child, this does not simply mean that all problems are over. The newly formed structures must be gradually incorporated in the field of competence of the child. In this way, the intermediate area remains accessible for the child (and, later, for the adult). I believe that the freedom of play depends on being able to reach that state where things are not definitely shaped, which corresponds to the stage in early childhood when the child has not achieved a final form for itself. As far as the healing process is concerned, this would mean that the disturbed person must find some way back to this state of formlessness, in order to form oneself anew.

In this view, play may contribute to the healing process, not because it deliberately provides lessons and experiences, but rather because it supplies that safe area, protected from encroachments and from the necessity to react. To engage in play is to submerge oneself temporarily into a region where things, as well as the subject itself, have not taken their final shape or been all thought through. This provides the subject with a new chance to reintegrate itself.

Determining the Model for Self-development

So far, we have dealt with play structures as if they were equivalent with developmental structures. What does development mean in this context? Development is understood here as a process of differentiation. It derives from relatively simple models which are probably biological in origin, and becomes more and more differentiated as development progresses, linking up the original simple structures. This results in a self with a networklike structure. This view implies the following:

1. One stage of development does not succeed and replace another. Instead, the network of related structures becomes more and more complex as development progresses.

2. When developments occur without emphatic contextual limits, the child can, at any specific point in life, refer back to the experience-structures of its life so far and employ them in the effort to solve a present problem.

3. If this is applied to the separation processes discussed above, it is clear that the structures acquired during that process can be employed in other separation situations occurring later in life. Thus, "ego-centeredness" and the dialectic of familiarity and strangeness, are not only processes of early childhood when relations with objects are established. In fact, they can recur whenever the question of object relations arises.

4. Developmental structures can, therefore, be described as highly complex patterns, in which past and present tasks connect to one another, in a self-organizing process.

5. The exact sciences postulate two different kinds of order: stable order and unstable order. Stable forms of order can be characterized by linear "if-then" propositions. Newtonian physics is an example of this kind of order. Examples of the unstable order are mainly found in multidimensional networks of relationships which are not in a state of equilibrium. In this state even very slight changes in the original conditions can lead to wide-ranging, quite unpredictable results. This unstable order can only be maintained if provided with a constant supply of energy. Most processes concerned with living appear to take this unstable order. These structures, then, are highly complex dynamic models which organize themselves into systems which persist in a state of unstable equilibrium.

From this view on development, consequences may be drawn for intervention in play. According to this view, although it is possible to influence the process of play, it is not possible to control it. This would be prevented by the process of self-organization and by the dynamic of unstable equilibrium. It would only be possible to control play if the complexity of the process could be reduced. Then, perhaps, the different points of influence might become clearly visible and individually controllable. However, even if this were possible, it would negate the specific *play* element in play.

Therefore, when intervening in play, one must regard the child as an autonomous subject, to whom one can offer something, but whom one cannot really influence. During play, the subject itself controls the models of how the self will develop in an open process. Here, an interesting distinction emerges between play as part of a healing process and the play of nondistressed children. When play is engaged in as part of the healing process, the subject requires some external support in order to get the process under way, and to deal with steps that might be too painful otherwise. In contrast, a relatively healthy ego is able to deal with this process by itself.

The Process of Complexity

Complexity can only occur as *process*. Only by engaging in a motion which embraces both conscious and unconscious structures (including those that have been repressed) can the various forms of experiences be integrated into subjective programs for action. This motion consists of repeatedly pursuing a chain of developmental steps, in the course of which the individual is brought out of a state of relative formlessness into an unstable order. This "regressive" process establishes the links of a network which connects the cognitive grasp of reality to the biographical, emotional, sensual and aesthetic structures. If we see the beginning of the individual's existence as proceeding out of the unity of psyche and soma, as Winnicott does, this suggests that the de-differentiation process may well extend (unconsciously, of course) into the sphere of psychosomatic processes and thus into the sphere of physical experience processes.

If the point of view proposed here is accepted, play always presents a challenge:

1. to generate complexity;

2. to engage in processes in which each subject organizes itself;

3. to avoid re-establishing balance where there is disequilibrium;

4. to support disequilibrium or even to bring it about as long as it remains bearable for the player(s).

In play, one can abandon oneself freely to this process of internal and external complexity. It protects one from the encroachments of reality and gives time to make repeated attempts to gradually approach one's own "core."

6

Imagery Techniques in
Play Therapy with Children

Dorothy G. Singer

Imagery-laden thought and its symbolic language is one of the human being's greatest gifts. But just as our thoughts can offer us solace and joy, our thoughts can also cause us pain and grief and become a curse. One task of the psychotherapist is to try and understand the hidden meanings that weave their way through a client's private thoughts and experiences. Sometimes, this jumble of images, perceptions, fantasies and memories, when tapped and brought to the surface through various techniques, can be fruitful in helping a client make connections between imagination and reality. Although many such techniques utilizing imagery approaches have been attempted with adults, there has been increasing interest in their application to young children. Those of us who engage in standard methods of play therapy realize that much of what we do is interpretation of the symbolic play of our clients who rely on imagery in their make-believe play. We see and hear these images come to life as children utilize materials, dress-up, change their voices and adopt the mannerisms or movements of the characters they become. A major component then of play therapy is the capacity of young children to actually experience symbolic or imagery-laden thought. As Hellendoorn (1988, 45) remarks: "In imagery interaction the therapist actively helps the child (a) to fully develop his or her own play themes, and (b) to work through those play themes, differentiating and shading them, and gradually influencing them in more desirable directions."

Definitions of Imagery

What do we mean by imagery? Images appear to be associated with the right hemisphere of the brain and its functions which include the visual and auditory imagery, spatial representation, pure melodic thought, fantasy and emotional components of ongoing thought (Singer & Pope 1978). Components of imagery such as kinesthetic/sensory, perceptual or structural, affective and cognitive, may all play a role in the forms of imagery expression. Thus in therapy, images can be described by words, through art forms, and through movement and dance.

Horowitz (1978) expanded on Bruner's earlier conceptualization of images (1964) stating that modes available for conscious expression are the enactive, image and lexical representations. Similar to Bruner's theory, enactive representation is based on memories of motor actions and the retention of imitative behavior of another person's actions. Enactive thought is thinking in action with concomitant sensing of different muscle groups that may signify covert trial actions. Both skeletal musculature and visceral neuromusculature are involved. Image representations are based on perceptions, memories, fantasies and are especially effective in yielding information about spatial relationships and forms. Emotional responses may be incorporated into images. When we inhibit or block image formation, the associated emotions may also be delayed. Finally, the lexical mode is characterized by Horowitz as the rational one dealing with abstraction and conceptualization. According to him, the enactive and image modes interact with the lexical mode, but with slight differences. While the lexical mode is a more organized, sequential method of representation, visual images process information simultaneously. Images also change over time and can become less vivid and less emotionally intense. Traumatic images, however, may remain quite vivid over a prolonged period of time. As a result, in therapy it may be difficult to label accurately or to categorize such images because of the intensity of the accompanying emotion.

Development Differences in Imagery

During the preoperational stage, ages two to three, some make-believe play develops, and within such play we see the rudimentary origins of imagery, reaching its peak at ages four to six when symbolic play (the substitution of objects for real things or persons) occurs with greater frequency (Piaget 1962). Now, the child's mental images are active and internalized imitation, with a close relationship existing among mental image, imitative gesture and graphic image (Piaget & Inhelder 1971). In addition to language, children now can represent their internal images through drawing or even movement such as imitating various animals or gestures of people.

In the stage of concrete operations, ages seven to twelve, children gradually move away from make-believe play to more games with rules, but they can also manipulate images more easily, and can use images for anticipatory ends. Language skills increase and for some children graphic expression is a favored mode. From ages twelve on, (the stage of formal operations), children can now "think about thoughts" with daydreaming playing an increasingly important role, especially during adolescence (Singer & Singer 1990). The images adolescents use revolve around future plans and the exploration of different roles in society. In this last stage, as in adulthood, individuals are processing external information into their private streams of thought.

Applications of Imagery Techniques in Psychotherapy with Children

Material that may be unavailable to children through the lexical system may emerge through images or through the enactive systems (see above for definitions). One major function of imagery techniques in psychotherapy is that it permits communication between child and therapist that may be blocked through verbal descriptions without this prior imagery release.

Before I turn to the different techniques that utilize imagery, some cautions must be considered. Rosenstiel and Scott (1977) outline four major points:

> (1) imagery scenes must be geared to the cognitive abilities of the child. Children aged six to eight can use complex images, while younger children may follow more simple directions such as thinking "fun" or sad thoughts; (2) the therapist should include children's naturally-occurring imagery as a basis for therapy. The child will be more interested if scenes are familiar and more real. Hypnosis and emotive imagery, for example, are especially adaptable to children's fantasies. Using familiar characters, superheroes, fairy tale characters, enables a child to image himself in settings with these "friends"; (3) attention to non-verbal cues such as flushing of the skin, increased

body movements, muscular tension, breathing patterns, and changes in facial expressions will enable the therapist to identify anxiety provoking images and when the child's anxiety diminishes; and finally, (4) attention should be paid to the descriptions and emotions aroused by an imaged scene or event. Questions should be asked about each segment of an image in order to assess the degree of comfort or discomfort.

The question of the ability of young children to use imagery effectively in treatment is still open to research. Studies indicate that five and six-year-olds do not use mental imagery in recall as well as seven and eight-year-olds (Purkel & Bornstein 1980). Lazarus and Abramovitz (1962) support the Rosenstiel and Scott (1977) argument that if children imagine themselves in the company of a favorite hero while encountering a difficult event, the visualization process is more meaningful.

Finally, the notion of narrative enters into the child's ability to translate the image into a story or script. The narrative account reflects the child's experience of historical truth that is colored by highly personal meanings. When images are produced and then reported to the therapist, the distortions, omissions, elaborations, or fragmentations are influenced by unconscious motives and feelings. Logical sequence may disappear as themes and fantasies of conflict and defense are visualized and verbalized.

Primary process material will appear in imagery as it does in spontaneous play, and the therapist must be able to make "the critical transition from assessment to treatment . . . creating and maintaining the necessary therapeutic environment to enhance and cultivate the unfolding of the child's narrative account" (Brandell 1988, 248-249).

Various methods utilizing imagery techniques have been used successfully with young children such as relaxation therapy, systematic desensitization, cognitive therapy, guided affective imagery, mind play techniques, art therapy and movement/drama therapy. For the purposes of this paper I will focus on those methods that I have found most beneficial with my clients and that also seem to be valuable on the basis of clinical and research literature.

Systematic Desensitization

A procedure that evolved from classical conditioning is systematic desensitization (Wolpe 1958). This method assumes that the imagined stimulus matches the real stimulus to such an extent that equivalent anxiety is induced. The belief underlying this form of treatment is that certain cues in the child's environment trigger anxiety or fear reactions. The fear can be reduced by conditioning an alternative response to stimuli or cues that are incompatible with fear responses. Relaxation and anxiety are considered to be incompatible states; therefore relaxation should inhibit the anxiety aroused by exposure to the cue or stimulus. Fear-eliciting stimuli are placed in an ascending order on the hierarchical list on the basis of their ability to arouse anxiety. They are paired with a relaxation response. First the child relaxes and is asked to imagine a scene with only some mildly anxiety-provoking stimuli. Deep breathing is encouraged, and as a result this should inhibit the mildly-arousing anxiety. Step by step, other stimuli on the list are introduced and paired with relaxation. The goal is to eventually eliminate the capacity of the stimuli to evoke anxiety. The child can now imagine an anxiety-provoking scene with relative calm. Hopefully, this relation and anxiety reduction should carry over into a real situation.

A six-year-old child, Meggin, was treated with a variety of approaches as part of an overall plan that included traditional play therapy as my main technique, the use of behavior modification for her enuresis and *systematic desensitization* for a phobia. Meggin's parents both worked, spent relatively little time with her, and left her in the care of a loving, but psychologically naive housekeeper. Meggin was particularly afraid of ceiling fans which were used instead of air conditioning to cool the house; Meggin's problems were not confined to this phobia. She was extremely shy, withdrawn, overweight, and to add to her difficulties, enuretic. To deal specifically with the enuresis, a behavior modification plan including an apparatus (the liquid sensitive pad and alarm similar to that proposed by Mowrer and Mowrer 1938), was used at night.

Systematic desensitization was utilized to help with the fan problem. It involved first teaching Meggin to relax and image a mildly anxiety-provoking cue that was paired with the relaxation. A hierarchy was then defined using the noise of Meggin's mother's electric mixer as least feared and the ceiling fan as the most feared. In addition, I asked Meggin to rate herself on a scale from 1 to 10 to describe her degree of fear as each item on the hierarchy was offered. This training continued for ten sessions with noticeable reduction of anxiety as we approached the fan item on the list.

Meggin was also encouraged to free-associate about the fan. She began to image "flying witches who whirled through the air," and told me about a "scary story" she heard in school before Halloween and at about the time her phobia began. Meggin had such vivid images and dreams about this flying witch that she had found it hard to separate the noise of the fan which was on at night when her parents were sitting in the kitchen from her images and dreams. Somehow the fan and the flying witch became one for Meggin and her fears began.

Through systematic desensitization, drawing pictures, and later her willingness to talk about her associations to the fan, Meggin was able to control her fears. If she entered the kitchen, Meggin used her deep breathing and image of a less threatening item on the list (such as a vacuum cleaner, or her father's car starting up) to cope with the fan's noise. Once this phobia was eliminated, Meggin was able to deal with some of her other issues in a more receptive way.

Cognitive Therapy

The value of this therapy depends on the ability of the client to change thought and image content while working on false appraisals of danger. Martin and Williams (1990) suggest that the imagery and automatic thoughts are warning signals, and that removing them would not diminish the fear of the situation. The client in cognitive therapy, however, learns that the warning system is "overactive and distorted" and that he must gain mastery over it which then provides him with confidence for "appraising more realistically the feared situation" and for coping with it (279).

Certain imagery-based procedures which rely on the client's production of thoughts and images have been summarized by Martin & Williams (1990, p. 279) as follows:

- *Turn-off technique*—the client is trained to turn off autonomous images or fantasies by increasing sensory input such as clapping hands, blowing a whistle.

- *Repetition*—by forcing repetitions of an image, the content becomes more realistic and anxiety may be reduced.

- *Time projection*—if the client can image a scene in the future when the troublesome event is past, he may be able to distance the self from current anxieties about the event.

- *Symbolic images*—symbols may be modified or changed. If for example, a client images someone attacking, a shield can be added to the image.

- *Facilitating change in induced images*—an anxious fantasy may be changed into a neutral or positive image by having clients imagine themselves painting an image of their choice.

- *Substituting a positive image*—the client images a comforting scene in a potentially anxiety-inducing situation and focuses on all sensory modalities involved in this image.

- *Exaggeration*—the client images a consequence worse than his or her own fears so as to put them in perspective.

- *Coping models*—the client images someone who is considered capable as coping with the feared situation and then models the behavior.

- *Imagery to reduce threat*—the feared stimulus is made less threatening through imagery (for example, imaging the doctor in a clown's suit).

- *Goal rehearsal*—the client images a new, frightening situation and then images ways to cope with it (useful for children starting a new school, or for a child afraid of the dark).

Repetition, substitution of a positive image, and turn-off techniques were successfully used in my work with an anxious seven-year-old child, Lori, whose parents were both well-meaning but rigid individuals who displayed very little overt affection towards their daughter. Lori was slow intellectually compared to a brilliant older brother. In addition to her cognitive disability, she had poor motor coordination, difficulty in making friends, was inappropriate socially (giggling to acting babyish) and had swings of moods from sadness and mild depression to anger and acting-out aggressive behaviors.

Lori had a particular fear of a "gorilla" who "sat on my bed at night" and who was "scary." The gorilla image was frightening; as a result, it was difficult for Lori to get to sleep at night. In the play room, we talked about the gorilla and what it could mean, but Lori still could not rid herself of this image. I decided to try relaxation exercises with Lori, and when she felt relaxed, asked her to image the gorilla. We did this often, repeating the gorilla image, until she could see it without the degree of anxiety that was initially in evidence. I then used substitution images, by asking Lori to picture an animal, object, or person she liked. Lori chose a particular doll in the playroom and we began exercises to help her image the doll sitting on her bed rather than the frightening gorilla. At night, there were times when the gorilla did come back, but Lori was able to use the substitute image practiced in the playroom to remove the gorilla image. I also gave her two turn-off techniques to use. Lori had a little "poem" she recited if the gorilla image reappeared: "go way, go away, I don't want you to stay." She clapped her hands twice as another turn-off technique. She felt in control now and was able to reduce the recurrent gorilla images.

At the same time that imagery was used to ameliorate her fear of the gorilla, we were able to play out some of the underlying causes of the gorilla image. The immediate effect of the cognitive imagery techniques was to help Lori get to sleep and reduce some of the anxiety surrounding the dark and bedtime. The issues dealing with the significance of the gorilla and what this symbol meant (the harsh, demanding, overbearing father was Lori's nighttime gorilla) took longer to work out through our play and through Lori's verbal recognition of this negative aspect of her father's personality.

Guided Affective Imagery

This is a psychoanalytically-oriented technique that is used with adults and children as young as six years of age. This method, utilizing imagery, differs from cognitive therapy in that the topics or *motifs* that are offered to the client are not directly related to the presenting disorder. Leuner and colleagues (1983) describe the procedure of Guided Affective Imagery, GAI, and offer numerous clinical examples in their book. Basically, GAI is a projective procedure; the client closes the eyes and projects images generated by the motifs suggested by the therapist. The child may lie on a couch or be seated in a comfortable chair and encouraged to relax with eyes closed. Observation of a child's facial expression, muscle tension, breathing can be indicators of the degree of relaxation. If there is difficulty in generating images, Leuner suggests offering some images of a meadow where one can rest after a long summer's walk or other such peaceful scenes.

When the therapist is assured that the child is completely relaxed, a choice from eight standard motifs are offered: the meadow, the ascent of a mountain, the pursuit of the course of a brook, visiting a house, an encounter with relatives, the observation of the edge of the woods from the meadow, a boat, and a cave. The meadow is usually introduced first.

Treatment consists of a fifteen to thirty minute duration period preceded by instructions concerning what the client will be doing during the imaging and then followed by a discussion of the scenes the client imaged. Steps consist of the relaxation, the starting point where the first motif is suggested (generally one or two motifs are used per session), the unfolding of the client's imagery or "waking dream," encouragement by the therapist with restatements or reflections, questions about the imagined scene, and occasionally suggestions by the therapist as to what the client may do during the imagery. I find it useful to ask the child to draw any image he or she desires, and then talk about it.

GAI was used with Jean, a seven-year-old child whose parents were recently divorced. The father has remarried and has a child by his new wife. Jean's mother works as a secretary and is a sensitive, caring person who expressed concern about Jean's depression, anger towards her, and Jean's desire to live with her father.

Jean is a pretty, dark-haired child with large brown eyes, but thin and pale. During the first weeks of therapy, her expression was usually sad and worried-looking. It was easy to establish rapport with Jean, however, and she entered into house and doll play quite readily. She told me that she wants to live with her father and "argues with Mommy all the time" but didn't seem to know why she was so angry. Jean told me she would say "I hate you" to her mother, but "I don't really hate her, its just that I don't know why I say that." Jean did bring a book about divorce to our second session and read it to me, but did not seem convinced by the story—mainly that parents can still love you even if they are divorced.

Since Jean seemed to enjoy puppet play and dollhouse play evidencing much imagination, I decided after a month of therapy to try GAI in order to help her uncover some deeper feelings and also to accept the finality of the divorce. I also planned to use GAI for only a small part of each session allowing her time to draw after the GAI and then to choose whatever game or activity she wished to play during the last part of the session. It was relatively easy for Jean to relax. She quickly got into the spirit of GAI and often while seated in a comfortable chair did move her hands and legs to help express her images. I started with the meadow motif and we stayed with that for two sessions when I introduced animals into the meadow as Leuner suggests. Jean made the cow (the mother symbol) a frightened animal who would run away whenever an elephant (Jean's own interjection of an animal) appeared. The elephant was "strong and big like my Dad—if you jump on my Dad with shoes on, it doesn't even hurt him." This elephant played an important role in subsequent GAI sessions where it chased the cow frequently, but as we progressed through the doll play that followed each GAI session, the cow and elephant became friends.

The cave motif was introduced and became a place where Jean could "hide," and where her "Daddy, king of the cavemen, could stop all the other cavemen from fighting." Drawings after the addition of the cave motif were generally of the elephant, the favorite drawing since the first introduction of it by Jean. I followed Leuner's use of the eight motifs, and presented them in the order he outlined. The use of imagery uncovered feelings about Jean's mother that were more tender than the way she was portrayed in doll play. Gradually, some of the cow's gentleness was transferred to a doll who earlier had been portrayed as the "mother-boss" who "got a divorce and chased the father" out of the house.

As imagery sessions progressed, each time followed by Jean's drawing of an image she liked, the doll play began to reflect direct changes. The father doll who was the "strong caveman" in the GAI became a more "polite Daddy" figure. Both mother and father dolls learned to become "friends" just as the cow and elephant learned how to "drink from the same pond" and play together. We had sixteen GAI sessions, carried out twice a week over a two month period. During this time, Jean's relationship with her mother improved. Jean was able to accept the finality of the divorce, and no longer needed to see her parents as battling. She was able to "come out of the cave" and face the "nice animals in the meadow," such as the "deer and birds" and even the "mean ones who chase you." She could accept her mother as capable of protecting her and loving her, while the "king" no longer needed to assert his power.

Mind Play Techniques

"Mind play" wherein directed imagery is the main focus can prove fruitful as an adjunct to the more standard play therapy techniques. Exercises or "games" such as described in *Put your mother on the ceiling* (de Mille 1973) can help children gain control over their fantasies, encourage belief in their own effectiveness and capacity for self assertion, and result in more positive self-esteem. Some of the exercises in that delightful book deal with images about mother, father, school, manners, food and pain. A child, for example, in the exercise dealing with parents is stimulated by such images of father and mother growing smaller, turning various colors, standing on the roof, going deep into a mine, having a dragon breathe fire on them, having a steamroller flatten them, and having the parents upset the steamroller. The game ends by having the parents "wink" at the child and asking, "What would you like to do with them now?"

Discussion following the exercises focuses on the images that were generated and encourages children to bring up fears or difficulties that were bothering them.

A fourth case involved application of the games selected from *Put your mother on the ceiling*. Daniel, a six-year-old child was referred because of aggressive behavior in school. He bit children, threw a chair at a teacher and often refused to comply with the teacher's rules, suggestions, or directions. His parents were divorced and were not on amiable terms with each other. Mother was a cold person who used intellectualization as her main defense. The father was well-intentioned but more lax and permissive than the mother in his discipline methods. This led to confusion, frustration, and anger on Daniel's part. The parents came for monthly counseling sessions in regard to Daniel, and generally argued with each other in my presence. They themselves were in therapy as well.

At about our eighth play therapy session, I introduced the imagery exercises from the book. These simple games allow the child to image people or animals in unusual positions or image strange things happening to them. Prior to the time of these imaging sessions, Daniel's play vacillated between attacking a Teddy bear with a toy syringe or cuddling it. He liked to curl up on the couch in a fetal position, thumb in mouth, or would build block structures that he knocked down with great shouts of glee.

We began the exercises with "animals" and when he seemed to enjoy these mind games, we moved on to "parents." He imaged his parents "growing smaller," being "eaten by sharks," "flattened out like pancakes," "run over by a steamroller," and growing larger again. He was permitted, according to the game, to also image his parents in any way he chose. Daniel's fantasies allowed him to gain control over his parents and in effect "punish" them for the divorce. Gradually, Daniel's play began to change. Images allowed anxieties, pent-up feelings and fears to come to the surface. The exercises were followed by discussions about his parents' divorce, his feelings of guilt about causing this, his desire to be a baby again like "I used to be," and then "everybody would love me." The aggressive behavior which was a reaction to the divorce slowly subsided as Daniel was able to verbalize his anger and distress. Daniel now "repaired" houses that he knocked down and played more gently with the Teddy bear. He gave up the babyish behavior, and no longer needed to lie on the couch sucking his thumb.

The use of imagery allowed Daniel to get in touch with his feelings, to self-heal and to accept the reality of divorce. He was able to understand that he was not the cause of the divorce and that his parents truly loved him. The parents began to work through their own anger with their therapists and to accept some of my suggestions for parenting skills. We continued using imagery throughout the remaining weeks of therapy with continued success as manifested by more appropriate behaviors both at home and at school.

Poetry can also be used to stretch a child's imagination and to give practice in imagery production (Koch 1970). In a short poem feelings can be expressed on a variety of topics. A stimulus word or phrase such as "wish," "dream," "baby," "the things I hear," "I seem to be/but really am," or "strange things" can tap into a child's unconscious and help reveal feelings and conflicts. Similarly, pantomiming images that pertain to emotions may help a child express fears or even joy and perhaps remove some blocks. *The magic if* (Kelly 1973) offers many suggestions and exercises that probe into a child's awareness and fosters imagination. Imitating a person's walk or movements, and facial expressions forces a child to concentrate and generate images pertaining to the stimuli. Children are encouraged to think about adaptation to another person's mood by imaging how the other person might look and act if a request were made. These exercises are useful when helping a child understand how to improve interpersonal relationships with peers, siblings, parents, and even teachers.

Words or phrases may also be used to stimulate drawings that express a child's feelings, or a drawing or color may be used to stimulate an image (Goodnow 1977; Wood 1986). Finally, the Mutual Storytelling Technique (Gardner 1983) is a method that encourages the child to tell a self-created story, and which permits the therapist to examine the psychodynamic meanings, and to create a responding story.

Art Therapy

There are two main approaches to art therapy: (1) the use of visual media with emphasis on the artistic aspects of the product itself with verbalization about the product as secondary; insight is not emphasized and the client's unconscious material is not uncovered or revealed directly to the client; and (2) the actual rendition of the product but with verbal free-associations. The first approach is applied usually as an adjunct to other forms of therapy. Here the therapist may simply want the child to find an outlet for expression, or to draw because the child is blocked in verbal expression. The second approach which may be called *art psychotherapy* relies on the rendered product as the sole approach utilized in therapy.

Rubin (1987) uses *art psychotherapy* in her approach. According to her, art can help a child uncover unconscious imagery, communicate, and express feelings. Art psychotherapy can be used according to Rubin in helping the child deal with defenses. The therapist asks open-ended questions, observes the child's nonverbal behavior during the art session, and encodes the child's symbolic expressions.

A child, Barry, with whom I worked in play therapy often made drawings, clay models, and even *papier mâché* volcanoes over a period of months while he dealt with strong aggressive impulses and anger towards his parents who not only were drug abusers, but had frequent violent arguments and fights. Through his art forms, play, and my interpretations, Barry began to understand his rage and inability to control his parents' behavior. The repetition of his volcano images helped him release tension and work through unacceptable feelings. When he finally learned how to express his anger through the use of words, the volcano-making subsided. Barry soon was able to recognize and deal with his sense of helplessness that had been manifested through the opposite emotion of anger. When children tell stories about their renditions as Barry did, they reveal some of the intrapsychic difficulties that are deeply hidden but emerge through their art images.

Summary Statement

I have attempted to trace definitions of imagery and theory to the practical applications of imagery in clinical settings. As has been pointed out there are numerous definitions, types of imagery, and a variety of methods utilizing imagery techniques with children. What is needed, it seems, is more systematic rigorous investigation of imagery methods with children. In addition, psychotherapists who use traditional play therapy might try to venture into this realm of imagery and pay more attention to the fantasy productions of their clients. In Jean's *fantasy* for example, mother was tender, but in her *play*, mother was portrayed as bossy and mean, the everyday realistic view of a harassed single parent. The images uncovered Jean's true feelings towards her mother, feelings she was afraid to show. Like Jean, in the "playground of our minds" we may find some answers that will make life more tolerable and perhaps more of an adventure into the possible.

/7

Indications and Goals in Imagery Interaction Play Therapy

Berendien L. van Zanten

Child psychotherapy never will be effective without a thorough assessment of both the child's and family's problems. Only on the basis of such an assessment can we draw up a treatment plan, which usually contains information on the indication, the goals and the strategy of therapy in a particular case. These issues relate to the start of a therapy, as opposed to issues like outcome criteria which concern mainly the end of a therapy. Up to now the subject of research has mostly been the effects of play therapy or of a particular method of play therapy, whereas treatment planning is still a process without adequate empirical support.

However, some descriptive studies have been published which illuminate this process. A few topics that were studied are: play therapy limits (Ginott & Lebo 1961; Rhoden, Kranz & Lund 1981), the expectations of clients about what will happen in therapy (Day & Reznikoff 1980; Adelman, Kaser-Boyd & Taylor 1984), the process of change in client centered therapy (Borke 1947; Moustakas & Shalock 1955; Mook 1982a, 1982b; Schmidtchen 1986) and others.

Researching the process of change, Schmidtchen (1978, 1986) also considered the *goals* of therapy. He is a strong advocate of individual goals and outcome criteria, tuned to the individual case. Illuminating is his distinction between *general* and *specific* goals. General goals have value for all clients, for example, self development, personal growth, self-actualization, emotional learning, creativity, greater autonomy, increased problem-solving ability, decreased anx-

99

iety and reduction of behavior disorders. Specific goals aim at diminishing individual behavior symptoms, such as bed-wetting, stuttering, social maladjustment or the working through of traumatic experiences, pertaining only to one specific client.

In the Netherlands, Hellendoorn (Hellendoorn et al. 1981; Hellendoorn 1985, 1992) emphasizes the importance of clearly formulating indications and goals in play therapy. Her method of play therapy, called Imagery Interaction Play Therapy, is based on the principle that the therapist does not talk directly with the child about his or her feelings or ideas, but rather about the play world the child creates, and about the play persons and their thoughts and feelings. Language is used in the sense that it structures and orders activities, feelings and meanings, even though these belong to the play persons (Hellendoorn 1988). In an explorative study on the practice of imagery interaction by Loeven and Harinck (1985), eighteen therapists gave extensive information by means of questionnaires on process variables as referral problem, indication, goals and strategy of therapy. The results of this study suggest (among other things) that planning of goals and strategy is worthwhile: therapists who carefully planned their goals and strategy showed a higher success percentage in their case load. Although some therapists expressed some reserve because of the possible inflexibility of an explicit treatment plan, most therapists stated that they felt free to change the original planned goals or strategies, if necessary on the basis of new information. Apparently these therapists did not think of goals only as the final product of therapy, but as a guideline which helps identify and clarify therapeutic change.

However, knowledge about therapeutic process variables as used by child psychotherapists is scarce. Consequently, questions such as: What goals can be set in what specific cases? What strategy should be chosen in case of specific family circumstances? How long will a given play therapy take? are very difficult to answer. This was the reason to start a descriptive evaluation study on imagery interaction play therapy in clinical practice.

Research Questions and Method

Elsewhere we reported on the design, procedure and some preliminary results (Hellendoorn, Riekert & van Zanten 1986; van Zanten 1986). To summarize: we chose a multiple case study in order to describe and explore individual cases as well as remarkable congruences and incongruences between cases. The therapists themselves were involved in collecting the clinical data. At the start, during and after the therapy they kept a detailed record file of their clients by means of standard forms on different aspects of therapy. In this report we present results concerning referral problems, indication criteria for imagery interaction play therapy, and the original goals of therapy as well as the changes in goals.

Participants in this evaluation study were eight female child psychotherapists, working in out-patient settings like a university clinic or a private practice. They all practiced imagery interaction play therapy, a method in which they had at least two years of training. They reported about twelve children, five male and seven female. At the start of the project the age range of the children was 3.7 to 10.9 years.

The research questions were:

1. What referral problems are formulated?

2. What relation, if any, does exist between the indication for imagery interaction and the global result of the therapy?

3. What therapeutic goals are formulated?

4. What goals are formulated or reformulated in the course of therapy?

To answer these questions we used data derived from two standard forms in the record files. On the first form therapists were asked (1) to formulate referral problems; (2) to state what indication they saw for imagery interaction play therapy and what basic conditions were present or absent in each individual child; (3) to set down their therapy goals for both the child and its parents.

According to the theoretical framework, six conditions on the side of the child (to be called: child issues) should be taken into consideration to indicate that imagery interaction play therapy would be the right therapy to start with. First, at least some part of the referral problem should be experienced by the child itself and not only occur as a result of the family interaction. Second, in order to profit from imagery interaction, play should be a modus the child likes and can work with. In practice this means that the child should at least show minor elements of imagination during the assessment phase. Third, the child should show a minimal degree of vital energy. Therapy, as most people know, can be stressful and the child must be able to bear that little extra. Fourth, the child should have a minimal capacity to integrate therapy experiences in daily life. For extremely chaotic children, for instance, this method is not deemed suitable. Fifth, there should be some sort of certainty about the child's future. If we want the child to work through past experiences and to grow towards new ways of living and behaving, with whom and in what environment will he or she do so? If, for instance, there is uncertainty about outplacement, about foster care or residential care, this is perhaps not the best moment to start therapy. Sixth, there should be some glimpse of motivation for therapy with the child: does he or she like to come? This question can usually be answered after the assessment phase, of which play assessment forms a natural part.

Apart from these child issues, therapists should also consider the willingness of parents to get involved in some guidance program as an important condition to decide on imagery interaction play therapy. For this purpose two more issues are added to the first form: the parents should show at least some capacity and willingness to change their behavior, and, finally, they need to be motivated (even if only slightly, and with much reserve) to discuss their way of child upbringing.

The second form was used by the therapists to summarize each play session with the help of questions which are meaningful for a description of the therapeutic process. One of these questions, about changes of goals in the course of therapy, we needed in order to answer our fourth research question.

A content analysis was performed to order and categorize the qualitative data of both forms. Data for the global results were collected by ratings on a three-point-scale indicating a positive, moderate or negative change of the child's problem behavior.

Results

The referral problems, as stated by the therapists, were classified in six clusters, as shown in table 7.1. The most frequently mentioned problems at referral were: behavioral problems at home (9x) followed by problems at school (7x); Cognitive problems and problems in the domains of interpersonal relationships and physical well-being all occurred three times. Finally, one therapist reported about problems due to personality characteristics. Except for the last cluster, these descriptions are mainly phrased in terms of observable behaviors.

Although emotional well-being is lacking in the clustering of the referral problems, the therapists were fully aware of it during the assessment period, as becomes clear in table 7.2, a summary of the

Table 7.1   Referral Problems as Stated by Imagery Interaction
Play Therapists

	REFERRAL PROBLEMS	IN NR. OF CASES
Behavioral	• Demanding behaviors	3
	• Sleeping disorders	2
	• Delay in speech development	1
	• Excessive eating	1
	• Lack of initiative to play	1
	• Extreme disobedience	1
Problems at school	• Low grades	3
	• Problem behavior	2
	• Lack of concentration	1
	• Lack of discipline	1
Cognitive / affective	• Loneliness	1
	• Low self-regard	1
	• Preoccupation with death	1
Interpersonal relationships	• Lack of contact with peers	2
	• Bad relation with foster parent	1
Physical*	• Losing hair	1
	• Swollen feet	1
	• Stiff legs	1
Personality	• Dysharmonious personality structure	1

* no medical cause known

basic conditions for indication on imagery interaction play therapy
for both the child and its caregivers. The first issue, the child's own
problem experience, was usually put in terms of expressing emotions. For instance, one therapist wrote: "anxiety, resistance to experience problems and a lack of trust in adults"; another remarked:
"sadness, not feeling happy." Besides the expression of negative emo-

Table 7.2 Basic Conditions for an Indication on Imagery Interaction Playtherapy and Global Results (N of clients = 12)

NR	PROBLEM SIGNIFICANCE			IMAGINATIVE ABILITY	VITALITY	CAPACITY TO INTEGRATE	FUTURE PERSPECTIVE	MOTIVATION	CAPABLE OF BEHAVIORAL CHANGE		MOTIVATION		GLOBAL RESULTS		
	ENE	NEE	IR						Father	Mother	Father	Mother	Therapist	Father	Mother
1	+			+	+	++	++	+	++	++	±	++	++	++	++
2	+	++	+	++	+	+	++	+	+	+	+	+	++	++	++
3	+			++	+	++	+	++	+	+	++	++	++	++	++
4		+		±	+	++	+	+	±	+	+	+	++	++	++
5	+			++	++	+	+	+	±	±	±	±	++	++	+
6			+	++	++	±	±	++	+	±		++	+	++	++
7		++	++		+	+	++	+	+	±	+	+	+	++	++
8		+	+	±	±	+	+	+	±	++	±	++	+	++	++
9		+		++	++	+	+	+	±	±	++	++	+	+	+
10		+		++	++	++	+	++	+	±	±	±	±	+	+
11	+	+		++	++	+	+	±	+	−	+	±	−	+	−
12	−	−	−	++	++	++	++	++	−	−	±	±	−	−	−

ENE = Expression of Negative Emotions; NEE = No Expression of Emotions; IR = Interpersonal Relationships

tions (ENE), therapists also noted an inability to express emotional experiences (NEE). A third distinctive cluster under this heading was the child's experience of difficulties in relation to its direct caretakers or peers (IR).

An independent judge categorized all basic conditions as positive (++), moderate (+), slight (+) or negative (-). Almost all child issues were judged as moderate or positive, which is rather favorable. Apparently, therapists do therapy only with child clients for which they think this method a suitable one. Only case 12 was a remarkable exception: the therapist found no problem consciousness with the child at all. The overall picture changes substantially, however, when we add therapist's judgments of the parental issues. Here we find more "slight" and even some "negative" judgments.

What about the outcome? The first three cases in table 7.2 are comparable in that all basic conditions were judged moderate to positive, with both therapist and the parents thinking of the play therapy as a real success. For cases 4 through 10 the picture is not that clear, although the global results are moderate to positive. However, if these cases are compared with cases 11 and 12, we notice an absence of negative judgements in cases 4 through 10, whereas cases 11 and 12 have some issues judged as negative. In both these cases the therapists were aware of a negative attitude of one or both parent(s) towards therapy, while in case 12 also the absence of any problem experience in the child was noted. According to the theoretical framework of imagery interaction therapy these negative judgements should have led to a contraindication. In spite of these findings the therapists started therapy, which failed at the end.

The therapists were also asked to formulate goals with respect to the individual child as well as goals pertaining to the parents. Here we present only those for the child. The number of goals for the individual child varied from two to five. All goals were qualitatively categorized into eight clusters (see figure 7.1): (1) cognitive goals (28 percent), (2) emotional goals (17 percent), (3) developmental goals (17 percent), (4) behavioral goals (16 percent); and clusters concerning (5) interpersonal relationships (12 percent), (6) the working through of specific life events (4.3 percent), (7) personality structure (4.3 percent) and (8) physical well-being (1 percent).

For the sake of a clear presentation a distinction was made between a cognitive and an emotional domain by categorizing those goals which clearly described feelings as anxiety, sadness or aggression into an emotional cluster. Aims such as self-confidence, insight or decreasing ambivalence were considered to be cognitive goals, since they refer to a processing of information. Since there is clearly

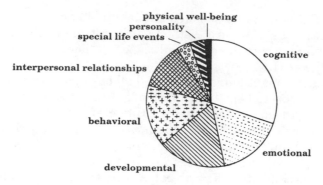

Figure 7.1 Clusters of Goals for Imagery Interaction
Playtherapy, as Stated by Therapists

some overlap in these domains, imagery interaction therapists usually speak of a cognitive/affective domain, which would account for 45
percent of all formulated goals. Including the behavioral domain, at
least 61 percent of the goals is related to the individual child.

The therapists also foster general development, mostly stated
in terms of "more exploration of the outside world" or "facilitating
development" or "daring to be a child." Whether the therapists do use
general as well as specific goals is shown in figure 7.2. A second order
classification resulted in a distinction of general and specific goals for
the cognitive, emotional, and behavioral domains. Two examples of
specific goals in the cognitive domain are "learning that it is possible to

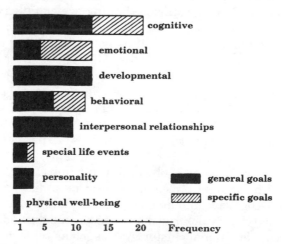

Figure 7.2 Frequency of General and Specific Goals for Imagery
Interaction Playtherapy

be naughty and loved at the same time" and "learning to be less ambitious and less willing to be her parents' pride." A specific emotional goal is "lessening fear of death," while specific behavioral goals are illustrated by "unblocking of speech" and "becoming less insistent."

Finally we explored the additions and changes in goals during the therapeutic process. The amount of additions/changes ranged from one to seven times per case. Many of these were intermediate goals, pertaining to the therapy sessions themselves: (1) goals concerning the therapeutic relationship such as "building up a safe working alliance" or "learning to feel safe and to relax while playing during sessions," (2) intermediate diagnostic goals, such as "trying to clear the meaning of the car accident," and (3) specific strategies as for instance "helping the child experience that it is possible to get overwhelmed by lots of sand, but that there are always people to help you." But sometimes there were (4) some new goals, whereas (5) some original goals were dropped in the course of therapy.

Conclusion

It appeared that the basic conditions to indicate imagery interaction play therapy, especially those pertaining to the child's problem-consciousness, imaginativeness, vitality, integrative ability and motivation, were useful in pointing out the chances of success or failure of therapy. However, the child's living environment with its parents seemed to contribute heavily to the effectiveness of therapy. Although imagery interaction theory and training has always been alert on this point, therapists in this sample did not always show the required critical attitude. In two cases, a negative motivation of one or both caregivers will probably have contributed to the failure of the therapy. This underlines the need for further research into the basic conditions for imagery interaction play therapy, especially with regard to the caregivers of the child in need of therapy.

Although behavioral problems were the main cause for referral, the child psychotherapists formulated their goals primarily in terms of cognitive and affective problems. This is in line with the principle of imagery interaction, which states that behavioral problems are the result of cognitive and emotional problems. Further exploration of goals within each play session and the strategies used can illuminate the therapeutic processes in relation to changes in the originally stated goals.

Besides dealing with problems, imagery interaction theory considers the fostering of normal growth and development as an important aspect of help. Therefore, it was rather amazing that in only 50 percent of the cases the therapists explicitly formulated goals in this domain. Other researchers also stipulate that the fostering of normal developmental processes should be part of any treatment plan (Rutter 1982; Harter 1983).

In congruence with the ideas of Schmidtchen (1978) and Hellendoorn (1985), two distinctions were made. First, a distinction between general and specific goals. A general goal can be conceived as a directive along which all therapies are expected to proceed (e.g., better self-actualization). These general goals may vary with the therapeutic theory favored by the therapist. Usually these general goals are not easily observable in clear final results. It may be easier to observe specific goals, because these relate more directly to individual problems observed in the child client. So the final result on specific goals is often perceived by all participants in the therapy. Second, there is the distinction between final and intermediate goals. Intermediate goals mostly regard the therapy sessions themselves and often represent stages in the therapeutic process. Final goals form criteria for possible termination. These distinctions between different kinds of goals are important when one plans evaluation studies or discusses the improvement of a child in treatment (Soudijn 1992).

Contrary to the findings of Loeven and Harinck (1985), the therapists of our study did not often change the originally planned goals. If goals were changed, this often concerned the addition of a new goal, usually an intermediate goal. Of course, when the therapist gets better acquainted with the child and his or her specific problems and possibilities during therapy, the therapist also may feel justified in further structuring the process by means of these intermediate goals which can serve as guidelines on the way toward the final goals.

PART 2

Play for Children with Special Needs

Over the last decades, research on play and development has accumulated. However, very little is known as yet about play in "special children." One of the reasons may be that there are so many kinds of "special children," all with their own specific handicaps and needs. In the next chapters, we will encounter some of them: children with communication problems, physically and mentally handicapped children, as well as children with multiple handicaps and autistic children. Can these children play and do they play? And if they cannot or do not, can something be done about that?

As recently as 1986, McConkey stated that many people were still convinced that mentally handicapped children are unable to play. Although this view was at that time already clearly outdated, its persistence is perhaps understandable: children with more or less severe mental handicaps are evidently unable to play on the level of their same-aged normal peers. However, if mental age (and not chronological age) is taken as the criterion for comparison, mild to moderately retarded children have been shown not to differ essentially in play behavior from normally developing young children (see Hulme & Lunzer 1966; Hill & McCune-Nicolich 1981; Hellendoorn & Hoekman 1992). Even so, in many handbooks on the development of retarded children there is no mention at all of play or fantasy.

Many deaf children too show a retarded play development, especially with regard to symbolic play and other more advanced forms of planned play activity (Gregory & Mogford 1983; Casby & McCormack 1985). But in more recent studies it appears that these children's play ability is largely related to other domains, notably their communicative ability and their relationship to supportive adults (Lyon 1990; Morshuis & Hellendoorn 1992). And again, handbooks on the development of deaf children, and of blind children for that matter, are notably lacking in mention of play.

Perhaps the central problem is that, for special children, play is not regarded as a natural or important part of their development. Other topics, notably the stimulation or compensation of the social and intellectual functions they lack, appear to be studied with much more interest by professionals and caregivers. The educational problems of special children are more often defined in terms of what they cannot do and what should be remedied than in terms of what they can do.

Consequently, parents, educators and caregivers encounter the additional problem of being left empty-handed. What do they need to know about special children's play in order to assess what their particular child is capable of? What can they do to help these children make better use of the play abilities they have, few though these may sometimes be?

In this section, different kinds of play interventions with special children are presented. It should be borne in mind that most of it is pioneer work, with as yet only minor theoretical and empirical foundations. So it is definitely still in the exploratory stage. Much more work has been done in the field of play interventions in regular education. There, as will become clear in the next section, the body of knowledge is now such that critical hypotheses can be tested. In the field of special education, this stage is still far ahead.

Therefore, all contributions to this section are necessarily exploratory. They present new ideas, tried out with small groups of children and their educators, which seem worthwhile to pursue. Some of them include research in the form of preliminary evaluation reports of play interventions, with little methodological sophistication, but which indicates new roads that are possibly fruitful.

Mentally handicapped children are most prominent. *Joop Hellendoorn* presents an imaginative play program for severely retarded children (mental age about two years). Her results indicate that these children are able to acquire new play skills, while almost all reach some level of pretend play. How to generalize these skills to other life situations is the next problem. In view of that, the pleasure most of the children exhibit in make-believe, once they grasp the principle, is encouraging.

Play pleasure is also one of the features of *Roy McConkey*'s innovative planning for play in families with handicapped children, particularly in developing countries. His starting point is that play helps the children learn basic skills like exploration, joint activities, turn-taking and problem-solving in a natural way. The parents and the local culture are actively involved. Starting with the games they are familiar with because they recall them from their own youth, many different play activities can be used to explore the learning value of joint play with their disabled children. The program is enhanced and made more interesting by video support. As McConkey himself says: with a world growing more open, planning for play should embrace all children.

For children with multiple handicaps, however, play sometimes seems an almost unattainable goal. *Han Nakken* and his colleagues try to bring it nearer, even for children who seem capable of very little indeed. Most important here is the way caregivers are trained to observe and involve the children in playful activities. Since in most residences little time is available for this sort of special help, structural measures have to be taken to implement these new ways to communicate with these profoundly handicapped children.

Jan de Moor and his colleagues report on a play program for differentially handicapped children. Their aim is to help caregivers create individually geared play learning opportunities. However, their outcome does not confirm any specific progress for the toddlers in their experimental group. A plausible explanation for this lack of success, as compared with other programs described in this section is perhaps that their approach is relatively unspecific. More goal-directed training activities might have given more improvement. But then one could ask (as de Moor does) whether such a gain would not be too much adult-initiated to generalize to other, novel activities.

The "Play Observation Kit" described by *Kay Mogford-Bevan* has been found useful in the assessment of children with communication difficulties. It was developed for systematically observing parents' play with their child. With the help of pre-coded checklists, detailed information can be gathered about the child's current level of play and about the parents' way of perceiving and communicating with their child. This forms the basis for an intervention plan, aimed at supporting or enlarging the child's communicative abilities in a playful interactive framework, with the parents as co-actors.

Specific problems are encountered in the play of autistic children. One of the symptoms of autism is impairment in imaginative activity. Pretend play is rarely seen. *Ina Van Berckelaer-Onnes* tried out a three-month twice-a-week training program involving simple manipulation, relational play, functional and imaginative play. Only a few children reach the imaginative level. Intellectual capacity and language development seem to play a prominent part in this transition from functional to symbolic play. All other children show some improvement in toy play behavior, which may contribute to their over-all development by extending the variety in their experience.

Common to most of these contributions is the emphasis on active intervention by stimulating adults, in contrast to "naturally occurring play behaviors." Does this mean that too much is "being done" to these children, and too little is left to themselves? This is a central problem when we are dealing with special needs children, because of their lack of initiative in many situations. While some of this is doubtless due to inherent inability (particularly so in profoundly and multiply handicapped children), lack of appropriate stimulation and early discouragement are also crucial factors. Finding the appropriate ways to help these children is no sinecure. Caregivers will need careful training and coaching in order to better observe each child's specific possibilities. Only if these are known, will "naturally occurring playful events" be recognized earlier and consequently be put to better use.

/8

Imaginative Play Training
for Severely Retarded Children

Joop Hellendoorn

Imaginative play is generally considered an important factor in the cognitive, social and emotional development of children (see, e.g., the reviews of Van der Kooij & De Groot 1977; Fein 1981; Rubin, Fein & Vandenberg 1983). Usually, the first signs of imaginative or symbolic play emerge at about eighteen to twenty months of age (Piaget 1962). At first, only simple transformations are performed of self-directed acts (e.g., eating imaginative food from a real plate with a real spoon). Gradually, symbolic acts are extended to others and to symbolic persons (e.g., doll or bear), and the number and complexity of transformations expand. According to Cole and LaVoie (1985) and Pellegrini (1985), three to four-year-olds are already able to play more elaborate imaginative stories with different roles.

What about the early play develoment of retarded children? Research in this field is relatively scarce, as compared to what we know about normally developing children. Results indicate that the early play development of children with mental retardation follows approximately the same sequence as that of normally developing children, but at a (much) slower rate. The same types of play and the same degree of play organization can be seen at about the same *mental* or *developmental* age, although calendar ages may differ widely (Hulme & Lunzer 1966; Whittaker 1980; Hill & McCune-Nicolich 1981; Odom 1981; Motti, Cichetti & Sroufe 1983; Cunningham, Glenn, Wilkinson & Sloper 1985; Hellendoorn & Hoekman 1992). As in normal development, the basic condition for the emergence of symbolic play in mentally retarded children is found to be a minimal mental age of about twenty months.

However, many retarded children who reach a mental level of about two years do not attain the corresponding simple symbolic play level. And if they do, their play may still be qualitatively different (Li 1985; Beeghly & Cicchetti 1987). How can this be explained? In general, children learn and develop by their interaction with their environment and in particular with the stimuli they receive from adults. This poses some basic difficulties in the case of retarded children. They develop much slower than other children. Motor handicaps may further impede their exploratory urge. They are slow to understand situations and relations between people. That is why parents with their customary pedagogic tools see little or no progress. If changes occur, these often go so slowly that caregivers have difficulty recognizing them and may easily become demoralized. This poses a definite risk of understimulation, with negative consequences for the child's self-image. Not surprisingly, many retarded children tend to avoid the unknown and keep to the few skills they have mastered. This, in its turn, may lead to repetitive and stereotyped activity or to passivity.

It seems to us that the play retardation of many severely mentally handicapped children (relative to their mental age) is only partly due to innate disability, but at least as much to lack of specific stimulation and training. Many adults have long given up encouragement and expectation of play and symbolic activity. About fifteen years ago, play pioneer Wehman (1977) already complained about the lack of knowledge and motivation among professionals regarding play development in these children. In many handbooks on mental retardation (Ingalls 1978; Payne & Patton 1981; Ehlers, Prothero & Langone 1982; Zigler & Hodapp 1986), mention of play is minimal or absent.

If imaginative play is acknowledged as an important part of total development (cf. the chapter by Singer, earlier in this volume), there is no reason to believe that this should not be true for mentally handicapped persons. However, if this kind of play does not emerge spontaneously at the appropriate mental age, specific individual or group training may be needed.

The research literature in this field, as far as known to us, is limited to one study only. Kim, Lombardino, Rothman and Vinson (1989) developed an imaginative play training for children with a mental age of about three years. Their program consisted of ten daily sessions of twenty minutes. During about half of this time, the trainer modeled, verbally and nonverbally, thematic play just above the existing imaginative play level of the child. Compared with non-treated children, at the end of the training a definite increase in quality and quantity of imaginative play was observed. However, individual results seemed rather strongly related to the child's motivation. It is a pity that longer term effects were not investigated, since in other (non-imaginative) play training efforts generalization of the newly learned skills was poor (Morris & Dolker 1974; Murphy, Callias & Carr 1985).

The Imaginative Play Program

At our department, an imaginative play program was designed for retarded children and adolescents with a mental level of two to three years, whose play level is lower, but who meet the preconditions for the transition to symbolic play: (1) they have some working knowledge of everyday objects and are able to manipulate and use these objects in functionally appropriate ways; (2) they show a beginning sense of object constancy; and (important for this project) (3) they are sufficiently other-oriented to enjoy doing something together and imitating others.

The program follows closely the way normal children develop symbolic play skills. Normally, the first make-believe acts are autosymbolic, that is, the make-believe is directly involved with the child's own body and behavior: pretending to eat or to sleep. Next, the child involves other actors, another person present, or a more or less make-believe person such as a doll or a bear, using the same simple enactive schemes. Gradually, the number of make-believe elements or transformations expands (McCune-Nicolich 1980; Singer & Singer 1985, 1991).

In accordance with this process, our program consists of eight play themes, each divided in six consecutive steps, leading from functional play via autosymbolic to (simple) actor-directed symbolic play. This developmental sequence is shown in figure 8.1. The play themes all refer to well-known everyday occurrences: hair combing, bathing, eating/drinking, brushing your teeth, dressing, going to bed, telephoning and going out.

The training itself is largely done by modeling: the play trainer takes the lead by modeling each consecutive play step, trying to awaken the child's interest, pleasure and activity, and gradually fading into the background as the child's own play competence and initiative grows stronger.

Each session starts with a pleasurable activity, for example, a familiar song or sensorimotor action in which the child can easily participate. This may also strengthen the child's feeling of togetherness with the trainer while at the same time heightening the basic

---

1. Functional use of play material, normal daily activity, no evidence of pretense.

2. Functional activity directed towards a symbolic person (doll or bear).

3. Introduction of a definite pretense element: a crucial play material becomes "make-believe" (e.g., bathing without real water)—autosymbolic;

4. Make-believe extended to symbolic person(s);

5. Expanding the number of transformations;

6. Relating one play theme to another, designing a play story.

Figure 8.1   The 6 Consecutive Play Steps

focus on imitation. Next, there are a few exercises in object constancy, mostly in the form of hide-and-seek games.

In our manual all exercises are described as well as the sequential order in which they are to be presented. However, the pace of passing through should be specifically geared to each individual participant. The same goes for the play exercises. The exact content of each session, therefore, is dependent on the child's personal play level as established in the previous session. A new step may only be introduced when the preceding activities are well played through, over at least two different themes.

In this way, we also hope to avoid a well-known pitfall in training programs for retarded children: their tendency to repeat familiar acts, rather like "tricks" to satisfy the adults instead of intrinsically motivated action (an essential characteristic of play). This danger is guarded against by introducing different play themes for the same level of symbolic development and by frequently changing from one theme to another.

One additional word of warning: Playing should be fun, relaxing and intrinsically satisfying. Can this be achieved in a *training* program, with necessarily extrinsic reinforcement? People working with the program should not just be interested in developing skills, but even more so in eliciting play pleasure in order to heighten the possibility of transfer and long term effects.

Research Method

Four small scale controlled effect studies have been performed. In all, thirty children and adolescents (sixteen female, fourteen male) from five to thirty years of age and with an approximate mental age of about two to four years old participated in the training. About half of them were living in residential care, the others visited day care centers while living at the parental home. All participants were individually trained during nine to fifteen sessions of thirty minutes each.

Before and after training, all children were observed during a special scoring session, with their play scored on the Play Observation Scale (POS; Hellendoorn 1989). This ordinal scale is an adaptation of the Free Play Scale by McCune-Nicolich (1980). McCune distinguished three play levels: manipulatory, combinatorial, and symbolic. In the POS, the first two were retained. McCune's first symbolic category (pre-symbolic play which was defined as functional use of play materials) was extended to a separate level with four categories, allowing for more differentiation in functional play. On the symbolic level, McCune's categories were largely retained, although some definitions were adapted. A further specification of the play behavior seemed warranted for use in a training or a stimulated play situation. Obviously, it makes a vast difference whether some specific play action is directly imitated, was strongly stimulated or comes spontaneously. Especially in the case of retarded children, this differentiation allows for more subtle distinguishing and measuring small changes.

For this project, the functional and symbolic level are the most relevant. These are shown in figure 8.2. The starting level of participants should be at least in the functional region and not too high on the symbolic level. The scale can be used for both spontaneous and guided play. Different kinds of scoring are possible: by time sampling or event sampling, modal score or maximal score. Interscorer reliability as measured by mean Cohen's kappa on five pairs of raters was found to be .60, which we deemed satisfactory for our exploratory purposes.

Pre- and post-training measuring sessions had a similar structure. During the first ten minutes, the child was shown a standard set of toys and was invited to pick them up and play with them. During the last ten minutes, the investigator took a more directive attitude, by modeling and stimulating trying to elicit higher play levels than the child had previously shown. The pre-training session was guided by the trainer, who at that time was not well-known to the children. The post-training session was led by another adult, who performed the training in another institutional setting and therefore was experienced in this kind of play but unknown to the children. She knew the purpose of this study, but had no knowledge

M SIMPLE MANIPULATION (seven ordinal categories)

C COMBINATORIAL (four ordinal categories)

F FUNCTIONAL (appropriate toy use, no pretense)

F-1 Functional body involvement (e.g., throwing, kneading, stroking)

F-2 Functional grouping (e.g., tables and chairs)

F-3 Functional dynamic action (e.g., rolling a car)

F-4 Sequences of two or more functional acts

S SYMBOLIC PLAY (pretend, make believe)

S-1 Autosymbolic single scheme

S-2 Single scheme symbolic play, other-directed

S-3 Repetition of same single scheme

S-4 Combination of different single schemes

S-5 Planned symbolic act

S-6 Combination of planned symbolic acts, play story

SPECIFICATIONS FOR LEVELS F AND S

IM direct imitation   ST after directive stimulus

DI deferred imitation   SP spontaneous

Figure 8.2 Play Observation Scale

of the children's previous play scores, nor of their belonging to the experimental or the control group. For twelve children an additional follow-up score is available.

The twenty-five control children (fourteen female, eleven male), matched as well as possible, were tested by the same adults and at approximately the same times as the experimental children, but in between they received no special play interventions.

Results

The results of pre- and post-tests are presented in figure 8.3. The scores given are the maximum scores attained by the children during the scoring sessions. To improve readability of the plot, the play levels are somewhat condensed, and the specifications are left out. For the control group, scores before and after clearly overlap. The children who participated in the training did not differ from the con-

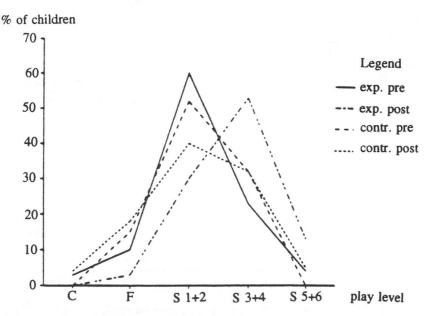

% of children

Figure 8.3 Frequency of Different Play Levels, Pre- and Post-Test (maximum score during test session)

trol group at pre-test, but after training there is a definite shift towards a higher play level.

Individual losses and gains in play level after the training period are shown in figure 8.4. Again, whereas the gains in the control group average zero, the mean gain in the trained children was a full play sublevel. All these differences are statistically significant.

For twelve children in the experimental group, a follow-up test score after three months was available. Figure 8.5 shows again the shift towards a higher play level after training, but it also shows that this gain was retained during follow-up time. At least there was no loss in play skill.

To summarize the results: many retarded subjects were well able to learn some new play skills and to demonstrate these to a strange adult. Not surprisingly, the play level during training itself, guided by the well-known trainer, was usually much higher than at the scoring session. At follow-up, again with a strange adult, most of the skills were retained. Bearing in mind the small number of training sessions (for some of the children only nine), this gain was remarkable. Over the same period of time, the control subjects (who did not attend the training) progressed very little or not at all.

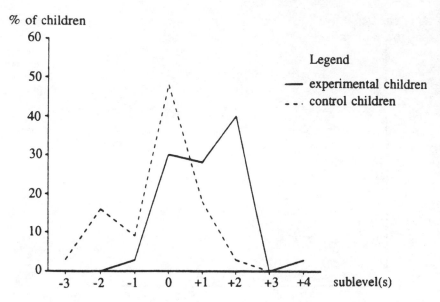

Figure 8.4 Losses/Gains in Play Sublevel After Training (maximum score during test session)

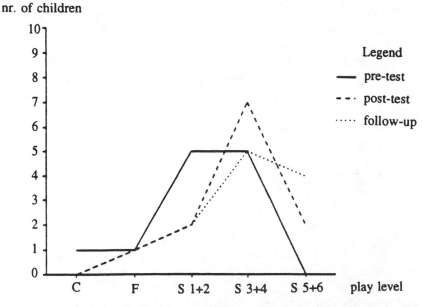

Figure 8.5 Frequency of Different Play Levels, at Pre-Test, Post-Test and Follow-Up (12 experimental children)

No sex differences were found in play levels or play gains. Encouragingly, it seems that play gains increase with the number of sessions. Nine to fifteen sessions is certainly not much for these slow learners, and it is recommended to lengthen the program to at least fifteen half-hour sessions.

Some of the experimental children seemed to improve somewhat in verbal production. However, on the Reynell developmental language scale this could not be confirmed.

But at least as important as the quantitative results was the evident pleasure of many experimental children in joint play and in imaginative activities. This may in time develop into the intrinsic motivation which characterizes play. Moreover, where no change in maximum play level occurred, we often saw a transition from imitated to more spontaneous play inside that level. This spontaneity and pleasure was reflected in the trainers' satisfaction: they liked what they were doing, and found the training provided a basis for good working relationships with their participants.

Generalization of Results

In all, our results are encouraging. However, one central problem remains: we have not yet been able to reliably measure progress in play in the daily living environment of the participating children. Generalization of the play skills seems still poor, even though at follow-up (with a different adult) in the same play room the children show they still master them.

Three main reasons may be responsible for this lack of transfer from the experimental to the natural situation.

1. Both in the training and test sessions the children experienced positive interaction with a stimulating adult. It may be argued that the children's higher responses in that situation were evoked rather than induced or newly developed. In that case, the children naturally would not respond as well in other (less stimulating) environments. Although this may be a valid argument, it should be pointed out that some of the higher scores during the post-test sessions were attained during unstimulated play, in which interaction was minimal.

2. In the living group, either in day care or in the residential homes, toys to play imaginatively are largely absent. Care-

givers are much more involved with the routines of daily life, such as drinking coffee and outside activities, or with developmental material, such as puzzles, building blocks etc., than interested in play with dolls, bears and houses. In the groups of retarded adolescents especially, caregivers may even reject such toys as inappropriate for their residents' age. However, we found that thirty-year-olds with a mental age of four years can play enthusiastically with little cars, dolls and imaginary water taps. This rather negative attitude of caregivers may be one of the factors that limit generalization of the trained skills from the play room to daily living environment.

3. The other essential factor to prevent transfer is, without doubt, the attitude of the retarded children themselves. Left to themselves, they tend to keep to the well-known, well-trodden paths and not to take new initiatives. This is a familiar problem for all kinds of training programs. These children need the continuing stimulating guidance of their caregivers to show the skills they are capable of.

That is why, at present, we extend the project to include caregivers in day care and homes, so as to incorporate the play skills and the fun of joint imaginative play in the regular day program. In one of the residential centers, play is going to be a new item in the caregivers' inservice training. In one of the day care centers, parents have become interested. This is important, because this new way of play may give a new dimension to overall development and the daily life of many of our participants.

By giving imaginative play its rightful place among the many guided activities in the day programs for mentally retarded children and adolescents, we can at least pass the message to them: Play is fun—and you can do it too.

9

Families at Play: Interventions for Children with Developmental Handicaps

Roy McConkey

Throughout the world, families play games. Whether it is the mother-infant games of finger rhymes and peek-a-boo, the rough-and-tumble play of fathers and toddlers, or children's chasing games and imaginative play (Sutton-Smith 1972; Grunfield 1982). Indeed, the earliest collection of European folk games compiled by the Castilian King Alfonso in 1923 contains many items which are familiar to twentieth-century children and their families.

Research in developmental psychology has documented the learning value of these games for infants and toddlers (Moyles 1989). Donaldson (1978), in her review, identifies three features inherent in many games which promote cognitive growth. First, the importance of *joint activities* between adults and children in establishing common references and shared meanings. Tizard and Hughes (1984) observed richer linguistic inputs in the homes of working-class mothers when reading books and playing cards with their daughters than provided to the same children by teachers in nursery schools.

Second, *turn-taking games* provide infants with opportunities to initiate routines and enable them to play an active part in communicative interchanges. Bruner (1975) analyzed the developmental significance of games such as peek-a-boo and Chapman's review of "motherese" research concluded that "it is the linguistically responsive environment, rather than the linguistically stimulating one which should accelerate language acquisition."

Third, Donaldson's (1979) own research stresses the value of *problem-solving* opportunities so that preschoolers can gain their own understanding of the world and relationships by discovering their own solutions ". . . not without putting forth some effort, not without difficulties to be mastered, errors to be overcome and creative solutions to be found."

These three attributes are to be found in many of the informal games which families have played in every generation (Marjanovic 1986). Indeed, the teaching opportunities offered by games are hard for nursery school teachers to replicate:

- individual tuition;

- models of competent performance given as the experienced players take their turn in the game;

- immediate correction of children's mistakes, often with an explanation;

- opportunities for repeated practice as many games involve repetition;

- intrinsic motivation for learners to continue with the game.

Thus, the conclusion reached by the Director of the Harvard Preschool Project, Burton White (1979), is hardly surprising: "We came to believe that the informal education which parents provide makes more of a total impact on a child's total education development than does the formal education system." This assertion echoes the findings of various British longitudinal studies which consistently demonstrate the dominance of family variables on children's scholastic performance (e.g., Davie, Butler & Goldstein 1972).

Play as a Means of Intervention

These insights from developmental researchers open new approaches to helping children who are at risk of developmental delays or with developmental disabilities. During the past twenty years, services have demonstrated that much can be done to ameliorate their handicaps through early intervention and stimulation programs (Mitchell & Brown 1990).

However, the specialist-led service programs which are now commonplace in industrialized countries are ill-suited to the developing world with its scarcity of personnel and resources to pay them

(O'Toole 1990). Yet ninety percent of the world's children with disabilities live there and at best only one in ten receive any form of help (WHO 1985). But even in industrialized countries, many families whose children are at risk of developing problems receive little or no guidance on how they could prevent or overcome these difficulties. Indeed many parents appear to have little appreciation of the influence they can have on their child's development (Goodnow & Collins 1990).

The solution of employing more professionals to do the job is unlikely to be affordable even if it were desirable. More attractive is an intervention strategy based on optimizing the naturally occurring interactions which all children the world over experience within their families and local community. In short, play would be the medium of intervention. This offers the following advantages:

- Games which parents and other family members are already familiar with reduce the need for training and the feelings of inadequacy which "professional exercises" often present to families. Families can more easily "own" and control the interventions, making it more likely that they will continue to use and adapt them (Baker 1989).

- Existing family routines are reinforced or extended rather than that families are expected to adapt to new procedures which may be impractical, given home circumstances and responsibilities (McConachie 1986).

- As the activities are drawn from the local culture, the ecological validity of the intervention is assured and the cultural identity of the children may even be strengthened (Ivic 1986).

- For the child with a marked disability play-based interventions could offer a better opportunity for successfully integrating them into the family and the life of the local community (Richardson & Ritchie 1989).

In addition to the conclusions emerging from developmental research which were cited earlier, a growing body of evidence has demonstrated that play-based interventions can enhance the development of children with mental retardation (Odom & Karnes 1988), can overcome language problems (Martin, McConkey & Martin 1984) and can enhance their cognitive maturity (Weikart, Epstein, Schweinhart & Bond 1978).

Making Play Work

Three steps are required in order to put play-based intervention into practice. First, identifying the existing games and play activities within a culture which are especially nurturant of children's development; in particular those involving joint activity, turn-taking and problem-solving. Second, establishing optimal interactions between adults (and older children) and children during play. Third, finding effective ways of sharing this approach with all families, especially those in developing countries.

Children's Games

Although attempts have been made to develop anthologies of children's games, the task has been beset with definitional problems compounded by the sheer volume of material to be catalogued (Marjanovic 1986). A more pragmatic approach has been to observe children at play. One of the most comprehensive studies of this kind was undertaken by Opie and Opie (1969) in Britain. However, they concentrated mainly on children's games outside the home. Similar small-scale studies, mainly carried out by anthropologists, have documented the activities of children in other cultures (Ivic 1986).

A third source of games and play activities can be found in the many books published in recent years aimed primarily at parents. Such "baby" and "toddler" guides may overemphasize certain types of play activities; for example so-called educational toys such as jigsaws, which may not be typical within a culture. A number of books also focus on play with children who have special needs (Riddick 1982).

The fourth approach is arguably the easiest and most effective. Adult members of the community are asked to recall the games and activities of their childhood and to report on those which their children play. This can be done with individual families but is more productive in group settings when participants have the chance to be reminded of activities reported by others. Their recollections can be supplemented by activities culled from other sources.

The resulting listings of games and play activities can be used by the group to explore the learning value inherent in common games. For example, they might chose a game from the list and analyze the skills needed by children to play the game. The ancient game of Tick-Tack-Toe (known as Noughts and Crosses in Britain when played with paper and pencil) requires players to take turns, draw symbols, plan ahead, change strategy, remember, count, and so on.

Different games will yield other listings of skills acquired as children develop physically, socially and cognitively: jumping and skipping games; throwing at a target; or pretend games. These skills can be linked to activities which are important in everyday life and valued by the group, such as writing, cooking, road safety, etcetera. In this way the value of play experiences is reinforced.

A further refinement is to arrange these games into *developmental sequences*; starting with activities which parents can use with babies. Then the games can be matched to the child's developmental level, irrespective of chronological age. Figure 9.1 is an example of a games list prepared in Uganda for use with video programs illustrating ways of helping the development of children with disabilities.

Parental Style

The learning value lies not just in the game but in how it is played. Particularly important is the way in which adults interact with children. For example, we know that children's language learning and usage is enhanced or hindered by the way adults talk to them. As Tizard and Hughes (1984) noted: "The kind of dialogue that seems to help the child is not that currently favored by many teachers in which the adult poses a series of questions. Rather it is one in which the adult listens to the child's questions and comments, helps to clarify her ideas and feeds her the information she asks for."

Young parents need to know that and practice doing it. There are many other pointers they can be given as well (MacDonald & Gillette 1988):

- Engage the child in play with no performance demands— act like the child, matching your actions to his/hers.

- Use an easy give-and-take style—relax and enjoy yourself.

- Show the child the next step and give him opportunities to copy you—but do not force him or her to imitate you.

- Let the child initiate actions to which you can respond.

- Talk in ways that describe the child's actions and current experience.

- Provide simple words for his/her nonverbal communications.

THINKING TOGETHER ACTIVITY SHEET

*Please note that these activities should be done
by all members of the family.*

EXPLORATION OF OBJECTS

Prop child up in cot—will he follow your face as you move from side to side? If the child cannot sit, make sure he can watch what is going on, both in the home and outside.

Play in front of the mirror—encourage the child to pat, kiss, etc.

Encourage the child to explore your face—wear hat and sun glasses—see if he will try to get them off.

As the child lies in bed, lean over and push the mattress so that he bounces up and down. Talk as you do it.

Take turns to pull the cloth off each other's face. Peek-a-boo!

Encourage the child to explore your face, hair, etc. Laugh, giggle, etc. as though he is tickling you.

Let the children share a bath. Encourage them to copy each other, e.g., pouring games, splashing, etc.

Massage the child's body with scented talc or oil.

Place rattles into the child's hand—then encourage him to shake.

Dangle toys over the child when he is lying down for him to try to swipe at or grasp.

Hold toys in front of the child and slowly move from side to side (a torch will do as well).

Rub the child's body with cloths of different textures—rough, smooth, furry, etc.

Gently blow the child's cheek or palm.

Tickle the child with a feather.

Put beans in a plastic bottle. Place bottle in child's hand. Shake to make a noise.

Have objects in the bath when you are washing the child. Show him how they bob up and down; or pour water with them.

Give the child a chance to smell the food before you start feeding.

Tie string to a small toy—dangling it close to the child's hand. When he grasps it, pull gently so that the child needs to hold on to it.

Collect 6 objects which feel very different and are of different shapes—leaf, paper, etc. Put them one at a time in the child's hand and see which one he holds longest.

Tie string to an object. Encourage child to reach for object when it's held above his head or to one side.

Put a small squeaky toy in the child's hand. Encourage to squeeze it.

Cut a piece from a plastic supermarket bag—make it a ball. Encourage the child to squeeze and make it crackle.

Dangle a balloon above the child's cot. Encourage to pat it with his hands.

Figure 9.1   A Games List Developed in Uganda

The foregoing may seem all too obvious to professionals involved with preschoolers but can be a revelation to many parents. But changing parental styles begs a number of important questions.

First, the cultural perceptions of disability. For example, Nguyen (1989) writing of the people of Southeast Asia: "Since people with disabilities are believed to be punishments to their families, the handicapped person is isolated from society, and is considered useless, worthless, a shame on the family. Nothing will be done for them. They have no future." Attitudinal change must therefore be a key element in establishing any intervention program; a process that has been ongoing in industrialized countries for the past thirty years but which has barely begun in some parts of the developing world. Yet as Walker (1986) notes in relation to West Africa, attitudes vary not only between countries but within countries.

An important finding from American studies is that the two most helpful coping strategies for families were (1) believing that the child's intervention program had the family's best interests at heart and (2) learning how to help their child improve (Gartner, Lipsky & Turnbull 1991). I would argue that play-based interventions which focus on developing basic skills fulfill both of these conditions.

A second obstacle could be the cultural acceptability of adults playing with children. Again this is not unique to the developing world but it may be more apparent there, given the work load which mothers especially bear to provide for their families. It is therefore even more crucial that interventions are family-centered and embrace grandparents and older siblings among the target audience. However, the attitudes of mothers and fathers can be influenced by the models and arguments of others in their community who feel they have benefitted from play-based interventions (Baker 1989).

Spreading the Word

Traditional ways of sharing knowledge—through talks and literature—are ill-suited to reaching families. However, modern technology in the form of video recordings does offer an attractive alternative and our research in Ireland has demonstrated its potential effectiveness (McConkey 1988). The advantages are easily summarized:

- *Visual*—Viewers can see play activities and interactive styles in action. A variety of games can be quickly displayed and, if need be, viewers can watch the sequences a number of times to reinforce their learning. Thus literacy and language problems are immediately overcome.

- *Culturally appropriate*—Local scenes depict the viewer's reality and emphasize that the activities are used by their countryfolk.

- *Local languages*—It is relatively easy to dub commentaries in local languages on to the video programs. This makes the training available to everyone and not just those who can read.

- *Easily transportable*—Videocassettes are easily taken or sent to any place which has video playback equipment. This is becoming more readily available throughout the world. Recorders and color televisions can be battery-operated.

- *Easily repeated*—The video programs can be easily repeated with different groups and although time intensive to make, they are very time efficient thereafter.

- *Enhanced status*—Portraying families and children with disabilities on video, can enhance their status within the community as the programs focus on what the children can learn to do for themselves, rather than on their handicaps.

Although video equipment is not commonplace in developing countries, it will become more so in the future. Even now, video equipment has been donated to organizations in developing countries but lies unused as local personnel are unsure how best to deploy it.

In 1990, the Special Education Section of UNESCO launched a development and research project to produce training materials aimed at families in developing countries who have young children with developmental handicaps. In particular, the project aims to evaluate the use of indigenously produced training packages, based around video programs recorded on location mainly in urban and rural homes. The videos focus mainly on naturally occurring interactions and play activities in the home and local community. UNESCO are sponsoring projects in Uganda, Malawi and Sri Lanka in order to:

- Explore the feasibility of local personnel in these countries producing video training programs and associated print materials aimed primarily at families. UNESCO consultants of which I am one, provide initial support and direction;

- Establish the usage of the packages and discover common problem and solutions;

- Determine the impact of the packages on family attitudes, understanding and practice;

- Discover the adaptability of this training model to local circumstances and the influences on style, content and implementation of the packages according to the agency (or agencies) involved in the production of the packages.

Video programs based largely around common play activities have been produced in the three participating countries and they are presently being field tested. The common aims of all the packages are (1) to promote enjoyable interactions among the family members and the child with a disability; (2) to illustrate the developmental progression in key areas of development, such as mobility, communication, use of hands and thinking; (3) to give ideas for play activities which families can use at home and in the neighborhood; (4) to provide models of adults (and older siblings) playing with rather than observing or "teaching."

As a participant in the recordings, I was left with three strong impressions. First, how the same game, or variants of it, occurs in different cultures—are there play universals? If this is the case, greater opportunities open for sharing training materials across cultures (Ivic 1986). Second, how easy it was to get families playing, even if it is not typical of their daily routine. Suggestions from visitors, demonstrations and the provision of simple playthings which were easily improvised, quickly got adults and children playing. Third, the pleasure which family members took in the child's achievements; and the fun extended to viewers watching the video recordings as laughter is contagious.

Equally striking with many parents was their low expectation that the child with special needs could learn. They would quickly discontinue an activity if the child did not succeed straightaway or showed signs of disinterest. Of course, few had been given any advice on how best to help the child.

And so we come back to where we started. Ninety percent of the world's disabled children and their families are still waiting for help. As the World Health Organization (1985) noted: "Fortunately most of the recent advances in education and training and in helping mentally retarded persons to develop their skills are comparatively simple and these techniques can be acquired after only a short period of training by most people irrespective of their previous experience. An urgent task facing all societies . . . is to devise a strategy for disseminating existing knowledge and skills to the hundreds of thousands of people who come into daily contact with mentally retarded people."

Play researchers and practitioners in affluent Europe have much to offer, as well as to learn from, the families and children of the developing world. Our thinking about play must embrace all the world's children.

/10

Play Within an Intervention
for Multiply Handicapped Children

**Han Nakken, Carla Vlaskamp
and Ruud van Wijck**

It is not easy to imagine the picture of a child at play, or of an adult playing with a child, when that child is profoundly and multiply handicapped. And yet, in this chapter we will discuss how to stimulate these children to activities and interactions with play elements, which is a new development in the care and education of profoundly multiply handicapped children. A central problem of profoundly multiply handicapped children is their inability to play or to interact with their environment in an active way. At the same time, parents and care staff in day and residential centers are often unable to help them find appropriate ways for exploration and play.

Ideas for the solution or reduction of this problem were combined in a program that was evaluated in four different educational centers for the mentally and multiply handicapped. Basic to this program is the stimulation of active play-directed and communicative behavior in the *care staff*, who are themselves guided by pre-formulated goals.

In the first part of this paper, the educational problems encountered in dealing with the profoundly multiply handicapped children will be analyzed. Next, the elements for a solution of these problems will be discussed. Finally, the design of our intervention and evaluation strategy is described, as well as the main results of our research.

Profoundly Multiply Handicapped Children
and Their Education

By "profoundly multiply handicapped children" we particularly mean children who hardly seem to function at all, as a result of severe brain damage before, during, or shortly after birth. Their cognitive development is profoundly retarded. In terms of DSM-III, this means an IQ/DQ of below 30 (Hogg & Sebba 1986). They are hardly capable of any form of movement (diagnosis often spastic quadriplegia). Additional sensory disorders regularly occur, even though these are not always easily detected because of the interaction of the disorders. Epilepsy is almost a common phenomenon.

This picture should be kept in mind when we discuss the education of profoundly multiply handicapped children. To prevent misunderstandings we name this group "profoundly physically-mentally disabled (PMD) children." We do not intend, however, to discuss in depth whether or not this group should be distinguished from other groups of profoundly handicapped persons. This discussion can be left to other forums (e.g., Wolf & Anderson 1969; Sontag, Smith & Sailor 1977; Nakken & Den Ouden 1985; Nakken 1990).

What are the educational problems of profoundly PMD children? To answer this question, let us look briefly at normal development from a transactional point of view (see, e.g., Sameroff & Chandler 1975), and at the consequences if this development fails or partially fails to occur (as previously described by Nakken & Den Ouden 1985).

Normally, children develop in active interaction with people and with objects and people. They explore their environment, they explore their relations with others, much of this in a playful way. They challenge adults to smile, to play, or sometimes even to punish them, and these reactions again rechallenge the child. These interactions between the young child and its environment influence the development of brain structure, which, in turn, influences the cognitive and affective abilities of the child.

What about these challenges and interactions in the care for children with profound multiple disabilities? The challenges are extremely difficult to understand and to react to. Adults often do not know how to communicate and how to adapt the environment to the child's abilities and vice versa. The child is hardly able to attract the attention of adults and to express its desires and feelings. A clumsy action does not elicit an appropriate response anyway. As a result, these children fail to take initiatives and have much less experience than other children. Unnecessary delays in their development and isolation can be the result (Le Gay Brereton 1972). Deprivation and degeneration are a real danger.

If the PMD child is fortunate enough to live at home, where parents see opportunities for creating an active relation with their child, deprivation can be prevented. Even though the child is apparently "capable of nothing," a communicative and therefore decent human existence is still possible. But many parents see little opportunity for the education of their profoundly PMD child, a problem often aggravated by the absence of home training programs and good day care centers. In consequence, a residential unit for the mentally handicapped is often seen as the only possible solution.

In these units both time and knowledge, necessary to work towards communication, are often lacking. Here, too, the above mentioned vicious circle in interaction may develop. Caregivers, however well-intentioned, may easily get disappointed about the child's reactions to their challenges and give up their attempts. The child ultimately also gives up its attempts. Consequently, care staff may assume that, apart from physical care, nothing else is possible. Working with this group becomes less interesting and less challenging, which diminishes the chances for establishing a relationship based on interaction and trust. The child appears well looked-after but is at the same time deprived, locked up in its own body and isolated as long as it lives, its right to human communication seriously jeopardized. These educational problems are summarized in table 10.1.

Looking for Solutions

In signalling these educational problems and in our search for solutions we take a normative position, already implicit in our discussion, which may be stated as follows. All children have a right to be educated in the broad (Western) sense of that word (see Nakken 1992). Education can be described as a living together of children and educators (parents, teachers, and/or others) who try to prepare the child, according to their own standards, for some sort of (if possible, independent) life in their particular type of society. In our society, the right to an education in the family or in a residential center implies the right to be taken care of, the availability of adults with whom you can share your emotions and who support you when you have problems, but also the right to learn everything you are capable of, the right to participate in social life, etc. (Hallahan & Kaufman 1988; Kiernan 1992).

Table 10.1   Problems in the Education of Profoundly Multiply Handicapped Children in a Residential Center

PROBLEM	PRESUMED CONSEQUENCES
The development of the child is deviant. As a consequence it cannot independently achieve exploration and play.	The child does not get any or hardly any experiences and suffers an unnecessary delay in development.
Child and care staff have difficulties in understanding each other or do not understand each other at all.	The child gives up possible attempts at communication, care staff give up misunderstood attempts at communication. The child lives in isolation.
Care staff lack ideas for a better education of the "unusual" child.	Care-staff do not "design" educational goals and means. They "just" take care of the child.
Care staff in the groups for profoundly PMD children search solutions for educational problems, managers of residential centers are concerned with physical care.	The discussions revolve around "more hands at the bed" (which cannot be supplied) and not about improving the educational help. There is a large care staff turnover.
The organization lacks a model for educating profoundly multiply handicapped children.	The groups are not regarded as an educational unit. No means are allocated for educational activities.

This basic position has the following consequences for solving educational problems in the residential care of profoundly PMD children:

a. Educational measures should not only aim at changing the behavior of the child. An educational problem is a joint problem of the child, the educators or caregivers and the living environment (the residential unit).

b. As almost nothing happens spontaneously with a profoundly PMD child, it is not enough to create a good home in which the child is challenged to explore. The child needs the intensive help of others to acquire experiences, to communicate and to play. Therefore, caregivers have to take the initiative.

c. In order to attune these initiatives to each individual child, goal-setting and goal evaluation are indispensable. After all, with profoundly PMD children, general goals valid for all children cannot be pursued as a matter of course. Working with individual goals and evaluating them by means of single case research (Hersen & Barlow 1986) has repeatedly been shown effective in stimulating development of children with mental and physical disabilities (see, e.g., Nakken & Den Ouden 1985; Schneider 1989; Vriesema, Miedema & Van Blokland 1992). Therefore, we assume them also effective when the emphasis will be on goals that apply to interaction and communication.

d. In the case of profoundly PMD children, the goals are to prevent isolation and to stimulate the child's activities and play. In doing so, however, one should not neglect medical-biological goals but rather integrate them in the educational goals as much as possible. For example, if one stimulates certain activities, one should take great care to help the child find a posture which facilitates these activities (Bobath 1967). Medical or physical care activities (for example changing and feeding) can also be used to communicate intensively with the child.

It is not a simple or casual task, however, to find or develop activities which stimulate the profoundly PMD child to action or to communication with others. To start with, we must find out what opportunities there are in any given situation. An example of an activity for Harry in interaction with a care staff member will illustrate this. Harry is a profoundly physically and mentally disabled boy, who is also deaf, figure 10.1.

Finding and presenting opportunities for the child to actively do something himself (to explore and to play) is illustrated in the next example with Tom, who is blind, deaf, and has profound physical and mental disabilities, figure 10.2.

Of course, these are not particularly impressive play activities. But whoever has sat with a PMD child will understand what effort and patience is needed to make anything at all happen. This means that the implementation or changing of an educational model such as this has several consequences for the care system.

As said before, such an intervention in residential care should not exclusively be directed towards training the child in particular activities. Children, educators, and living environment should be

Goal:	To acquire knowledge on how Harry makes eye contact in this situation.
Activity:	Lying with Harry on the mat (red mat in the play corner)
Time:	In the afternoon
Situation:	Red mat in the play corner
Duration:	± 15 minutes
Materials:	None
Execution:	Make sure there are no toys in the play corner within Harry's field of vision. Place the mirror with the reflecting side turned away so the play corner is separated from the rest of the group. Put Harry on the mat in such a way that he cannot look into the living room. Lie beside him on the mat. Play with him, *without* materials.

> For example: • lie beside him
>
> • have him sit between your legs in front of you, facing you

Make sure your attention is completely focused on Harry while you are busy with him and *watch Harry's eyes!!*

Report on:	1. duration of eye contact
	2. actions that lead to eye contact

Figure 10.1 Example of an Activity Plan for Harry

simultaneously influenced. This can best be accomplished by working intensively with the (substitute) educators, the care staff. In addition, this should be done in close cooperation with the therapeutic staff and the unit (middle) management which is, after all, responsible for managing the educational program. In Dutch residential centers for PMD children, this middle management usually consists of the unit head, an educational psychologist (or a comparable professional) and the unit physician.

Implementing an Intervention Program

With the previous points in mind an intervention program was developed for use in residential centers for the mentally and multiply handicapped. This program consisted of (a) training courses on "working with an educational plan," given to care staff, therapists and middle management teams; (b) on-the-job-training for all personnel and

Goal:	To offer opportunities for Tom to manipulate materials
Activity:	Placing materials in Tom's hands
Situation:	Tom sits in his wheelchair (in a way that is suitable for him)
Time:	About 9:30 a.m.
Duration:	Variable, sometimes as long as an hour
Materials:	• telephone flex
	• rattle with a good handle
	• "fiddle apron" (an apron containing all kinds of tactile materials)
	• piece of "fluff rope" (sisal rope)
	• other materials Tom is capable of holding well
Execution:	Place the materials in Tom's hands and observe his reactions
Report on:	1. possible preference for materials
	2. reactions: • fiddling • smiling
	• no apparent reactions

Figure 10.2   Example of an Activity Plan for Tom

(c) evaluation of effects on the children, on care staff and management team. Our *questions* were: (1) is the implementation strategy effective?; (2) are the evaluation procedures implemented; and (3) what are the effects of the intervention on the behavior of the residents, on the communication between residents and care staff/therapists and on the behavior/ideas of all personnel about education?

We will briefly describe some central features of the program, the training course and the evaluation procedures. Next, the implementation of the educational model and its ensuing intervention is discussed. Finally, some general results will be mentioned.

Intervention Program

The intervention program is implemented at four levels of instruction: information, training, support and written directions. Information is provided during a four-month course and consists mainly of aspects of educating the profoundly mentally and physically handicapped and to the principles of program-evaluation. In this course we also present our working model. In this model, both theory and experiential knowledge (step 1) is used as a basis for drawing up an educational perspective for the resident (step 2). A perspective means: to state a desired situation or development in the future for an individual resident. A perspective should be valid for a period of about one to two years. In most perspectives for profoundly multiply handicapped, emphasis will be on improving interaction and communication. Perspectives related to cognitive development will not be feasible in most cases.

The main goal (step 3) is directly deduced from the perspective and is a joint goal for every professional concerned with the care for this particular resident. Of course, more than one main goal can be deduced from the perspective. A main goal is mostly drawn up for a period of four to six months. To draw up a short-term goal is step 4. Deduced from the perspective and based on the main goal, all professionals concerned have to draw up short-term goals with which they can work for a short period of time. In a short-term goal is stated what can be achieved within a period of two to four weeks.

The fifth step consists of an exact description of the activity needed to reach the short-term goal. This includes detailed information on how, when, and who is to perform this activity. Details must be given on the context in which each behavior, vocalization or gesture takes place. To draw up items to report on regarding the performance of these activities is the sixth step. This can be viewed as a daily evaluation. Decisions about the progress observed and about the choice for a next short-term goal depend largely on these reports.

The seventh step is drawing up a goal attainment scale. A goal attainment scale is a useful instrument to verify whether the intended goals are indeed attained.

Next, we start to work on the short-term goal. At a previously set date we evaluate. Evaluation is the eighth and last step of the scheme. We evaluate both short-term and main goals at a previously fixed time. Subsequently, a next short-term goal is chosen, activities and report items are stated, and a new goal attainment scale is drawn up, figure 10.3.

During training, the emphasis is on setting short term goals. Support will be given to participants who encounter difficulties in performing these activities to reach the determined short-term goals or in dealing with other problems related to this method. Management receives support in coaching care staff and therapists in their educational activities and in the use of program evaluation procedures. Written directions are provided to all participants in the intervention program and will be used both as a support by drawing up goals and as a reference.

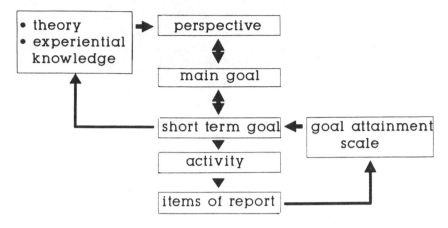

Figure 10.3   Goals and Their Evaluation

Implementation

To start with, an analysis is made of the initial situation. This comprises: (a) behavioral assessment of the profoundly PMD residents, (b) educational problems as reported by care staff, but also (c) appraisal of the capacity for change of care staff and middle management, in relation to (d) the organization model (Van Wijck, Vlaskamp, Nakken & Smrkovsky 1991).

In addition, instruments for effect-measurement are selected and a pre-test takes place. Effects are measured with respect to job satisfaction, knowledge about and abilities to work with goals, particularly with respect to problems in residential care.

Next, the program (course, on-the-job-training, and evaluation procedures) is implemented during four months. During this period management team and care staff together analyze their initial situation, and design perspectives and long-term goals for each resident. During training, the emphasis is on setting short-term goals and designing activities to reach them. Care staff execute these activities (in which play is an important element) with the residents.

All goals are recorded and evaluated at a fixed time. The entire intervention process is carefully recorded, thus enabling a "program evaluation," which may lead to changes in both form and content of the program (Van Wijck, Vlaskamp, Nakken & Smrkovsky 1991). At the end of the intervention period the instruments for effect evaluation are administered again, as well as four months and eight months later.

What makes this intervention program innovative is that such a program has never been applied to this specific population of residential PMD children. This also means that no previous investigations have been done on its effectiveness (Rossi & Freeman 1989).

Results

At the start of our research project we used a quasi-experimental design: a variation on the pre-test post-test control group design (Cook & Campbell 1979). However, as a consequence of our program evaluation strategy, our research design changed to a multiple case study, in which each case consists of the evaluation of an intervention.

Preliminary results show that we are well on our way to establish a useful program for the education of and association with the profoundly multiply handicapped. Firstly, the program is valued positively by the whole care staff because it allows them an appreciable degree of self-management: the program generates information on children that they themselves can translate into new perspectives and goals.

Secondly, nearly all caregivers report behavioral changes in all residents, based upon intersubjective judgement. These changes are in accordance with the proposed working goals. According to self-report, communications and interactions between the residents and care-staff have improved. The whole care staff reported that their problems in those areas have been reduced, figure 10.4.

Thirdly, by using the program, the educational needs of all the profoundly PMD children involved become more distinct. A high percentage of positive Goal Attainment Scale scores (80 percent, which is far above criterium value) indicates that after training care staff is able to adequately design working goals. Daily routines are changed and the whole care staff is more aware of their motives in interactions with these children. During the intervention period, their knowledge about educating the profoundly handicapped has improved and ideas about these children's possibilities have changed in a positive direction.

Finally, almost certainly as a consequence of the above mentioned changes, job satisfaction for all members of the care staff has increased. Initial problems with respect to residential care and residential education change, become more concrete, and sometimes even diminish after intervention.

For Harry and Tom, results can be summed up as follows. For Harry, the main goal for the four-month period was to identify and understand his communicative behavior. Through a series of short-term goals, care staff were able to recognize and attend to the context and meaning behind Harry's efforts to communicate. They have moved through successive stages of observing, understanding and participating in Harry's communicative behavior. Right now, Harry's regular playtime (half an hour daily) is a high point for both Harry and the care staff.

Tom's handicaps are very severe and his inert behavior had previously led the care staff to believe that they had better not touch Tom. He was considered to be happy if left alone. By drawing up a perspective and main goal, aimed at increasing Tom's experiences, the focus of the care staff shifted to attempts to recognize his needs for basic experiences. After a series of short term goals, in which Tom was offered a variety of simple experiences, including physical experiences (see the example given above), his caregivers are now able to hold Tom on their lap on a regular basis. They are still amazed to see how much he enjoys this.

Figure 10.4 Evaluation of Goals for Harry and Tom

These results warrant the conclusion that this educational approach to profoundly multiply handicapped children is effective in stimulating exploration and play as well as communication between children and care staff. Thus, it contributes to a more humane living and working climate in the residential center. However, results are only lasting if the (middle) management actively takes over the goal-setting and evaluation procedures.

/11

Effectiveness of Play Training with Handicapped Toddlers

Jan M. H. de Moor, Betty T. M. van Waesberghe, and Han H. L. Oud

At the moment there is no unequivocal empirical evidence that play training with handicapped children stimulates cognitive development. The purpose of our study is to examine whether a play training program with handicapped toddlers fosters play development and improves attention behavior during free play. According to Piaget, play as well as language and deferred imitation are regarded as simultaneous manifestations of underlying semiotic function.

Because we used play as a diagnostic for cognitive progress, our first problem was to find out for Dutch children whether the occurrence of a detailed sequence of play behavior categories may be used as a reliable and valid indicator of cognitive growth. The selection and definition of the observation categories was based on the previous studies of Belsky and Most (1981), Largo and Howard (1979) and McConkey and Jeffree (1979). We predicted that there is a developmental progress from exploratory behavior with objects like mouthing, visual examination and simple manipulation to pretend play.

An effective play training depends on the content of the instruction program of the toddler teacher. Therefore our second problem, preliminary to the main question of the study, was focused on testing this program. Previous studies have demonstrated that attention-focusing behaviors of the mother, parental responsiveness and postresponse feedback of the mother promotes infant functioning, especially play and attention behavior (Belsky, Goode & Most 1980; Filler & Bricker 1976; Riksen-Walraven 1978). Based on these studies concerning effective parental behavior we composed the instruction program of the toddler teacher.

Infant Free Play Behavior: Development of an Observation System

In a cross-sectional study with forty nonhandicapped toddlers, an observation system was constructed for measuring the frequency and duration of play behavior during individual play. We investigated free play behavior in the presence of the mother. In free play neither the mother nor the experimenter initiated interaction with the child. The mother was asked not to provide the child with ideas or directions about what to do with the toys.

The toddlers were divided into eight age groups of fifteen, eighteen, twenty-one, twenty-four, twenty-seven, thirty, thirty-three, and thirty-six months respectively. The child's play was recorded by means of videotape and coded (from the transcriptions) in the different categories of play behavior. In addition to the category nonplay behavior, thirteen categories of play were selected, which were hypothesized to form a developmental sequence of thirteen steps (Belsky & Most 1981). These categories were all extensively operationally defined and subdivided into four groups (figure 11.1).

The overall reliability evaluated for three observers varied over sessions and pairs of observers from .83 to .94 (with a mean of .88), the reliability per category varied from .68 to 1.00 (mean .88) (Cohen's kappa).

For the validation of the observation system trend analyses were performed on the total frequency and total duration for each category and group of categories (de Moor, van Waesberghe, van der Burg & van den Bercken 1993). The total frequency and duration of exploration (cat. 1-5) decreased linearly between fifteen and thirty-six months of age. After an increase over the period between fifteen and twenty-seven months the total frequency and duration of functional and/or relational play (cat. 6-8) decreased somewhat (a curvilinear relationship). The total frequency and duration of pretend play increased over the entire period. The resulting developmental trends for Dutch children were very similar to those found by Belsky and Most (1981). In the course of development we see that on the one hand indiscriminate handling of objects (exploration) decreases and that on the other hand knowledge of object properties increases and

Exploration (categories 1-5)

(1) Mouthing: indiscriminate mouthing of materials (e.g., the child grasps an object, brings it to his mouth, then licks, mouths or chews it)

(2) Visual examination: the child inspects the object by turning it round in his hand and looking carefully at it

(3) Simple manipulation: exploring objects by indiscriminate manipulation (e.g., holding and shaking an object or banging it against a surface)

(4) Specific manipulation: exploring the function and possibilities of the object (e.g., spinning wheels of a toy car)

(5) Relational manipulation: bringing together two or more materials in an inappropriate way, that is, a manner not initially intended by the manufacturer (e.g., puts spoon in bath)

Functional-relational play (categories 6-8)

(6) Functional play: visually guided manipulation with an object that is used in a functionally appropriate way (e.g., rolls car, takes off clothes of doll)

(7) Relational play: bringing together and integrating two or more objects in an appropriate manner, that is, in a manner intended by the manufacturer (e.g., set cup on saucer)

(8) Sequential-relational play: a sequence of play behaviors inside a common framework (e.g., the child puts the pan on the stove, brings the pan to the table, empties pan onto plates and finally brings spoon to the mouth of the doll)

Pretend play (categories 9-13)

(9) Enactive naming: approximate pretense activity but without confirming evidence of actual pretense behavior (e.g., touch cup to lip without making drinking sounds, tilting head back)

(10) Pretend self: pretense behavior directed toward self in which pretense is apparent (e.g., drinks from cup, making drinking sounds)

(11) Pretend other: pretense behavior directed away from child toward other (e.g., feed doll with spoon)

(12) Substitution: a. using a "meaningless" object in a creative or imaginative way (e.g., eating a block); b. using an object in a pretense act in a way that differs from how it was previously used by the child (e.g., use hairbrush to brush teeth after already using it as a hairbrush); c. without material: a pretense act with gesticulations and/or verbalizations (e.g., picks up doll from bath, pretends taking a towel and dry the dolls hair saying "drying, drying")

(13) Double substitution: pretense play in which two materials are transformed within a single act into something they are not in reality (e.g., cuts pizza with knife while the bottle is the pizza and the handle of the pan the knife)

Non-play behavior (category 0)

(0) Non-play behavior: all behavior with material not applicable to one of the 13 play categories (e.g., touching a toy, pointing at toy)

Figure 11.1 Hypothesized Sequence of Play Categories

schemes are applied to the different features of objects (functional and/or relational play). Finally, with functional and/or relational play increasing between fifteen and twenty-seven months, the mental representation of an act is also becoming more important than any toy characteristic, and helps to initiate play activities. This is demonstrated in pretend play.

Developing and Testing an Instruction Program

Next, an instruction program for changing teacher's play behavior was developed and tested. First of all we constructed an observation system. Six categories were used to refer to attention-focusing strategies of the toddler teacher.

1. *Point / reposition*: the toddler teacher points to a toy to draw the child's attention or moves it so that a child can grasp it.

2. *Demonstrate*: the toddler teacher models to the child how something works or shows an appropriate play action or sequence of play actions.

3. *Physical guidance*: the toddler teacher moves the child's hand to make appropriate play actions (e.g., assisting the child to push a car).

4. *Question / instruct*: verbalization which focus a child's attention on a toy (e.g., "Is your doll sick?") or encourage play actions (e.g., "The doll wants to eat" or "Put the car in the garage").

5. *Highlight*: the toddler teacher describes a unique characteristic of the toy (e.g., "The ball can roll").

6. *Name object / verbalize play actions*: the toddler teacher names the object toward which she is focusing the child's attention or verbalizes the child's play actions (e.g., "That's a car" or while child is putting the doll to bed "Doll is going to sleep").

Three categories were used to describe the toddler teachers behavior which occured after children's response.

1. *Positive verbal feedback*: the toddler teacher provides a positive reinforcing statement about the child's play behavior (e.g., "That's great") or she repeats the child's verbalizations (parallel talking).

2. *Positive physical feedback*: the toddler teacher responds with a potentially reinforcing physical contact like hugging or kissing.

3. *Responsiveness*: any time the use of attention-focusing strategies and positive feedback is judged as response-contingent upon the child's behavior the category responsiveness is scored.

Reliability was assessed for the combined observation data of six sessions. The mean reliability (Cohen's kappa) over pairs of observers for attention-focusing strategies was .69, for positive feedback .69, and for responsiveness .68.

Next, the effect of the instruction program on the behavior of the toddler teacher in the play situation was tested. The dependent variable was measured by means of seven criteria of positive teacher play behavior (e.g., criterium five: "When the child demonstrates nonplay behavior the teacher uses one of the attention-focusing strategies"). These criteria were based on the nine observation categories described above. The score of the teacher's play behavior was calculated from the frequence of noncompliance to these criteria during the whole session (five-second intervals).

The instruction program aimed at adapting the behavior of the toddler teacher to the play level and the play behavior of the child and to its specific characteristics like motor abilities and attention. It consisted of two parts. Firstly, an individual meeting with the toddler teacher was arranged in which information was given on the succesive levels of play development and the different strategies to enhance it. This information was supported by discussing play fragments of her behavior that had been videotaped. At the end of the meeting objectives for her behavior were formulated. Subsequently, direct feedback on these objectives was given by means of an earphone ("bug in the ear") during five play sessions.

To test the efficacy of the training, a multiple-baseline design across subjects was used. The subjects were three toddler teachers working together with one toddler each. One child was diagnosed as having cerebral palsy, two had mental retardation. The results show that the instruction program was effective: after two or three feedback sessions the play behavior of the toddler teacher improved and met the criteria. These results clearly indicated that it is possible within a short time to modify the play behavior style of the toddler teacher and to teach her behavior strategies that are more appropriate to the child's play.

Effect Evaluation of Play Training with Handicapped Toddlers

In this study we tried to determine the effect of play training on the children's play development and on their attention for play objects (van der Burg, de Moor & van Waesberghe 1992). The training was carried out by an instructed toddler teacher. Specific questions were: (1) Does play training increase the frequency and duration of functional-relational play and pretend play and does it decrease exploration? and (2) Does play training increase attention behavior, operationally defined as the amount of time that the child remains focused on the play materials presented?"

The subjects were sixteen handicapped toddlers. Eight of the children were diagnosed as having cerebral palsy and eight had Down's syndrome. The children with celebral palsy attended three rehabilitation centers for physically handicapped persons with an early intervention unit and the Down's syndrome children were enrolled in four day care facilities for mentally retarded children. The children's chronological age ranged from twenty-five to fifty-four months (with a mean of forty-one months); their developmental age and developmental quotient as measured by the Griffiths Mental Development Scales ranged from twenty-five to fifty-four months (mean twenty-five months), and from thirty-five to 110 (mean sixty-four), respectively.

We used a pretest-posttest control group design with matching and randomization. In addition to the matching on the clinical characteristics of the groups mentioned, the matching variables were: developmental age as measured with the Griffiths test, and play age as measured by the Symbolic Play Test (Lowe & Costello 1976). The play training program for the experimental subjects consisted of twenty-five play sessions, two or three times a week and each lasting approximately twenty minutes. The instruction program for the toddler teacher included three parts:

1. A general course with group discussion, role playing and video illustrations. Two weeks before starting the play training, the toddler teachers got detailed information about the successive levels of play development, the different types of attention-focusing strategies and positive feedback during play training, the importance of responsiveness to the child and the negative effect of disturbing strategies on the child's play. All these issues were illustrated with video fragments. At the end of the course the toddler teachers practiced what they had learned by role playing.

2. An individual meeting with the toddler teacher just before starting the play training. Video fragments of her behavior during play were analysed and discussed, and either two or three instructional goals were chosen to be reached within the first three sessions. We also talked about the child's play characteristics and how the child's play behavior could be guided and structured.

3. Feedback following each play session.

During the entire play training period the toddler teacher got regular feedback on her behavior. In the beginning (the first four to six sessions) we gave advice and suggestions after each session; from the sixth session onwards feedback was given only after one out of three sessions. The instructional goals and the way to handle special play characteristics of the child were changed, if necessary.

The sixth play session was used to code whether the behavior of the toddler teacher was adapted to the child's play. We defined seven criteria based on the categories of the teacher's instruction program mentioned above. Prior to all data collection the overall reliability (Cohen's kappa) over all the criteria together was .81; the reliability per criterion varied from .66 to .100. The results showed that after six play sessions with feedback all the toddler teachers, except one, met the criteria and were very sensitive to the child's play behavior.

The experiment had two groups of dependent variables: (1) variables of the child's exploration and play behavior: frequency and duration of exploration, functional-relational play and pretend play as coded according to our observation system; (2) variables of the child's attention-focusing behavior: total amount of seconds the child was engaged with play objects, mean length of the two longest unbroken play periods and three measures of play involvement: "Unfocused behavior," "Extended exploratory bout" and "Very lengthy exploratory bout." The code "Unfocused" was assigned to any period of five seconds or more in which the child was not engaged in focused exploration of the toys provided. "Extended exploratory" designated any period of focused exploration of more than two and less than eleven consecutive ten-second intervals. The code "Very lenghty exploration bout" was used for eleven or more of such contiguous ten-second intervals.

We collected pretest, posttest and follow-up data in the experimental and the control groups before and after the training period, which consisted of twenty-five play sessions (during a mean period of 2.5 months). For each measurement and with each child we video-

Problem

Lucy was a thirty-five-months-old cerebral palsy child, enrolled in a special class for physically handicapped toddlers. Her developmental level varied from twenty-four to thirty months; age scores for language production and reception were both thirty months and the play age as measured by the Symbolic Play Test was twenty-three months. Analysis of the child's free play showed that Lucy's play was characterized by visual examination, specific manipulation and relational manipulation (categories two, four and five), little functional and relational play (categories six to seven) and no symbolic play. In addition she lacked attention-focusing behavior and had a tendency to stereotypic behavior. Analysis of the behavior of the toddler teacher showed that she did not comply to criterium 2: following the child's lead.

Objectives for the child

(1) Extending functional and relational play (categories 6-7) and starting sequential relational play (category 8);
(2) Improving the child's attention for play material and facilitating varied play actions;
(3) Providing equipment to maintain a good sitting and standing position.

Objectives for the toddler teacher

(1) Following the child's lead;
(2) Using attention-focusing strategies (especially nonverbal) when the child does not play or persists in stereotypic behavior.

Program

The play training consisted of twenty-five play sessions of twenty minutes each and lasted 2.5 months. To ensure a good sitting position, the first step in the program was supplying an adapted chair. The choice of the play material was determined by Lucy's severe spasticity, her distractability and stereotypic behavior. Therefore, the teacher chose adapted play materials, limited the number of play objects and varied the play themes together with the play materials. The toddler teacher got feedback on her behavior after each session. The feedback aimed at the way the toddler teacher adapted her behavior to the play level and play behavior of the child especially by using attention-focusing strategies like pointing/repositioning, demonstrating and physical guidance and following the child's lead. From the sixth session onwards feedback was given once a week. After twelve sessions the objectives for Lucy had to be changed and the teacher had to give special attention to improve symbolic play.

Figure 11.2 A Practical Example

taped two ten-minute play sessions. All sessions took place in a quiet and isolated part of the child's own classroom. The child was stimulated to play freely on the floor or on the table with a fixed set of toys. Teachers were instructed to respond to the child's appeals but not to elaborate or initiate interaction or to demonstrate play activities. The play sessions were transcribed and the coders scored them in terms of the thirteen play categories and the one nonplay category and finally classified them as: exploration, functional-relational play or pretend play. To test the inter-rater-reliability, the scores of two observers on fifteen ten-minute transcriptions were calculated. The overall reliability (Cohen's kappa) varied over sessions from .78 to .96 (median .83). The median values of the reliability per category ranged over sessions from .64 to 1.00.

To examine the effect of the play training the experimental and control group means were compared, both at pretest and at follow-up. Because the matching and randomization over the experimental and control groups did not account for the differences in pretest scores of the dependent variables, we undertook analyses of covariance with the pretest scores as a covariate. The results of the analyses revealed that play training did not increase the frequency and duration of higher play levels; neither did it decrease exploration. Scores on the attention behavior variables also showed that play training was not effective, neither for the total experimental group, nor for either of the two clinical groups. In spite of the different nature of the two clinical groups (cerebral palsy and Down's syndrome), table 11.1 shows that there was no significant interaction between play training and clinical group. The table indicates that for functional-relational play of children with cerebral palsy there is a significant difference between the experimental and control group but the results are opposite to expectation: the control group made progress, not the experimental group. Because of the large amount of tests we do not attach much meaning to this difference.

Discussion

What reasons could be responsible for the lack of success of the program? One reason could be the short training period (mean period: 2.5 months). The findings in the first study with non-handicapped children suggest that the sequence of play categories progresses concurrently with cognitive development. Therefore it is conceivable that mentally retarded subjects (mean DQ: 64) with a very slow rate of cognitive growth need a more intensive training to improve their

Table 11.1   The Effect of Playtraining on Posttest Scores, Using Analysis of Covariance with Pretest as a Covariate.
N = 16, Down's syndrome (N = 8) and cerebral palsy (n = 8)

VARIABLES	TOTAL GROUP		CEREBRAL PALSY		DOWN'S SYNDROME	
	F(1,13)	p	F(1,6)	p	F(1,6)	p
Play behavior						
exploration						
frequency	0.00	.96	0.69	.44	0.03	.87
duration	0.28	.61	0.00	.98	0.11	.75
functional—relational play						
frequency	0.27	.61	7.59	.04*	0.76	.42
duration	0.02	.88	9.29	.03*	1.51	.27
pretend play						
frequency	0.67	.43	1.53	.27	0.01	.91
duration	1.19	.30	2.80	.16	0.20	.67
Attention on play objects						
amount of sec. engaged with play objects	0.02	.89	0.54	.50	0.00	.94
mean length of the two longest unbroken play periods	0.49	.50	2.42	.18	0.00	.97
play involvement unfocused	0.04	.85	0.09	.78	0.01	.94
extended exploratory bout	0.34	.57	0.00	.95	1.16	.33
lengthy exploratory bout	0.01	.93	a	a	a	a
Exploratory competence	0.18	.68	0.65	.46	6.60	.05

* p < .05

a) These values were not calculated because we could not test for homogeneity.

play behavior and to reach a higher play level. Another possible reason is related to the content of the training program. The program stimulates the child to initiate and to continue play and the teacher to follow and to structure the play. Perhaps a goal-directed way of play training could be more successful. This is reported by Wehman

(1975, 1977). He chose an approach in which "play behaviors" are trained using various behavior techniques. Although he and his colleagues have produced more purposeful play behaviors, one important drawback of this approach is "that any resultant gains are adult-initiated and usually adult-maintained. There is little evidence of generalisation to novel contents" (McConkey 1986, 100), a problem which is also recognized by Hellendoorn and by Van Berckelaer-Onnes, elsewhere in this volume. Further, negative findings could also result from the style of behavior of the toddler teacher during the training sessions which was quite different from that during the posttest and the follow-up test. During the play training the toddler teacher was instructed to stimulate the child's play and to respond to its play behavior; during the test sessions, however, this was not allowed. It might be possible that this unexpected change in teacher behavior did disturb the child's free play. Finally, one cannot exclude that play development is simply not trainable in an essential sense. According to Piaget (1962, 162) play in the first place has a consolidating function: play is "assimilation for the sake of assimilation with no need for new accomodation." However, more research is needed to confirm such an important hypothesis.

/12

Play Assessment for Play-Based Intervention: A First Step with Young Children with Communication Difficulties

Kay P. Mogford-Bevan

This paper describes the play assessment which is used as a first step in helping young children with a variety of communication impairments. Before discussing the assessment itself, the intervention program to which it is the prelude will be briefly outlined. This will emphasize the need for assessment of play development.

The Context for the Play Program

The play program is used in the treatment of children with a variety of communication impairments who attend a once weekly clinic which also provides opportunities for training of speech and language therapists at the University of Newcastle upon Tyne in Great Britain. Most children attending the speech and language clinic are identified as needing assessment, diagnosis and intervention when speech and language fail to develop at the expected age, in the normal way, and there is no obvious explanation for this. Alternatively, a child may have already been diagnosed as suffering from a condition, part of which is a communication impairment or delay, e.g., Fragile X syndrome or hearing impairment.

The children attending the speech and language clinic will have a communication disorder which fits one of the following descriptions:

1. The child is able to understand spoken language better than (s)he can command verbal expression. Expressive language may be sparse or unintelligible. This might happen either when a child's problems are confined to language acquisition in the main and no other disability is involved or when a child is suspected of having a speech disorder of motor origin.

2. The child is unable to respond appropriately to verbal communication but is able to interact appropriately where communication addressed to him is nonverbal. A hearing impairment may be responsible or a central problem in processing auditory language signals.

3. The child has delayed understanding and expression of language and presents the picture of a younger child in all aspects of development.

4. The child has a communication impairment linked to a psychological condition where the child is withdrawn and unsociable, e.g., in autism or related syndromes. When this happens, preverbal as well as verbal communication is poor. The formal aspects of language, grammar and phonology, may be acquired without difficulty but the ability to use forms meaningfully and skillfully is impaired.

5. The child's communication impairment reflects the tempo of the child's activity, ability to listen and attend to language models. Little mutual attention between parent and child is observed and the turn-taking structure of exchanges frequently breaks down. Sometimes the child may seem to be able to express meaning verbally better than he seems to understand speech.

All these difficulties are normally recognized in the second year of life so that children are referred to the clinic for help as young as eighteen months to two years, and invariably before the age of four years.

Whatever the nature of the communication impairment, the greater part of intervention will be accomplished through the medium of play, because the children are so young. The play program principally involves the child's parents at home, but may also include other professionals working in an educational or remedial context.

A second reason for intervening through play is that the speech and language therapist seeks to ensure that the child experiences an effective and optimal language learning environment. This is in addition to measures that may be taken, where this is feasible, to treat or eliminate factors responsible for the communication disability. Interactive play provides an exchange in which the child is fully involved, emotionally and intellectually. This ensures that the speech and language heard and used appropriately matches the events and meanings that hold the child's immediate attention. Language experienced in this way is comprehensible and functional. It arises during events in which players share mutual attention and meaning. The child, being highly involved and excited, expresses feelings and reactions which provide cues for parents to respond to. Parents can also put into words the feelings that the child expresses in actions. In addition, the child may be more willing and able to attempt expressive communication in play which is not focused primarily on the adequacy of communication.

In shared activity the child's attempts at communication are more likely to be recognized and acknowledged because they are supported and made intelligible by the shared context. When this leads to successful understanding, further encouragement to communicate often follows. This positive spiral can replace the discouragement of previous failure in communication for both parent and child. A further benefit of basing intervention on play is a high degree of repetition which is characteristic of play so that successful communication can be repeated and rehearsed.

Characteristics of Play Intervention

The main characteristics of the play intervention are outlined below. Space does not allow a theoretical justification although it owes a great deal to the work of Bruner and Vygotsky. For a fuller account of the theoretical basis for the role of communication in the socialization of thought and development, see Wood (1989). Any shared activity provides opportunities for communication. Successful communication reinforces the framework of social exchange on which language acquisition is based and also creates the cultural framework on which further intellectual and linguistic development can be based.

Because the child's difficulty lies in developing communication skills the program encourages play with social interaction rather than solitary play. The interactive partner is usually an adult, the child's parent or primary caretaker, but other family members, particularly older siblings, may also be involved. The child's interactive partner may act mainly as a facilitator and commentator or play an equal and reciprocal part in the play activity.

Play intervention is planned and designed to meet the needs of individual children within a specific framework, the main points of which are now outlined.

In young children with communication impairments or delay, interactive play is reported by parents to be difficult and solitary play tends to predominate in the child's experience. Certain kinds of play and activity, looking at picture books and other symbolic activities, are specially identified (Liddle 1991). In some cases any kind of interactive play has been abandoned altogether by a family. The initial cause of the difficulty probably lies in the child's lack of communication skills, particularly of joint visual attention, listening and turn taking. Where interactive play has been abandoned the program aims to reestablish it, particularly in the symbolic activities mentioned above. Where parents are successfully persisting with interactive play more variety and developmental progression may be encouraged.

The program sets out to stimulate developmental progression, increase the frequency of play, facilitate interaction and encourage a full range of different types of play although the precise form of play activity is not prescribed. Although materials may be lent to the family and different ways of using them suggested to parents, no parental script is given, leaving parents freedom to use their communication skills to respond appropriately to their child's lead in play. The abilities that may be developed through play with a toy or game will be discussed with the parent, and their relevance to speech and language development explained. Ways of introducing play materials, demonstrating their play potential and attracting the child's participation may also be discussed.

It is important to distinguish clearly between providing opportunities, props, and strategies for engineering certain kinds of play experiences and intervention methods which dress up therapeutic exercises or training drills as games. This latter approach is not implied in play intervention. The assumptions of this approach are:

  a. it is possible to specify a range and variety of play experiences and the stages through which ordinary children progress in play;

b. different kind of play experiences enable children to develop and perfect abilities involved play, and that these abilities contribute to the more "serious" use of the abilities in functional terms;

c. although children vary in their preferences for certain kinds of play, most children experience a broad range of play;

d. children with disabilities tend to have a more restricted range of play experiences by virtue of their disabilities. Those experiences that are missed out further undermine their functional competence. There is some evidence of the restriction of play experience in disability (e.g., Hewitt 1970; McEvoy & McConkey 1983). In interactive play parents can scaffold experience in ways that permit competence and experience that would otherwise be inaccessible (Mogford 1979a).

It follows that intervention should aim to restore experience and prevent restricted accessibility to the range of play experiences available to the ordinary child. Where an aspect of play is relatively underdeveloped, encouragement starts at the developmental level appropriate to the child. This may be difficult for parents to determine if the activity is not one they have tried or have abandoned. If they have successfully hit upon the appropriate level they may need reassurance and encouragement to continue their effort, especially when the level is well below that normally associated with their child's chronological age.

Intervention is accomplished through the loan of play materials from a toy store or library, or through suggesting activities with materials that are already available at home. The type of activity is selected to encourage particular aspects and levels of play, after some experimentation to determine which particular toys are attractive and appealing to individual children and parents when introduced in an appropriate way. Such preferences will depend on the child's previous experience, the novelty of materials and individual interests.

The toy library includes items which provide opportunities at a range of developmental levels and across a variety of activities. Lending items helps to overcome lack of appropriate play resources and expands parents' ideas for games and activities, providing a variety of different materials where activities need to be repeated, and so varying the vocabulary and language used.

The Case for Play Assessment

Central to the play program is the need for a form of play assessment. This is essential if the program is to meet individual needs and to match play activities to the appropriate developmental level for each child.

The observational play assessment described is used as part of and continuous with the play program, that is: assessment in play for intervention through play. In the setting described it is also used for diagnosis and for assessment of early educational needs. It is still in the process of being developed and refined.

Various guides and schemes of observational assessment of children's play are available but they are not suitable for this purpose. For example, Newson (1979) described a play-based assessment but this is not sufficiently structured to ensure systematic investigation of different types of play, is relatively time consuming and labor intensive, and lacks an explicit framework for interpreting observations. Other observational play assessments are designed for use in nursery classes (Sylva, Roy & Painter 1980), and for different age groups. They rely on eliciting play with materials that do not appeal to all children with the special needs described above, assess a limited range of types of play (Westby 1980; Lowe & Costello 1976), or apply schemes of interpreting observations that rely heavily on the judgment of the observer. Other schemes lack attention to detail or fail to provide adequate criteria that can be used to interpret the developmental level and significance of observations. None of these assessments can be used easily for the intervention purposes already described. The new assessment has been developed after many years of use of an earlier form of the method: the Observational Play Repertoires (Mogford 1979b).

The play observation assessment needed in the program described above should sample the different types of play activity to be encouraged in intervention through the parent-child interaction.

Guidelines are needed for the observer on which aspects of the play to attend to and how to interpret these observations in developmental terms. If the technique is to be used for diagnostic and assessment purposes it should also provide systematic ways of looking at the quality of play and exploration.

All these requirements are more easily met if standard play materials are used, provided that these materials are suitable for all the children who need to be assessed, that is, they should be attractive as well as physically and intellectually accessible. Another advantage of using the same materials each time is that the user becomes increasingly proficient at observation and interpreting observations. This is particularly valuable in a training context.

Using an assessment that structures observation makes it both more systematic and reliable. Opportunities are offered for the same range of play behaviors to be observed on different occasions and different observers can attend to the same aspects of the child's play.

Without these guidelines and structure, observational play assessment relies heavily on the judgment and experience of the observer to relate the observed behavior to developmental sequences in play. Being able to relate observations directly to sequences and stages in play development allows play needs to be matched to play opportunities for individual children. This last feature is essential if the assessment is to provide guidance for intervention.

Principal Features of the Play Observation Kit (PoKIT)

This assessment method is designed for use with any children who have developmental disorders of known or unknown origin and who are chronologically and/or developmentally below the age of four years.

The Play Observation Kit (PoKIT) uses the child's *spontaneous* play with a standard set of toys. It is based on observation of parents playing with their own child. The presence of an adult is usually needed to initiate and sustain the young child's play but it also stimulates the situation which will be used to assist development. PoKIT involves the child's parents in the assessment and they provide their own evaluation of the child's play at the end of the assessment session. The parent's participation in the assessment procedure helps to sensitize them to their child's developmental achievements and supports the validity of the activities which are subsequently recommended.

As well as indicating developmental progress, PoKIT provides qualitative information on how the child approaches and communicates with play partners and approaches the physical environment. For example, it encourages the observer to note reliance on others for initiating and prompting play, and to note the knowledge and previous experience which the child brings to exploration. It also allows the observer to note how the child combines different abilities to solve problems thrown up by the play materials. The assessment can lead directly to intervention strategies in that examples of the more developmentally advanced and successful play and interaction can be used to suggest play materials and aspects of play to be encouraged and developed.

The assessment requires a minimum of special knowledge and skills to use. A manual (in preparation) will describe the developmental play sequence characteristic of each toy used in the assessment. Checklists for each toy help observers to notice and record significant play items. Assessment summaries for each toy help to bring out qualitative as well as developmental information.

PoKIT currently consists of four toys and assorted picture books. These toys are the Galt's pop-up men, Escor Roundabout, Merit pop-up cones, and a set of toys for pretend play (pretend set) which consists of a clothed doll, bed with pillow, mattress and cover, and a tea set and telephone. The five picture books range from simple books with no text and no story, through to books with a well-developed story and several lines of written text per page.

Also parts of the kit are:

1. A preliminary questionnaire to measure the child's familiarity with the play materials, explore play preferences and opportunities for play at home. This also investigates any problems that the parents have experienced in playing with the child.

2. Detailed checklists for recording observations of the child's play which can be filled in either from a video recording or from notes made from direct observation of the play session.

3. A questionnaire to rate parent's perception of the child's play during assessment. This simply asks parents to say whether with each of the toys the child performed as expected, better or worse. They are also asked to comment on play which surprised them or was in any way untypical, and to indicate any alterations to the circumstances which they would recommend and any comments they wish to make.

4. A manual containing details of procedure and instructions for use.

Use of PoKIT

Table 12.1 indicates the range of abilities that can be assessed. The range of toys and play sampled have been chosen to be relevant to communication development. First, different forms of symbolic and

Table 12.1 Range of Abilities to be Observed

| | TOYS IN THE PLAY OBSERVATION KIT | | | | |
	ROUNDABOUT	POP UP MEN	BOOKS	POP UP CONE	PRETEND
Abilities observed:					
Developmental level	•	•	•	•	•
Attention	•	•	•	•	•
Communication	•	•	•	•	•
Listening			•		
Persistence	•	•		•	•
Variation in play	•	•		•	•
Representation	•	•	•		•
Pretend/thematic					•
Sensory/motor exploration	•	•	•		•
Hand/eye coordination, manipulation	•	•		•	
Conceptual development	•	•	•	•	
Word knowledge	•		•		•
Problem solving/learning				•	
Literacy awareness/ book handling			•		

representational play are included. Second, provision is made to observe types of play that develop relatively normally in children with communication impairments. If only symbolic and representational play are assessed, play development that is unaffected by disability is not revealed, causing an unbalanced profile of play development.

The particular items used in the assessment were chosen after many years of experience in using a variety of toys with the target age group. The toys were finally selected because they proved to be classic, unlikely to go out of production, and because they appealed to boys and girls across the age range. A pilot study confirmed that they were attractive to the age range, to children from a variety of social backgrounds, and accessible to children with a variety of disabilities.

Procedure

The first questionnaire is completed with the parents before the assessment play session and they are shown the toys to be used. The parent is given instruction on how the toys work and then asked to encourage the child to play with the toys and books in any way they think appropriate, in any order, so that a typical sample of play and picture book reading can be observed. The parent is reassured that if their child does not seem interested in any particular item they should move on to others, as it is likely that it will be returned to spontaneously later in the session or can be tried again on another occasion. The parent (or other familiar person) is then given time to introduce the toys to the child and encourage him/her to play. The session lasts until the child has been encouraged to play with each item and it is felt that some sequences of spontaneous play have been observed. This usually happens in twenty to thirty minutes. The second questionnaire is then completed and the parent's views and comments recorded. Further observation of the child playing alone can be made while the parent is occupied with the questionnaire. This is useful with parents who have adopted a highly controlling style in interactive play and allows some observation of the child's undirected approach to the materials.

The whole assessment may be carried out at one session, or on different occasions if this is more appropriate. It can be done in a clinic, nursery, or the child's own home. Toys which are novel for the child at the first session can be used again after an interval to see how much of the child's initial discovery of the toy's features is retained and to check the reliability of observations if required.

In addition to the play observation, the initial parental interview provides insight into existing provision for play in key areas, and may reveal particular problems that need to be solved before provision for the child's play can develop further. For example, attention may be poor so that little successful interactive play has been attempted. In such a case, ways of getting, maintaining, and developing attention can be discussed, tried and modelled as necessary.

The Checklists

The checklists are the unique feature of the assessment. Each checklist, one for each toy or set of toys, lists a wide range of play behaviors that have been recorded from observationvideos of upwards of fifty nondisabled and disabled children ranging in age from six to forty-eight months. The items are arranged in sections concerned with a particular aspect of the toy. The sections on the roundabout are as follows:

> Play immediately after demonstration
> Spinning roundabout
> Assemble/dismantle - Top from Bottom
> Removing pegmen
> Replacing pegmen
> Manipulation of pegmen
> Hand/eye coordination and grasp
> Representation and pretending
> Communication
> Concepts of color and number
> Assembling/dismantling - parts of toy

And for the Picture and Story books:

> Book handling
> Attention and story/book integrity
> Response to parent/Receptive communication
> > a) Imitates
> > b) Answers questions
> > c) Out of book context
> Conversation skills
> Initiates
> Concepts
> Words
> > a) for quality and quantity
> > b) grammatical
> Listens
> Literacy awareness

Within each section, related behavior items are arranged in developmental order, that is in the order that they appeared in the observation of ordinary children. See the examples given below which are extracts from the checklists for the roundabout and picture books.

Roundabout: Spinning Roundabout

> 13. Accidentally discovers that
>   roundabout turns   06-09 m

14. After discovering spinning turns deliberately	10-12 m ->
15. Spins roundabout deliberately	10-12 m ->
16. Maintains spinning as it slows	06-09 m ->
17. Spins and stops deliberately	10-12 m ->
18. Feels roundabout with fingers as it spins	22-24 m ->
19. Deliberately turns fast	19-21 m ->
20. Deliberately turns slowly	25-30 m ->
21. Varies speed of turning	25-30 m ->
22. Varies direction of turning	25-30 m ->
23. Spins roundabout by flat of hand on the top	10-12 m ->
24. Kicks or turns roundabout using feet	10-12 m ->
25. By pole of horse or seat	13-15 m ->
26. By the knob provided	19-21 m ->
27. Uses two or more means to spin roundabout	31-36 m ->
28. Turns fingers on the top edge so hand moves in circles	43-48 m ->

Roundabout: Replacing Men

56. Places man on the top or on the base	16-18 m
57. Swaps pegmen on a seat or a horse	16-18 m
58. Attempts to replace man on seat but falls	13-15 m*
59. Attempts to replace man on horse but falls	31-36 m*
60. Succeeds on seat	16-18 m ->
61. Succeeds on horse	22-24 m ->
62. Replaces all 4 men	49 m ->

*items that allow observation of persistence

Picture Books: Book Handling

1. Explores book with mouth	-> 10-12 m
2. Fingers pages	-> 10-12 m
3. Wipes hands over surfaces	-> 10-12 m
4. Flaps or waves book	-> 10-12 m
5. Throws book	-> 13-15 m
6. Visually inspects (briefly)	13-15 m ->
7. Upside down or any other orientation	-> 13-15 m
8. Corrects orientation of book	25-30 m

9. Holds book on lap or other part of body	16-18 m
10. Holds both sides of closed book	16-18 m
11. Holds both sides of open book	16-18 m
12. Opens book from the back to start "reading"	-> 31-36 m
13. Opens book in the middle to start "reading"	37-42 m
14. Opens book at beginning to start "reading"	37-42 m ->
15. Turns two three pages without passing	13-15 m
16. Turns a sequence of pages until end of book	13-15 m ->
17. Turns several pages in one go	-> 16-18 m
18. Turns pages one at a time	16-18 m ->
19. Turns pages backwards and forwards	16-18 m
20. Turns a page after discussion or comment	22-24 m ->
21. Turns back a page to check none missed	31-36 m ->
22. Flattens or smooths book open	37-42 m
23. Lifts flap in flap book	22-24 m ->
24. Closes flap carefully before turning the page	31-36 m ->

KEY. The same age bands are used for each checklist. These are given in three month bands from six -> twenty-four months and six month bands from twenty-four to forty-eight months. The ages given indicate when these items have been observed in the children in the pilot studies and are given as guidelines to assess developmental progress.

-> 3-5 m means that an item has been observed in children up to this age band but not beyond.

13-15 m -> meant that an item has been observed from this age onwards but not before this age.

16-18 means this item has been observed so far only in this age band.

The checklists deliberately contain detailed items, because small details of behavior give valuable insight into the child's development and understanding which if missed may lead to an incorrect assessment of the child's development. Consequently, play intervention may be at an inappropriate level. The degree of detail also helps to improve the reliability of identifying behavioral items.

The observer records items of behavior displayed during play on the check-lists. An assessment summary, at the end of each checklist, records qualitative aspects of the child's play as a basis for diagnosis, report writing, and intervention.

Example of the Assessment in Use

Jenny was seen for reassessment at the age of four years and six months. Jenny has a specific delay in expressive speech in addition to a general delay in development. She was first seen at two years and has attended a daily class for children with similar disabilities during the last twelve months. Jenny's mother initiated the play assessment because she wanted confirmation of the suitability of Jenny's educational placement. She also wanted further suggestions for play activities to help her daughter's development at home. Jenny now attends a mainstream nursery class in which several other developmentally disabled children are integrated.

The first play assessment session was in the playroom of the pediatrics department at the local hospital. At her parents' suggestion a second session was carried out at home two months later. At the first session Jenny played mainly with books and the pretend toy set. The extract given below is taken only from the completed checklist for the picture books.

> *First play assessment session*—Jenny, four years and six months.
> Jenny began with the books which she selected herself and then climbed into her mother's lap. Her mother held the books and turned pages. Jenny chose four books, ranging from the simplest with little or no story or text, to two books with stories and text. The simpler books were completed but the more complex books were not. Items recorded for Jenny on the checklist are given for each section, with the most developmentally advanced items indicated with age levels.

Book handling
Holds books on lap or other part of body
Holds both sides of closed book
Holds book at the beginning to start reading (37-52 m ->)
Turns pages one at a time
Lifts flap in flap book
N.B., book was always held in correct orientation

Attention and story integrity
Closes book before end is reached. (Lost attention to books with story and more text). Completes whole book - attended every page (two books: (a) simple story book with one line of text per page (b) book with photographs which share a theme but no text). Accepts closing book at the end without comment (43-48 m ->)

Response to parent / reception
(All verbal responses limited by poor intelligibility)
Imitates: Imitates partner's label for picture
    Imitates partner's previous utterance (31-36 m)
Answers questions: What does X say?
    What is it?
    Who questions (37-42 m)
    Yes/no questions
    Indirect suggestions to lift flap covering picture
    Where questions
    Other questions
    (All questions answered appropriately)
Out of book context: Responds to questions referring to events
outside present context (37-42 m)

Conversational skills
Completes word or phrase started by partner
(But failed to respond to request for clarification)

Initiates
By turning page
Instructs partner to turn page
Indicates picture using exclamation
Names character on book cover (31-36 m)
Names picture
Comments on picture (not naming)

Listens
As partner reads title
As partner paraphrases text (N.B., also if attention lost while
text paraphrased)
Listens as parent reads text (one line per page) (22-24 m)

Developmental level indicated (by taking the most advanced items
in each section): 22-24 m 25-30 m 31-36 m 37-42 m 43-48 m ->
No: of items   1   0   2   3   1

This was used to suggest to Jenny's mother that in her nursery
placement she was suitably placed and could benefit from the
curriculum offered to children at a similar developmental level.
These were currently the younger children in the group.

The discussion with her mother after the assessment on picture
book reading centered around the choice of books. As Jenny is one of

four children a variety of play materials and books are available at home. It was noted that picture book reading had been most successful where the story was simple and repetitive. Jenny's attention had been held when the book provided something to handle and investigate as well as opportunities to look and listen. It was suggested that development might now be possible in the amount of text available rather than in books providing only opportunities for naming and identifying pictures. However, it was probably better to choose books with familiar characters and a simple but strong story line, probably with considerable repetition in the text. Her mother was encouraged to build on Jenny's growing ability to relate the context of books and pictures to previous experience and perhaps to develop story cohesion by asking Jenny to predict what would happen next in the story. It was explained that this could to lead to language use that was not limited to "the here and now."

Summary

Children under the developmental age of four years who are referred to the University speech clinic with communication impairments are assessed as a basis for intervention through the medium of play. Intervention is continuous with assessment and both processes involve the child's parents. The aim of intervention is to establish the basic skills needed for communication and learning in an interactive framework. Language acquisition is facilitated when a sound and enjoyable communicative framework is established. An essential feature of the program is that toys and play activities are provided or suggested for parents which match the child's current level of play development. Few direct instructions are given on how to speak or what language to use. The example given above shows how directions given can build on exchanges that are already established parts of parent/child interaction. Techniques to introduce toys, to simplify and make them accessible to individual children are used, but the toys and play activities themselves provide a focus and structure for parents' playful interaction, providing appropriate communicative experiences for the child. Help is directed towards solving problems which parents may have, and encouraging forms of play in interaction that are underdeveloped or have been neglected.

/13

Play Training for Autistic Children

Ina A. van Berckelaer-Onnes

In the revised DSM-III (Diagnostic and Statistical Manual of Mental Disorders III-R, APA, 1987) the description of the pervasive developmental disorders (which includes autism) has been clearly broadened and enlarged. Where previously it spoke of an absence or a very serious deficit in contact, now "a qualitative impairment in reciprocal social interaction" is mentioned. This description does more justice to the group in question, since many children suffering from these disorders (including autistic children) certainly make contact. The quality of that contact, however, is different: the other person is often used as an instrument in order to reach a goal or as a sounding board for long-winded monologues on specific subjects (e.g., stars, dinosaurs or motorways). The disorder in communication is enlarged upon and described as "an impairment in communication and imaginative activity." The addition of disorder in imaginative activity has been supported by the work of Lorna Wing et al. (Wing, Gould, Yeates & Brierly 1977). They investigated the symbolic play in severely mentally retarded and in autistic children. Their study confirmed the opinion often found in the literature, that autistic children rarely show symbolic play (see, e.g., Bender 1956; Rutter 1974). In recent years, more and more specialized research has been done on the play behavior of these children.

The third criterion mentioned in the DSM III-R is "a markedly restricted repertoire of activities and interests." Beside these three basic symptoms (qualitative impairment in reciprocal social interaction; impairment in communication and imaginative activity; restricted repertoire of activities and interests) a number of associated behavioral characteristics are described for which we refer to the DSM III-R (APA 1987).

In this chapter we will focus on the disorder in imaginative activities, in particular the toy play behavior in autistic children. The way in which these children play with toys is very different when compared with children who have other developmental disorders, as described in other publications (Baron-Cohen 1987; DeMyer et al. 1967; Sigman & Ungerer 1984; Tilton & Ottinger 1964; Ungerer & Sigman 1981; Weiner, Ottinger & Tilton 1969).

Play Development

In our study we enlarge upon the publications of McCune-Nicholich (1980) and Ungerer and Sigman (1981). Ungerer and Sigman compared the play behavior of autistic children with that of retarded and nonhandicapped children. In order to do so they used a play development scheme which seems also suitable for our investigation. This scheme contains the following four phases of development: *Simple manipulation* (I). This type of play develops during the first year of one's life, as the child begins to play with his/her fingers, reaches for objects, brings them to the mouth, etc. At about twelve to thirteen months the child begins to combine toys, called *Relational play* (II). This still happens in a very exploratory manner: banging objects together, or stacking them: putting one object inside the other, and so on. Slowly *Functional play* (III) develops: a cup is related to a saucer (object-oriented); the child combs his/her hair with a comb (self-oriented), or combs a doll's hair (doll-oriented), or another's hair (other-oriented). This play form increases linearly and qualitative and is clearly the forerunner of *Symbolic play* (IV). This latter type of play develops from the eighteenth to the twenty-fourth month onwards. When children reach this level, they are no longer dependent on the material actually present, but can pretend, for instance, that they comb their hair or drink out of a cup. In symbolic play they can change the world: a box can become a house; a doll can become the doctor. This level requires a mental age of at least twenty months (Wing et al. 1977). Mentally retarded children functioning on a lower level are not capable of symbolic play.

Play Investigation

In our research we are working on the assessment and treatment of children, adolescents and adults suffering from autism and related developmental disorders (in short, the whole group of pervasive developmental disorders). The addition of the diagnostic criterion "impairment of imaginative activity" has led to the play investigation. Play observation has been one of the diagnostic means which we use when assessing these children; not in the hope of being able to observe imaginative play which can be interpreted, but as support for the classification of autism and related developmental disorders. The way in which these children use play material is so different that it contributes to the recognition of the autistic syndrome. We also want to enlarge our insight in the nature of play (especially toy play behavior) of these children in order to develop programs for further stimulation. This study aimed at two goals:

1. Description of toy play behavior by comparing it with the play of other groups of children (deaf, hearing-impaired, mentally retarded children, and children without handicap).

2. Design of a training program in order to stimulate the play development of autistic children.

The first goal was tackled by an observation study. Four student observers investigated the way in which various children interacted with the play material, using an observation schema developed by Ungerer and Sigman (1981). During a twenty-minute session, the children were shown different toys in a predetermined order. The child was sitting at the instructor's table and was offered the objects one by one. The child could do with them whatever he or she liked. A second observer was present in the same room and scored the child's (re)actions on the standard observation list. The four types of play were subdivided as follows (Ungerer and Sigman 1981):

Simple manipulation	Fingering
	Banging
	Mouthing
Relational play:	Combining 2 or more objects in a non-functional manner
	Putting one object inside another
	Stacking
Functional play:	Object-directed acts
	Self-directed acts
	Doll-directed acts
	Other-directed acts

Symbolic play: Agent play
                                    Substitution play
                                    Imaginary play

The various play objects could evoke the actions described. In addition, a number of other behavior variables were described: imitation, perseveration, curiosity and social interaction.

The research group consisted of sixty-four children, twelve of whom were autistic. In table 13.1 the distribution of children is given. We made comparisons between the groups and between autistic and nonautistic children, as all the nonautistic groups showed many similarities. In this paper, I will restrict myself to some general information on the outcome of this part of our study, in order to leave more room for the training program we developed as a consequence.

Our conclusions are based on the frequency of the recorded actions and on a qualitative analysis of the play activities. The most striking observation was that on all levels of play the autistic children showed less variation in activity. Their number of actions within functional play was higher than expected, but remained restricted to stereotyped object use, such as: putting a cup on a saucer; a lid on a pot. These actions seemed to be almost mechanical. The results about the play of autistic children when compared with that of the other groups can be summarized as follows:

Simple manipulation: less variation, one child bangs, the
                                    other licks;
                                    repetitive and perseverative actions;

Table 13.1   The Research Group in the Play Observation Study

GROUP	N	BOYS	GIRLS	VERBAL	NON-VERBAL	AGE RANGE
Non-handicapped children	28	11	17	23	5	15-65 months
Mentally retarded	12	8	4	6	6	35-70 months
Learning impaired	12	7	5	3	9	36-58 months
Autistic	12	9	3	6	6	17-83 months
Total	64	35	29	38	26	15-83 months

Relational play: fewer variations;
                       stereotyped combinations;
                       inadequate relationships (at an age
                       when these should be adequate).
Functional play: more restricted use of objects;
                       more object-oriented play than doll- or
                       other-oriented;
                       inadequate doll-play;
                       stereotyped play;
Symbolic play: generally absent; when present (only
                       in two children) poor of content.

Although the number of children in this investigation is too small to determine the reliability of these results and to generalize, we still found them marked enough to formulate three hypotheses to explain the differences between autistic and non-autistic children.

a. Autistic children have missed the variety of experiences which a healthy child gains in the first two years of life by simple handling and combining of objects. This handling and combining of objects is restricted to a number of stereotyped, perseverated actions (tapping with a stick, turning a knob, fiddling with a cord, banging two blocks against each other).

b. Autistic children have learned the actions which are characteristic of functional play, but mechanically, so that a type of automatic action has developed which is associative in nature; lid —> pot. The actions seem to be isolated and not part of a meaningful whole (e.g., cup —> saucer —> tea —> drinking —> etc.).

c. The "play" experiences which autistic children have on the manipulative, relational and functional level, are so limited and bereft of a healthy desire to explore that they cannot be in that form the forerunners of imaginative play.

Play Training

The play training program was based on the three hypotheses formulated above. It seemed important for these autistic children to go back to the very beginning of play, even for those children who were able to play functionally. Therefore, we started with training manipulative play, then went on with relational play and, next, functional play. In the experimental phase (in which research results were important) we kept as much as possible to the standard procedure given below. The length of the program in this research phase was kept short, only eleven weeks, with two twenty to thirty-minute sessions a week. This choice was arbitrary and based mainly on practical grounds after consultation with the day-care centers participating in the research.

The program has been divided in the following steps:

Phase I

Simple Manipulation: duration two weeks (four sessions).
Materials: Four sets (A, B, C, D) of twelve different play objects, varying from a ball, a cork, cotton wool, dinky car, etc.
Method: The toys were presented to the child one by one (with little verbal introduction). First the trainer observed what the child did spontaneously with the object, then she demonstrated what could be done with it (rolling, turning upside down) and then she gave it back to the child. In this first phase exploration of the materials was more important than meaningful use of them. In view of the very limited interest shown by autistic children in play objects, the tempo was kept fairly high (twenty to thirty minutes per session), in order to retain the child's attention as much as possible.

In the first session Set A was offered twice; in the second session Set A was followed by Set B; in the third session Set B and C, and in the fourth session Set C and D. In this way the child was offered every toy twice.

Phase II

Relational play: duration four weeks (eight sessions).
Materials: Eight sets (E-L), two objects per set. Four sets contained unrelated pairs (e.g., pencil and tomato-cutter; cloth and ball, etc.) While four other sets contained meaningful combinations (shaving cream and brush; string and beads; box and block).
Method: The same method was used. The first session began with Set D from Phase I, in order to facilitate the transition, followed by Set E. In the second session first Set E and then F was offered, and so on. Half of the sessions were devoted to nonfunctional and half to the functional pairs.

Phase III

Functional play: duration three weeks (six sessions).
Materials: Six sets of play objects which could evoke functional play. The sets varied in orientation. The first set contained materials that evoked object-oriented activities, the second doll-oriented, the third self-oriented and other-oriented, whereas the last three sets contained a combination of these. In this phase, again, two sets were offered together in the same way as in the previous phases.

The different types of play activity (object-oriented, doll-oriented, etc.) were equally divided over the sessions. Each set was offered twice, while the last two and a half sessions were devoted to the combination, especially directed towards the transition to Phase IV.

Phase IV

Imaginative Play: duration 2 weeks (4 sessions).
Materials: Four different sets of play objects which could evoke imaginative play. Some of the materials from the previous phases were utilized.

"Agent play" (doll drinks its bottle), "substitute play" (a block is a piece of soap), and "imaginative play" (child makes sipping noises while pretending to drink) were directly stimulated. However, only a start was made in this phase (during four sessions only) in order to see whether the child was capable of any imaginative play.

The choice of materials was varied and focussed on stimulating the different sensory stimuli (soft and hard materials, colored toys, noisy toys, etc.).

For the execution of this experimental training program, again we were able to utilize student trainers who had experience with autistic children. Twenty-four autistic children (between three and seven years old) took part in the research project. Thirteen of them attended a day-care center for mentally retarded children and the other eleven a day-care center for children with social and emotional problems.

For all these children, their level of functioning was determined with the psycho-educational profile (PEP) of Schopler and Reichler (1979). They all scored above the twenty-four-month developmental level, which we took as the minimum requirement for the ability to show pretend play. Special test sessions were set up before and after training.

Results

In the pretest session one child was able to carry out some symbolic activity, but only to a very limited extent, and the other children not at all. After training, still only four of the children were able to do so. These four children had also progressed in play behavior outside the training. Their parents stated spontaneously that the children showed more variation in their choice of toys, less stereotyped behavior and were able to play better and more often with their siblings. It must be pointed out that three of these children were, intellectually speaking, those who functioned best of the group. The fourth child had a delay of one year, but seemed to develop quite well. All these four children were able to talk.

The other children made no spectacular improvement, but still there was some progress. They manipulated more extensively and were able to combine more different toys. Four children (functioning at the lowest level, MA twenty-five to thirty months) improved only on the first two developmental levels of toy play. The other sixteen children also showed progress in the functional play. They were still more object-directed than doll or people directed, but could comb the hair of the doll, or brush the teeth of the doll. However, they did not make the step into symbolic play.

Discussion

These results suggest that intellectual capacity and language play are important variables in the transition from functional to symbolic play. A number of studies come to the same conclusion, including that of Ungerer and Sigman (1981). They found a high correlation between language comprehension and symbolic play in autistic children. This confirms the opinion that autism involves a general disorder of symbolic activities (see also Rutter & Schopler 1987; van Berckelaer & van Engeland 1986). Sigman and Mundy (1987) described the symbolic processes in young autistic children. They saw the core deficit in childhood autism at the intersection of symbolic representation and social experience. Studies of Baron-Cohen (1987, 1989), Frith (1989a, b) and Leslie and Frith (1988) emphasize the lack of spontaneous pretend play as a prominent feature of autism. Copying of other people's actions may be present but without real understanding of its purpose and meaning. To understand this failure, Frith (1989a) refers to Leslie's developmental theory of first- and second-order representations. First-order representations are what the mind makes of real states in the world, while second-order representations are what the mind makes of these first-order representation (Frith 1989b, 48). Pretending that an empty cup is full, is an example of a thought process that would not be possible without second-order representation.

Let me give an example. John was a three-year-old autistic boy, functioning at a cognitive level of twenty-eight months. He spoke just a few words, although his language comprehension was higher. John was focused on everything that could spin and whirl. He followed the training program and improved in the first three levels. After training he was able to execute some doll-directed activities, could dress a girl doll and comb her hair. However, he was not able to let her drink out of an empty cup, pretending that it was full. If we gave him a cup with water, he let the doll drink, but he was astonished that the doll did not really drink the water, that she did not swallow it. When the trainer drank the water, he followed her actions but did not understand why she drank it and the doll did not. Summarizing, we see that the boy was able to comb the dolls hair (first-order representation), but not to let her drink playfully out of an empty cup, pretending that it was full (second-order representation).

If, indeed, autistic children have a deficit in their capacity to form second-order representations, this should imply that the play training can only improve the first three levels: simple manipulation, relational play and functional play. The question is whether the symbolic activities, which four children showed, can really be considered as second-order representations or rather as copied activities of other people (first-order representations). We scored their activities as pretend play. These four children were able to drink out of an empty cup, pretending that it was full. Two children even made "swallow-noises." Even though this had the appearance of real symbolic play, it is still possible that the children copied these actions from other people. They showed some symbolic activities, but did not play a scene like a tea party. More research has to be done to investigate the theory about a deficit in the second-order representation system.

Although we presume that autistic children will seldom reach the symbolic play level, we believe that the play training in this study is helpful in stimulating the first three levels. The fact that the children developed a broader interest in toys and showed less stereotyped behavior, is an important improvement. Regarding our three hypotheses, we can say that the play training gives the children a variety of experiences in simple manipulation, in relational and functional play; experiences which they missed before. They are not able to catch up with normally developing children, but they can improve to an extent. Play training is one of the possible ways to help autistic children. However, because autism is a complex syndrome, play training or any other treatment should always be embedded in a broader treatment program.

$$\Large /\;\textbf{PART 3}$$

Theory and Research on
School Play Intervention

At issue in this section is whether or not play can be used as a form of training with educationally valuable consequences. In the last decades, a lot of research studies have been devoted to this question, some with favorable, some with less hopeful results. People who idealize play as a fundamental human resource welcome the idea that play might help children to learn better. *Peter Smith* approaches the problem through an overview of the biological evidence on play, in particular with regard to parent-infant play among primates. He introduces us to the sound consideration that whatever its uses may be, play can also be of some risk to those who participate in it. Play is perhaps, as Smith says, a relatively safe place for the practice of skills, when you contrast it with learning those skills through actual fighting or actual flight from predators; yet in its own right it must contain some of the exciting arousal of those adaptive activities or it has no motive. And in this arousal, which often requires risk and uncertainty to sustain it, lies the possibility of both danger and defeat.

The problem for human curricular play for children, however, lies at the other end of the dimension of danger-safety. It contains little risk and therefore may become no more than a boring imitation of play itself. Fortunately, what such school play has going for it, is that normal school processes are often even more boring than these domesticated playway forms of learning. *Peter Smith* and *James Christie* detail for us some of the procedures that they and others have pursued in both skeptically investigating and yet positively exploiting these kinds of domesticated play in schools. Their papers are cautious in their assessments and certainly give cause to think carefully before we rush to any judgment about the benefits of play.

In general, it seems that curricular play is likely to be a positive addition to the school curriculum, even though its actual success in directly promoting academic learning remains questionable. Perhaps it is unfortunate that most research work in this field has been done within the cognitively focused approach to childhood of the past twenty years. Consequently, there have perhaps been too many attempts to find play useful for children's development in representation or literacy or narrative or science, whereas the major function of play in relation to school (or in relation to life in general) may well be found within ontological rather than such epistemological considerations. Play may have more to do with one's self esteem and one's motivation for life in general than with the specifics of academic knowledge. This is indeed the focus of most of play therapeutic activity and also forms the major argument for specially helping handicapped children acquire play skills (as discussed in the previous parts of this book). *Waltraut Hartmann* and *Brigitte Rollett*'s use of play and toys as a regular classroom leisure opportunity illustrates this point of view. Their "free play intervention" seems to have improved the relations between teacher and children and between the children themselves and their prosocial behavior, as well as their pleasure in school and school activities. However, there was no direct effect on scholarly performance.

Does this mean that researchers as well as school administrators need to reconsider their reasons for the inclusion of play in school curricula? Maybe, maybe not. As *James Christie* points out, at least it is questionable whether all curricular activities called play deserve that name. Moreover, the links between play on the one hand and cognitive and social behavior on the other, are still far from clear. Play's ability to improve academic performance is in doubt, although it may be a mediator for language and social skills. Rather, time and space for play (including the child-oriented attitude from which these spring) may help form a school climate in which children like to be, where they find out things that are interesting to learn, and where their interaction with each other and their teachers is not limited to scholarly subjects. But beware of the "play ethos" and of the possible abuse of play for adult ends.

/14

Play Training: An Overview

Peter K. Smith

In this review I shall discuss the possible benefits of play training, both for the recipients (usually children) and for the trainers (usually teachers or parents). This area is not free from preconceived notions and assumptions. It may help to take a broad perspective on the topic. Certain concepts from the primate literature may be helpful to us before moving on to considerations of human play. I shall then consider the distinctively cultural aspects of human play, the possible benefits of play training, and the role the "play ethos" has had in influencing research and thinking on this topic.

Mammalian Play

Fagen (1981) provides a thorough and exhaustive review of mammalian play. Most play in mammals takes the form of physical activities, either solitary (such as lambs gambolling) or social (such as play fighting or sparring between pups or cubs). The social forms of play are mainly between age mates or litter mates, that is, mainly peer-peer play. However, adult-young play (normally, parent-offspring play) does occasionally occur.

There are a variety of hypotheses as to the functional or adaptive value of animal play (which may anyway vary for different forms of play, and between different species), but probably the hypothesis with the most support is that play generally provides safe practice for skills, such as fighting and predation skills, which will be important for the animal later, but for which direct practice could be particularly dangerous (Smith 1982). A young animal which practiced actual fighting might be badly injured; in playfighting, it is argued, it can get practice in many aspects of fighting without much danger. The playful nature of the bout is signalled by a play face or play gambol, and participants do not use full strength in a play bout.

This approach to the value of play can explain many findings, such as the forms of play (usually such as to be good practice for later skills), variations between species (such that skills used by adults in that species are practiced), and sex differences (similar to those in adult use of skills such as fighting and hunting).

Primate Play

Primate play takes a wide variety of forms. It includes the physical play, playfighting and chasing characteristic of many mammals, but also may include exploratory and object play, especially in the ground-living monkeys such as macaques and baboons, and in the apes. In general, it seems that primate play helps young monkeys learn about their environment—both social and physical.

Amongst the mammals, primates are characterized by: small families, typically having one infant at a time with a year spacing between births; a long life span and a long period of immaturity of the infant; a relatively large brain size, and more variable (plastic) behavior and a greater ability to learn; and, as a natural consequence of all these, greater parental investment. "Parental investment" here refers to the time, energy, and possibly risks which parents may incur in feeding, protecting and caring for their offspring.

The long period of immaturity in primates, and their relatively complex brains, suggest that play may be especially important as one way of learning about the particular environment in which the young monkey finds itself growing up. Most primate play is peer-peer, with other infants of similar age in the social group. However, not infrequently an infant or juvenile may play with someone older. The older person may be the mother, or more rarely a more distantly related "aunt" or adult female; sometimes an adult male (most often, one who has a high probability of being the father of the young monkey); or, not infrequently, a sibling who may be one or two years older.

These instances of play—usually playfighting—with an older individual, could be considered instances of "play training." The older and, hence, more experienced individual is providing play opportunities and practice for a younger one. It is unlikely that the older individual gets practice benefits from these play bouts, but the younger one may well do so, especially as its older partner will be restraining or "handicapping" itself to provide the younger one with a reasonable chance of winning (i.e., getting on top, pinning the other down) as well as losing. Given the benefits of play experience for the younger participant, this could be considered a form of helping behavior by the older partner, or, for mothers and "likely fathers," a form of parental investment. The play may be a "cost" for parents (in terms of time and energy), but this could be worthwhile as a benefit for their offspring.

While most parent-infant play is probably of this altruistic kind, play can be used for other ends by primate parents. For example, a mother may play with an infant as a distractor to stop persistent suckling, or to stop two infants squabbling. Such instances have been described by Brüggeman (1978) in rhesus monkeys and by Lawick-Goodall (1968) in chimpanzees. Their accounts show that an older individual may use play for their own purposes; that is, play can be used manipulatively by older individuals for their own ends and not necessarily in the interests of the younger individual who is persuaded into playing.

Four ideas, relevant to our general theme of play training, have emerged from our brief survey of primate play:

1. the benefits of play are probably related to practicing important skills for later use, and learning about the environment one is growing up in;

2. most play is peer-peer, but some is with older individuals, usually parents or older siblings;

3. these latter forms of play may be considered forms of helping behavior or "play training" by the older individual;

4. but, more rarely, may be examples of manipulation of a younger individual by an older one.

Human Play

Among the primates, humans have an especially long life span, long period of immaturity, large brain size, large learning capacity, small families, and extensive parental investment. Forms of play, while including physical and rough-and-tumble play, are more varied;

besides exploratory and object play, symbolic play forms occupy much time in early childhood (Bruner 1972). Symbolism and the transmission of cultural symbols from one generation to the next, particularly mark out the human species from all others. Cultural transmission is relevant to our discussion of play training in two most important respects:

a. Play may assist in cultural transmission—hence a greatly increased role for adult-child play, and for play training (which may be mainly helpful and cooperative, but also possibly manipulative, so far as the child's interests are concerned).

b. Cultural factors will themselves influence the values put on play, necessitating consideration of the ethos of play and how it may benefit various subgroups within a larger society.

An Increased Role for Adult-Child Play, and for Play Training

Given the tremendous amount of learning which must take place in human infancy and childhood, and given the amount of cultural learning (of language, tools, customs and morals), the role of the adult, whether parent or teacher, has always been of obvious importance. While children can learn a lot from peers, and from observing older persons in their culture, enculturation is greatly enhanced by active adult-child interaction. This can take the form of play, as well as more directly of learning and instruction.

Parent-child play is common in infancy and early childhood (MacDonald in press). In infancy, such play often takes the form of physical activities such as bouncing, tickling, etc., or a bit later, rule-governed activities such as peek-a-boo, rolling a ball between partners, etc. This play provides stimulation for the child and practice in conversational or game formats (Bruner & Sherwood 1976). Parent-child play becomes more varied in the later preschool years, and some parents may encourage forms of fantasy and sociodramatic play with their children at home (Newson & Newson 1970).

Adults can also enhance play by providing special toys and play environments. One example would be the Montessori apparatus which Maria Montessori recommended for nursery and infant classes (to encourage exploratory play, although not to encourage fantasy play in Montessori's case; see Kramer 1976). Another example would be play with computers (Simon 1986).

At nurseries, play groups and infant schools, adults and teachers can structure play for children, not only by providing a suitable physical environment and array of toys, but also by directly encouraging certain kinds of play. The idea of "structuring play in the early years at school" (Manning and Sharp 1977) is well established in many nursery and primary schools. In Israel, Smilansky (1968) has pioneered the idea of "play tutoring" in fantasy and sociodramatic play, encouraging such play in children who (perhaps because of home background) do not show such play spontaneously to any great extent. This has been taken up in the United States, in the United Kingdom, and other countries.

Benefits of Adult Intervention and Play Training

We have good reasons to expect that adult intervention in children's play, or the various forms of "play training" (whether by parents, by teachers or other adults, or by older children such as siblings) could enhance the practice or learning benefits that children would anyway get from play.

For example, Vygotsky (1978) postulated the importance of the "zone of proximal development" (ZPD) in understanding how children entered into a social and cultural world. The ZPD is the difference between what the child can achieve unaided, and what he or she can do with the aid of a more experienced, probably older, person to help. This argument has been developed by Wood, Bruner and Ross (1976). Using the metaphor of "scaffolding," they have described just how a more experienced person can help; for example, by pointing out salient features of a task, breaking up a large task into smaller components, helping with sequencing, and so on. If operating within the ZPD, or scaffolding slightly more difficult play, the adult can help a child learn more and play at a more complex level.

This important and helpful role of the adult in children's play—and especially the role of the parent—has been emphasized by MacDonald (in press). He argues that high parental involvement in children's play is a form of "parental investment," which is of fairly recent cultural origin. He contrasts the high investment in parent-child play in high SES (Socio-economic Status) groups in modern industrial societies, with the relatively low investment in parent-child play in lower SES groups, and in many tribal societies, which have a greater emphasis on "sibling rearing." He goes on to argue that: "the movement to encourage higher levels of parent-child play among lower class families . . . is . . . an attempt to modify parenting practices toward a high involvement, high investment parenting style which is ideally suited to life in an advanced post-industrial society."

The role of the teacher in play training has been similarly emphasized by other researchers. As envisaged and promoted by Smilansky (1968) and others, this involves enhancing fantasy play, thematic fantasy play, and sociodramatic play via such means as modelling, verbal guidance, thematic-fantasy training and imaginative play training (Christie 1986).

Such kinds of play training or tutoring are thought to be especially useful for those children who show little such play, perhaps those from lower SES groups whose parents have not encouraged such play at home (Newson & Newson 1970).

Evidence for Benefits of Play Training

Considerable evidence accumulated over the last twenty years suggests that there are indeed benefits to children from play training. Some of this evidence relates to parent-child play, suggesting benefits for children's social and emotional development. For example, Parke, MacDonald, Beitel and Bhavnagri (1987) and MacDonald and Parke (1984) found that if parents engaged in physical play with their children in sensitive, responsive ways, their children were more likely to be popular with peers.

So far as teacher-child play and play tutoring is concerned, a notably strong line of applied research has originated from the work of Sara Smilansky (1968; Smilansky & Shefataya 1990). Smilansky argued that sociodramatic play was the most advanced form of play in the three-to-six year age range, and that it was the basis for practicing and developing cognitive, socioemotional and academic skills. She also claimed that many children, especially those from less advantaged backgrounds, showed little or qualitatively poor sociodramatic play. This naturally led to intervention and play training as mentioned earlier.

Using a conventional research design, researchers such as Freyberg (1973), Lovinger (1974), Rosen (1974), Saltz and Johnson (1974), Fink (1976), Saltz, Dixon & Johnson (1977), Udwin (1983), Li (1985), and others have reported that children who experienced play tutoring showed gains in areas of social, linguistic and cognitive competence. They interpreted this as supporting the particular benefits of sociodramatic play hypothesized by Smilansky (1968). This interpretation is open to question: if proper "skills tutoring" groups are used, these make similar gains, as will be discussed shortly. But these studies with better control groups do nevertheless confirm that play tutoring brings benefits; the disagreement is about precisely what causes these benefits and whether play training has any unique role in providing them.

Manipulation of Play

However, we must bear in mind the possibility that the more play is "trained" or "tutored" and controlled by adults, the more scope there is for the manipulation of play for the benefit of the adult(s) rather than for the benefit of the child. Two examples will be mentioned here.

First, teachers may encourage play with toys and quieter forms of pretend play rather than "rough" play (such as playfighting) which they find noisy and disruptive. Yet, children may enjoy rough play and indeed get physical and social benefits from it (Pellegrini 1987; Smith 1989).

Second, teachers may use tutoring in fantasy/sociodramatic play as a vehicle for transmitting values of the teacher's cultural group, which may not necessarily coincide with the values of the child's cultural group (Sutton-Smith 1986). This may particularly be the case when teacher and child come from different socioeconomic or ethnic groups within the larger society. The teacher is mainly concerned with the child's adaptation to the classroom, but from the point of view of the children's interests we should also bear in mind their relationship to the SES and/or the ethnic group of which they will continue to be a part outside school.

The Influence of Wider Cultural Values

Because individual parents and teachers think and act within a larger cultural milieu, we need to take account of how these wider cultural values impinge on play and on adult's views of play. Adults themselves might be "manipulated" by societal norms to act in ways which do not always coincide with their own interests, any more than the interests of the children in their care.

So far as play is concerned, I have argued (Smith 1988, 1990) that the predominant value system we need to take account of in western societies over the last sixty or seventy years is the *play ethos*. This is epitomized in the following quotation:

"The realization that play is essential to development has slowly but surely permeated our educational system and cultural heritage" (UK; Department of the Environment 1973).

This play ethos has been very influential from the 1920s and 1930s through the 1980's. It can be traced back at least as far as Susan Isaacs' view that "Play is indeed the child's work and the means whereby he grows and develops. Active play can be looked upon as a sign of mental health, and its absence either as a sign of some inborn defect or of mental illness" (Isaacs 1929, 9). These views have undoubtedly nurtured the development of the play tutoring and training programs to augment fantasy/sociodramatic play in schools, as already discussed.

Indeed, the idealization of play has even sometimes led to a preference for "free play" over "structured play." This would be associated with libertarian views which extol the values of freedom of choice by the child, rather than any kind of coercion by adults. Such a preference is not obviously justifiable on educational grounds; it may have some force if one is concerned about the manipulation of play by adults, and wants children's play to be "natural," following their own wishes and uncontaminated by adult judgments of what is best for them (Sutton-Smith 1986).

Usually, however, the play ethos has emphasized the educational significance of play. A case can certainly be made that the play ethos has influenced the way research has been done on play in general, and on play training in particular. In a review (Smith 1988), I suggested that the research on the educational and developmental benefits of play has been characterized by selective interpretation of results, effects of experimenter bias, and use of inappropriate control groups. The last criticism applies particularly to the research on play training/tutoring.

The first generation of studies on play tutoring, cited earlier, essentially concentrated on following an experimental group which received the play training intervention. The control groups used were inadequate (or even absent). These studies found very widespread benefits of play tutoring. However, the benefits could have been due to either the increase in sociodramatic play (the Smilansky hypothesis), or the increase in verbal stimulation obtained from a tutor (the "verbal stimulation" or "tutoring stimulation" hypothesis). To discriminate between the two hypotheses, it is necessary to use nonfantasy play or skills-tutored groups, with an equal amount of verbal stimulation and tutor contact. The control groups in the earlier studies generally had unspecified amount of adult interaction, often apparently minor (e.g., "the experimenter led each control group in activities, often involving toys, to communicate that adults are interested in and supportive of children's play activities"; Rosen 1974, 922). Later studies with adequate skills-tutoring control groups have, in contrast, tended to find equal benefits to both kinds of tutoring (Smith & Syddall 1978; Smith, Dalgleish & Herzmark 1981; Hutt 1979; Hutt, Tyler, Hutt & Christopherson 1989; Burns & Brainerd 1979; Brainerd 1982; Christie 1983; Christie & Johnsen 1985).

It should be noted that this does not deny the pragmatic value of play tutoring to the nursery school teacher. (In addition, the above studies sometimes report that play tutoring increases social participation more than skills tutoring, although this may merely reflect the rather nonsocial sorts of skills tutoring used). The main findings do, however, challenge the idea that play tutoring is necessarily any better than other kinds of tutoring for educational purposes. In their latest discussion of this, Smilansky & Shefataya (1990, 211) cite the pragmatic argument (of equal attainment by play and skills tutored groups) in favor of play tutoring, but do not really tackle the conceptual issues involved. Their defence of the control groups used in some earlier studies lacks details and conviction: even where control groups were used, they did not match (or there is no evidence of matching) the levels of adult involvement and stimulation in the play tutored groups (226).

The play ethos has had wider ramifications, which are really outside the scope of this discussion unless one construes "play training" very widely. It can be argued that, when coupled with the commercial interests of capitalist societies, it has helped lead to the enormous production and marketing of toys and playthings which often greatly exceeds what might be in the interests of children or parents (Sutton-Smith 1986). To some extent at least this is more in the interests of toy manufacturers and advertisers. The most contentious issue in this domain has been that of war toys, often highly promoted by television series, which many parents find morally objectionable (Carllson-Paige & Levin 1987).

Summary

The possibilities for both the use and abuse of children's play by adults are exemplified in play training and in the influence of the play ethos on practice and research.

On the one hand, play training may be seen as enhancing the developmental value which play has, adapting forms of play optimally to the needs of postindustrial society (MacDonald 1992). This view is supported by the theoretical viewpoints of, for example, Vygotsky and Bruner, and empirically by the results of many play training studies (even though the conceptual arguments for the reasons why play training may work are still under dispute).

On the other hand, play training may be seen as a subtle way of using play for adult ends. It may do so, for example, by emphasizing adult-preferred to nonpreferred kinds of play (toy over physical play; accepted forms of play within the adult culture). Undoubtedly the research justifying play training has been influenced by the play ethos. And at a wider level, the play ethos has helped emphasize the special world of children as separate from adults, and the "consumption" of toys (Sutton-Smith 1986). Thus, questions of values inevitably come into consideration when debating the positive and negative aspects of play training and tutoring.

It is surely true that (in most people's value systems) some forms of play training will be helpful in many situations—indeed that they are a natural part of human cultural evolution, as are other forms of education. From this perspective, play training is indeed to be welcomed, encouraged and enjoyed. Equally, however, we need to be aware of the potential for adult manipulation of play for the ends of adults (or other segments of society) rather than for the children themselves, whenever we are practicing play training or doing research on play training.

/15

Play: Positive Intervention in the Elementary School Curriculum

Waltraut Hartmann and Brigitte Rollett

Increasing emphasis on formal learning and highly structured curricula in elementary school have reduced children's learning motivation considerably, and not exclusively in the industrialized countries (Rollett 1989). The same phenomenon can also be observed in developing countries (UNICEF 1990). The alarming expressions of this development are lack of concentration, a rise in aggressive behavior, discontent and school absenteeism on the part of school children.

In several countries, classroom trends show the endeavor to bring about integration of children's natural inclinations toward free play into curricula designed to further all the children's potential: not only their intellectual capacities, but also emotional and other personality-related faculties (Hartmann 1989, 1991).

International research results agree that children's play is not only a source of pleasure but has surplus value in that it reduces stress and enhances children's intrinsic motivation to learn, provided that educators refrain from controlling free play and from misusing it for their own purposes (Einsiedler 1985; Hartmann et al. 1988; Schmidtchen & Stüwe 1989; Sutton-Smith 1988, 1990).

While play activities and toy equipment play a central role in preschool curricula, they are generally frowned upon and minimized as an elementary school fact of life. The tremendous increase in research on play (as reviewed by Johnson et al. 1987; Einsiedler 1990; Christie 1991) elucidates the beneficial relationship between play programs and child development. There is no evidence that the positive impact of play on cognition, language, social skills and the emotional adjustment of children ceases in the early school years. On the contrary, the sudden curtailment of play in the elementary school curriculum leads to a "work-play dichotomy" (Torrance 1963) which hampers creativity and may, in the long run, cause an impaired identity formation (Erikson 1963; Hetzer 1969; Eichler 1979; van der Kooij 1983).

Practical experiences in everyday school life show that free play as well as the teacher guided play are integrative parts in all innovative forms of curricula like open classrooms, individualized instruction, cooperative learning or interdisciplinary instruction.

A Play Intervention Program in Austrian Elementary Schools

There were several reasons why the Viennese school authorities advocated the integration of play into the existing elementary school curriculum: the debilitating influences on children's cognitive, emotional and social development, the rising rate of aggression in schools and of school failures in classes with a high percentage of multi-ethnic, multilingual children and of pupils of low socioeconomic status.[1]

The experimental group consisted of twelve elementary classes. They were provided with a rich assortment of pretested toys, replenished at the beginning of each school year. The teachers were instructed in the pedagogy of play.

The approved set of toys consisted of:

- Stuffed animals

- Dolls and accessories

- Make-believe sets

- Puppets like Punch and Judy

- Miniature toys (houses, people, animals, cars, train sets)

- Wooden blocks

- Various plastic construction sets

- Flexible street plan with cars, traffic signs, houses and people

- Board and table games, jigsaw puzzles, didactic games designed to train memory, language, concentration, cooperation etc.

In each classroom four specific play areas were defined: a housekeeping area, an area for constructive play, a table-toy area and an area for dramatic play (especially for Punch and Judy). This ensured a sheltered atmosphere in which several small groups of children could devote themselves to the activity at hand, something crucial for the attainment of the program's goals: concentration, cooperation, creativity.

In order to integrate the play sequences into the daily schedule, teachers were counseled to schedule a total of about four hours a week of free play

- upon arrival at school before classes began,

- at recess,

- selectively when the children requested a play session ad hoc, or

- when the children became restless or tired.

The teacher guided play was usually of a didactic nature, tailored to reinforce the learning process. It was scheduled (cf. Hartmann, Neugebauer & Rieß 1988):

- for individualized instruction,

- for learning by doing in science and mathematics,

- to reinforce learning processes, like visual discrimination, concentration or memory,

- for remedial instruction.

The Evaluation Study

From 1983 to 1987 a longitudinal empirical study was conducted to assess the long term effects of the Viennese Play Curriculum (Weickl 1988; Fürnwein 1992; Konvalina 1992; Sevcik 1992). One of its main goals was to investigate the effects of play and games on the *normal curriculum* of elementary schools. The school authorities proposed specific questions for each school grade, which became the focus of interest for this investigation (cf. table 15.1).

In the first two grades, the Austrian primary school curriculum envisages the establishment of a satisfactory working atmosphere and an acceptable emotional climate among students and teachers. In the second grade, special attention is devoted to developing social behavior. In the third grade, students should have a solid command of the main subjects and a positive attitude towards academic performance. Moreover, they are expected to show responsibility for their own achievement. In the fourth grade, students should have learned to work on their own.

In addition, this study intended to show whether students from the experimental groups displayed more creativity than those from the control group. Finally, another focus of interest was to develop practical guidelines for integrating games and toys in the classroom.

Twelve Viennese elementary classes, with a total of 289 students, took part in the play program. These classes were deliberately chosen because students came from a predominantly low socioeconomic background and because of their high rate of children of foreign nationality. They were compared with twelve control classes (N = 266) matched in age, gender, IQ and socioeconomic status. In the experimental group, however, the rate of students of foreign nationality proved to be higher than in the control group. In the statistical analysis this fact was taken into consideration.

During the four year study, children of both experimental and control groups were regularly tested. In the successive grades, four different domains were studied: emotional attitude toward learning, social behavior, achievement orientation, and creativity. All instruments were standardized and well tested procedures that proved particularly successful for these specific inquiries in primary schools.

Results

Results will be presented on all four domains. First, children's and teachers' *emotional attitude towards school*. To assess the students' attitude towards school the "School Attitude Questionnaire" (Knaak & Rauer 1979) was handed out in the second grade. Two areas were studied: "Contentment with School" and "Adaptation to School." The ratings on "Contentment with School" were significantly higher among the children of the experimental group than among the controls (p = 0.005). Items such as "feeling happy in the classroom," "in

Table 15.1 Overview of the Instruments of Assessment Employed During the Four Year Study

STUDENT'S AND TEACHER'S EMOTIONAL ATTITUDE TOWARD LEARNING	SOCIAL BEHAVIOR	ACHIEVEMENT MOTIVATION	CREATIVITY
1st grade: • Content analysis of teacher's reports **2nd grade:** • School Attitude Questionnaire (Knaak & Rauer 1974) • Content analysis of teacher's reports **3rd grade:** • Dortmund Scale for rating teacher's behavior (Masendorf et al. 1975)	**2nd grade:** • Scale for Rating Students (Hanke et al. 1980) • Systematic observations of pupils' behavior	**3rd grade:** • Ambros' pictorial adaptation of the "AVT," Effort Avoidance Test (Rollett & Bartram 1981) • General Scholastic Achievement Test for the 3rd grade, "AST 3" (Seyfried 1978)	**4th grade:** • Divergent Thinking Test for grade 4-6 (Mainberger 1976) • Content analysis of students' ideas for a lesson without teacher

student-teacher exchanges," "in doing school work" and "in thinking of school" are some of the descriptors. As was expected, the children of the experimental group were considerably happier in school than those of the control group. A striking example: children of the control classes showed much higher agreement with the statement "I do not want to go to school" ($p \leq 0.001$) than the children of the play-enriched classes, as the study by Fürnwein (1992) demonstrated. The ratings in the factor "Adaption to School" showed no difference between the experimental and the control group.

There was an interesting difference between the ratings of the Austrian children and the non-Austrians in both experimental and control groups: children of foreign nationality showed higher ratings on the factor "Contentment with school" than the Austrians (p ≤ 0.012).

A content analysis of the reports of teachers who taught the experimental classes showed frequent expression of positive emotions like good mood, satisfaction with the toy equipment, or play pleasure (17.8 percent). Of all statements, 16.5 percent fell in the category "Interest in the individuality and in the problems of students" and 14.7 percent in "Stimulation and promotion by the teacher." Only six percent of the emotions expressed were negative, for example, frustration, helplessness.

This result concurs with the significantly higher ratings (p ≤ 0.009) given by the children of the experimental group, compared to those of the control group, to their teachers under the heading "being in a good mood" of the Dortmund Scale for Rating Teachers' Behavior (Masendorf et al. 1975). On the other hand, students in experimental classes felt that teachers' praise was used more sparingly for their school work than did the controls. Apparently, the children in the play classes, more content in the classroom setting, were more highly intrinsically motivated and not in need of excessive external reinforcement.

With regard to *social behavior*, teachers' ratings of their students' behavior in the second grade (Scale for Rating Students, Hanke et al. 1980) confirmed the positive effects of the play curriculum: teachers in the experimental classes observed behavioral changes along the lines of being "more candid, straightforward," "more companionable," "less aggressive," and "having fewer behavioral disorders."

These results were confirmed by a systematic observation study of students' behavior. During recess the social behavior of ninety-one children (four per class, in the experimental and control groups respectively) chosen at random was recorded by two independent observers. Time sampled observations were made in five minute blocks, according to a randomized schedule. Each individual child was observed four times.

The main results were the following. In the play-enriched classes, more cooperative contact with the teachers (p ≤ 0.03) and less rough-housing and competitive activity (p ≤ 0.002) were observed. While the controls were observed to spend their recess time more often in activities like eating, indulging in sweets or "horsing around," the children in the experimental group more frequently spent their recesses playing.

With respect to *achievement motivation*, no differences were found between the two groups on the factor "effort avoidance." However, children in the experimental group rated significantly higher ($p \leq 0.002$) on the dimension "conscientiousness" (i.e., doing practice exercises and homework), thus demonstrating a greater identification with academic goals.

Moreover, a paired comparison of scholastic achievement between control and experimental children (matched in age, gender, nationality, social class, parents' level of education, position in order of siblings, and number of siblings) could dispel any misgivings on the part of educators and/or parents that the four hour per week trade-off of play for formal instruction might result in a learning deficit. No differences ($p \leq 0.3$) were found on the General Scholastic Achievement Test for the Third Grade (Seyfried 1978) between experimental and control group subjects. Both groups achieved equally well.

The play program also seems to enhance *creativity*. In the fourth grade, the Divergent Thinking Test for Grades Four to Six (Mainberger 1976) was administered to the children to evaluate divergent thinking. As table 15.2 shows, the difference between the experimental and control groups was significant. The Austrian as well as the non-Austrian students in the play-enriched classes more often found novel, creative ways to solve problems.

To investigate the difference between the two groups in producing divergent ideas in real-life situations the following question was posed: "Imagine your teacher leaves the class for an hour. What would you and your schoolmates do?" A content analysis of the answers showed significantly more ideas about activities in the experimental classes: creative activities (inventing a story, making a poem, dramatic play) as well as motor activities (running, gymnastics, doing stupid things). The controls produced more ideas in the category "Passive behavior" (staying quiet, being good).

Table 15.2 Divergent Thinking Test: Comparison of Means Between Experimental and Control Groups

	N	MEAN	SD	p
Experimental group	207	104.96	15.71	$\leq .000$
Control group	241	95.76	12.97	
Total	448			

Summary and Conclusions

In summary, the play intervention program in the Viennese elementary school curriculum can be considered a success. Children in play-enriched classes expressed more contentment with school than the controls. In their reports, teachers of the experimental group frequently emphasized their joy, good mood and satisfaction with children's play and toy equipment. They rated their pupils as more companionable, more candid and straightforward, less aggressive, and they observed fewer behavioral disorders.

The children in the experimental groups more often spent their recesses playing and in active, cooperative interaction with their teachers, instead of eating, indulging in sweets or horsing around like the controls did.

Moreover, all of these benefits for the play-enriched classes were obtained without any forfeits in scholastic achievement. Students who could devote themselves to play activities showed a more positive attitude toward learning and a greater intrinsic motivation than the controls. Children of the play group found more divergent ways to solve problems and produced more creative ideas for organizing a school lesson without a teacher.

In 1987 the concept of "Learning through Play" was introduced as a recommended form of learning in the school curriculum for Austrian elementary schools. School authorities now are beginning to appreciate the value of play in elementary school. Teachers who are interested in play are invited to seminars on play and open education. A teacher's guide to the didactics and methodology of play in elementary school has been worked out by Hartmann et al. (1988). These developments mark a milestone on the way towards a humane school that does justice to the child. A school in which, apart from academic demands, there remains room for the child's individuality, emotional life and imagination.

/16

Academic Play

James F. Christie

Play has long had a major role in early childhood education, serving as a general means to facilitate young children's development. In recent years, there has been a push to expand play's role to include the teaching of specific academic skills and content. Academic play experiences are being recommended in such subjects as reading, social studies, mathematics, and science (Block 1984; Hartmann, Neugebauer, & Reiss 1988; Manning & Sharp 1977; Moyles 1989; Wassermann 1990). Advocates claim a number of advantages for instructional play, including increased motivation and interest, meaningful contexts for learning, opportunities for children to construct and perfect their own concepts and rule systems, and encouragement of risk-taking and innovation.

One factor propelling this academic play movement is the growing influence of constructivist theories, such as those of Piaget (1973) and Vygotsky (1978), which maintain that children acquire knowledge through active experimentation and social interaction, rather than by passive absorption. These theories have been buttressed by an extensive amount of recent research on play's role in children's social and cognitive development (Christie & Johnsen 1983; Johnson, Christie, & Yawkey 1987; Rubin, Fein, & Vandenberg 1983). This research, while not establishing clear causal links between play and development, has produced considerable evidence that play activities are a *context* in which cognitive and social growth can occur. As a result, many early childhood educators have adopted some tenets of the experimentalist philosophy of education (Glickman 1984), particularly the belief that learning is best accomplished by means of active, playful, child-centered activities rather than by teacher-led instruction.

The academic play movement, however, faces stiff opposition from two very divergent forces. The most formidable of these is the essentialist philosophy of education that is currently embraced by the general public and by many school administrators (Glickman 1984). This philosophy, which underlies the ongoing "back-to-basics" movement, maintains that the primary purpose of education is for teachers to transmit essential knowledge and skills to students. Direct instruction has long been the method of choice for accomplishing these essentialist goals, whereas play has been dismissed as being inefficient and frivolous—or, to use the essentialist terminology, as "off task" behavior. As a result, teachers face pressure to replace play-oriented activities with more direct forms of instruction.

The other source of opposition consists of play proponents who deeply believe in the value of free, uninhibited, "natural" play. These play advocates worry that play is perverted and distorted when used to achieve academic ends (e.g., Götz 1977; Sutton-Smith 1987b). Sutton-Smith has been one of the most vocal critics of instructional play activities. He recently commented, "It is better to encourage children to play amongst themselves than to infect them with our own didactic play bumblings" (Sutton-Smith 1990, 5).

The forces opposing academic play raise contradictory objections. Play proponents claim that activities in these programs are not really play, whereas many school administrators and members of the public worry that these same activities are too playful and are a waste of time. This paper examines both of these issues: (a) Do the activities in academic play programs possess the characteristics of play? and (b) How effective are these programs in promoting the learning of essential concepts and skills?

Is Academic Play Really Play?

While a precise definition of play continues to elude researchers (Vandenberg 1982), progress has been made in identifying traits or dispositional factors that set play apart from other behaviors (Garvey 1977; King 1979; Rubin et al. 1983; Smith & Vollstedt 1985). These characteristics include:

1. *Nonliterality.* Play events are characterized by a play frame within which internal reality takes precedent over external

reality. The usual meanings of objects are ignored, new meanings are substituted, and actions are performed differently than when they occur in nonplay settings.

2. *Positive Affect*. Play is usually marked by signs of pleasure and enjoyment. Smiles, laughter, and joking are some of the most obvious signs that play is occurring.

3. *Flexibility*. Children are more apt to try novel combinations of ideas and behaviors while playing than when engaged in nonplay activity.

4. *Means over ends*. When children play, their attention is focused on the activity itself rather than on the goals of the activity. In other words, means are more important than end products.

5. *Voluntary*. Play is spontaneous and freely selected by children.

6. *Internal Control*. In play, the players are in control and determine the course of events.

Smith and Vollstedt (1985) found that the first four characteristics (nonliterality, positive affect, flexibility, and means over ends) were useful and reasonably reliable indicators of play behavior. King's research (1979) has revealed that the last two (free choice and internal control) have an important role in determining whether kindergartners perceive school activities to be play or work. Children considered an activity like block building to be play if they chose to do it. The same activity was considered to be work if it were assigned or controlled by a teacher, as, for instance, when she asked the children to count the blocks.

In order to examine the playfulness of academic play programs, the activities in several programs designed to promote reading and writing will be briefly described and analyzed in terms of the above criteria. These programs were selected to illustrate the diversity of activities that fall under the rubric of academic play.

1. *Sociodramatic play interventions.*
   Sociodramatic play training, originally developed by Smilansky (1968) in Israel, uses theme-related props and teacher involvement to encourage group-dramatic play (Christie 1982). This strategy has been modified recently by several American and British investigators to focus on reading and

writing (Christie & Enz 1991; Hall, May, Moores, Shearer, & Williams 1987; Morrow & Rand 1991; Neuman & Roskos 1990). Theme-related literacy materials were placed in dramatic play areas, and teachers used suggestions and modeling to encourage children to use these materials in connection with their play. For example, a housekeeping center might be equipped with pens, pencils, phone message pads, self-adhesive notes, phone books, cookbooks, newspapers and other literacy items commonly found in homes. If several children had taken on the roles of parents and were planning a trip to a nearby store center, the teacher might suggest that they write a shopping list and leave some written instructions for the baby-sitter. Results have shown that these interventions are very successful in getting many children to incorporate literacy behaviors into their dramatic play.

2. *Thematic-fantasy play*

   Thematic-fantasy play (TFP) involves teacher-guided enactment of fairy tales and stories. The teacher first reads the story to the children, assigns roles, and helps the children re-enact the story several times (with diminishing guidance). This strategy was initially developed by Saltz and Johnson (1974) as a general means to promote cognitive growth, but it has been recently used successfully to promote two important literacy skills: story comprehension and knowledge of narrative story structure (Pellegrini 1984; Pellegrini & Galda 1982; Silvern, Taylor, Williamson, Surbeck, & Kelley 1986).

3. *Play-Debrief-Replay*

   Play-Debrief-Replay, originally developed to teach primary-grade science (Wassermann & Ivany 1988), has recently been extended to other curriculum areas, including literacy instruction (Wassermann 1990). Children, working in small groups, choose activity cards which give instructions for "play" activities. Following the play period, the teacher asks children questions which cause them to reflect upon their play. They then are encouraged to engage in similar activities with new materials or with a new focus. In the activity "Words and Sounds," for example, children are given a number of cards, each with a word containing a long *a* or a long *o* sound (*may, say, sleigh, weigh, boat, load, code, hope*). They are instructed to make some observations about the words and to group them. During the debrief phase, the teachers asks questions such as: "How were some words alike? How were they different? What groups did you make?" (Wassermann 1990, 158). For replay, it is suggested that children do the same activity with new word cards featuring other letter-sound relationships. They can also engage in "creative play," pantomiming the words on the cards or scrambling the letters in the words to make new words.

Research on the playfulness of these three academic play programs is, to the best of my knowledge, nonexistent. An examination of the activities involved in each program, however, reveals that large differences are likely to exist in the extent to which these programs possess the characteristics of play (see table 16.1).

This informal "task analysis" indicates that the sociodramatic play interventions are the most playlike of the three programs. These interventions occur in the context of self-selected (voluntary) dramatic play which, by its very nature, involves nonliteral role taking and make-believe transformations. There is likely to be considerable flexibility in children's behavior as they enact their dramatizations, and it is well established that children consider dramatic play to be an enjoyable activity. The literacy products (e.g., scribble writing and pretend reading) that are produced are of little importance to

Table 16.1 Play Characteristics of Three Literacy-Oriented Academic Play Programs

	SOCIODRAMATIC PLAY INTERVENTIONS	THEMATIC FANTASY PLAY	PLAY-DEBRIEF-REPLAY
Nonliterality	+	+	−
Positive affect	+	+	?
Flexibility	+	?	−
Means over ends	+	−	−
Voluntary	+	−	+
Internal control	?	?	−

+ = Likely to possess this characteristic
− = Unlikely to possess this characteristic
? = Variable

children other than as a means for acting out their stories. Thus, the means over ends criterion is satisfied.

The only questionable characteristic is internal control. The extent to which this criterion is met depends on how the teacher interacts with children during sociodramatic play interventions. Schrader (1990) found that teachers' involvement in dramatic play could be characterized as being either *extending* or *redirecting*. In the *extending* style, the teacher took cues from children's ongoing play activities and suggested a literacy activity that matched the child's current play interests (e.g., the shopping list/baby sitter suggestions mentioned earlier). The children were free to accept or reject the teacher's suggestions, so they remained in control of the play episode. This style of interaction seemed to have no negative effect on the children's play and was quite successful in getting children to incorporate literacy into their dramatizations.

Redirecting interaction, on the other hand, occurred when the teacher took over control of the play and imposed a literacy activity which bore little if any relationship with the children's current play. Schrader gave an example of how a teacher approached several children playing in a housekeeping corner and asked one of them to write a letter to the Easter Bunny (which had nothing to do with the children's ongoing domestic drama). Schrader found that redirecting style of interaction was ineffective, often disrupting the "play frame" and causing children to stop playing altogether.

Thematic-fantasy play, with its teacher-directed enactments of fairy tales, is inherently nonliteral. Researchers have also reported that children "enjoyed themselves tremendously" while engaging in these dramatizations (Galda 1982, 55), so this strategy also scores high in terms of positive affect. Little emphasis is placed on a polished performance, so means are more important than ends. However, the fact that the teacher supplies roles and a ready-made plot lessens the control children have over the activity and reduces the flexibility of their behavior. The extent to which internal control and flexibility are reduced depends on the style of involvement used by the teacher. If teachers adopt a *directive* role and use narrating and prompting to make sure that children act out all parts of the story accurately (Silvern et al. 1986), there is likely to be little internal control or flexibility in behavior. On the other hand, if teachers adopt a *facilitative* role and allow children to choose their own roles and make variations in the story, then these criteria are at least partially met. In all the studies to date, thematic-fantasy play has been a teacher-mandated activity, so the voluntary criterion is not met.

The play-debrief-replay strategy is clearly the least playful, satisfying only the voluntary criterion. Children do choose to participate and are allowed to select their activity cards. The extent to which the activities produce positive affect is unknown and is likely to vary. Some of the activities, particularly those in the science area, appear to have high enjoyment potential; others, such as the "Words and Sounds" activity described above, are much less likely to be enjoyed by children. The activities in this program are grounded in reality, and the end products (learning specific concepts) are of considerable importance. The students' actions are dictated by directions on the activity cards, minimizing internal control and flexibility.

This task analysis is, of course, informal and not research-based. It was conducted to show that considerable variation exists in the playfulness of academic play programs. Future studies of play programs would do well to include some objective measures to substantiate the degree to which their activities conform to play criteria. Several procedures are currently available for this purpose. Smith and Vollstedt (1985) have ascertained that even untrained observers can achieve reasonable agreement on whether or not activities possess the characteristics of nonliterality, positive affect, flexibility, and means over ends (least reliable of the four). Trained observers would likely be able to make even more reliable observational judgements. Gehlbach (1980, 115) has pointed out that the other two criteria (voluntary and internal control) can be "negatively operationalized" by excluding barriers: "For example, the voluntary character of play may be specified objectively . . . by excluding authoritative directives by non-players as the basis for children's initiation and maintenance of play in the target settings."

By addressing play criteria directly, curriculum designers and researchers could legitimate their use of the label *play*. Such procedures might also lead to the selection of more appropriate labels for the didactic, teacher-led activities found in some so-called play programs.

How Effective is Academic Play?

The essentialist philosophy that permeates many schools is a powerful force working against play-oriented activities. The only way to counteract this force is to prove that play experiences are effective in promoting the learning of academic content and skills. Glickman (1984, 268) explains the situation in United States schools:

The political and social climate is one of fiscal austerity and accountability for predetermined ends. Schools have been reduced in budget, staff, and materials. Schools are being asked to limit their purpose and to focus on reversing declining achievement scores. Unless research can show the benefits of play to such goals, it will not find a place in today's schools.

Several studies have compared play interventions with alternative treatments. Smith, Dalgleish and Herzmark (1981) and Christie (1983) found that sociodramatic play intervention and skills tutoring produced similar gains for preschoolers on a number of cognitive measures. Research by Silvern et al. (1986) and Pellegrini (1984) revealed that thematic-fantasy play was as effective as teacher "read alouds" and teacher-led discussions in promoting kindergartners' and first graders' story recall. In both studies, however, thematic-fantasy play proved to be less effective in promoting comprehension with older, second- and third-grade students. Thus, the evidence regarding the comparative effectiveness of play programs is restricted to the early childhood level.

There is a pressing need for research comparing the effectiveness of play programs and direct instruction in promoting academic achievement, particularly in the elementary grades. Such studies must, of course, feature implementation checks and extensive experimental controls. Several other features will enhance the likelihood of these comparative studies' success:

1. *Use long treatment durations*. As Martin and Caro (1985) have pointed out, many theories stipulate that play is likely to have delayed, long-term effects on development. Short-term experimental studies are unlikely to be able to detect these effects (Smith 1987). Take, for example, sociodramatic play interventions. If preschoolers engage in emergent forms of reading and writing in connection with their dramatic play, this provides valuable opportunities for them to experiment with the structure of print and to receive feedback from peers. Such experiences could, over time, enable children to hone and perfect their self-generated rule systems for writing and spelling. It is highly unlikely that these play experiences would have immediate effects on children's literacy behavior. Comparative studies involving play programs should feature lengthy treatment durations (lasting several months or years) so that play treatments have a chance to have a noticeable effect on children's development.

2. *Use an expanded range of dependent variables*. In order to

justify play's existence in essentialist schools, comparative studies must include measures of traditional academic outcomes. At the same time, investigators need to guard against the possibility raised by Smith (1987), that play programs may have effects that cannot be detected by traditional assessments. In the literacy domain, for example, it is possible that play activities might foster positive attitudes toward reading and writing and might increase children's self-confidence in being able to succeed in these activities. These types of outcomes should be assessed as well as the more traditional ones (e.g., recognition of the letters of the alphabet). Attitude surveys and observations of children's self-selected literacy activities during free-choice periods would be possible means for measuring these alternative outcomes.

Alternative outcome measures can be of considerable importance in cases where direct instruction and play programs bring about similar gains on traditional assessments. If it can be shown that play experiences promote comparable growth in academic learning plus superior gains in children's attitudes, self-initiative, creativity or other play-related outcomes, this would make a strong argument in favor of using play programs.

3. *Investigate possible subject x treatment interactions.* Research has shown that thematic-fantasy play has differing effects on children's story comprehension, depending on their age and ability. Silvern et. al. (1986) found that this strategy was more effective with kindergartners and first-graders than with second- and third-graders. They conjectured that, on the average, older children have better developed concepts about narrative story structure than younger children and, therefore, have less to gain from thematic-fantasy play experiences. However, the children's ability also needs to be taken into consideration. When Williamson and Silvern (1991) reanalyzed the data from their initial study, focusing only on second- and third-graders whose reading comprehension was below average, the results indicated that thematic-fantasy play did bring about significant gains in story comprehension. They commented that, if ability is not taken into account, a "masking" effect may occur. In their original study (Silvern et al. 1986), all the older primary-grade students were grouped together so that the lack of impact on the average and above average students masked the treatment's effect on the less able students. In order to guard against this, future comparative studies should utilize age and ability as independent variables. It is quite possible that the effectiveness of play and direct instruction treatments may vary, depending on these two factors.

Conclusion

This paper has examined two issues connected with academic play programs. The first concerned whether or not the activities in these programs deserve to be called play. The informal task analysis presented above indicates that academic play programs differ considerably in the extent to which their activities correspond to the characteristics of play. Some programs, such as well-executed sociodramatic play interventions, are very playful in nature and are likely to be perceived by children as being play. Others, such as the Play-Debrief-Replay program, have little in common with free play. This is not to say that such programs are undesirable or ineffective. I would simply suggest that these programs not use the label *play*. Using the term *play* in connection with activities that are teacher-directed, reality-bound, and outcome-oriented is likely to confuse children and adults alike. This mislabelling may also result in these didactic programs being used as a substitute for more playful classroom experiences.

I would also like to emphasize that, no matter how well academically-oriented play experiences conform to play criteria, they should not be used as replacements for the free play that occurs during school recess periods. Sutton-Smith (1987b, 289) has commented that this type of unguided play "abounds with the opportunities to try on powers, risks, deceptions, and skills and to share these with others." This rambunctious play tends to be incompatible with indoor classroom situations. Academic play programs should not be used as an excuse to eliminate recess, as has been the case in some schools (Sutton-Smith 1987a). Children can profit from teacher-guided play activities, but they also need opportunities to play on their own without adult interference.

The second issue concerns educational accountability. Comparative research studies, such as those recommended above, may show that some of the better academic play programs can produce larger academic gains than direct, teacher-led instruction. If this occurs, these play programs will undoubtedly find a permanent home in the elementary-grade curriculum.

The possibility also exists that these play programs may not prove to be very effective in promoting academic achievement. In this case, educators will need to consider the wisdom of allocating large amounts of precious time for play activities in the elementary-grade curriculum. There is a wide consensus that play should have a major role in early childhood programs. However, Sutton-Smith (1987a) may be correct when he asserts that, at the elementary-grade level, the best place for school play is on the playground during recess periods.

The most likely scenario is that comparative studies will result in a "tie," with play programs and direct instruction bringing about comparable gains on traditional academic measures. In this case, nontraditional outcome measures are of the utmost importance. If the play programs truly possess the characteristics of play, then it is possible that these programs will result in more positive attitudes toward academics, increased self-initiative, elevated self-esteem, and enhanced creativity. In this case, play programs would definitely be the method of choice for use with children at all grade levels.

EPILOGUE

Joop Hellendoorn, Rimmert van der Kooij
and Brian Sutton-Smith

Play and intervention. At the start of this book this may have seemed a contradiction. Perhaps to some readers it still is. Is it not the popular view in Western culture that play is (or should be) characterized by its essential freedom, whereas intervention implies some sort of control by others (cf. Huizinga's classical *Homo Ludens* 1955)? However, the contention that any form of intervention detracts from play's real value is not tenable. Play is always influenced, in one way or another. By the available space and materials, and most of all by the players: as soon as there are more players, freedom of play will of necessity be limited. Giving and taking, waiting for one's turn, and, particularly in rough-and-tumble play, physical toughness, play their own part. Moreover, as Sutton-Smith has repeatedly pointed out, play is not always fun: children can hurt each other, can fall out of trees, can exclude some players or always relegate them to the underdog role, and so on.

　　Many of those who work with children's play, under the power of Western culture's work ethic (including the view that play can hardly be serious business) tend to overreact defensively by sacralizing and idealizing play. They act as if the admission of play studies and techniques to serious society must be accompanied by serious idealization. Historically speaking, play is more noted for its excitement, risk taking, passion and brutality. It has very often been a powerfully motivating phenomenon in human affairs, but not always a peaceful one. In many of the contributions to this book some of this idealization can be seen, when play is said to contribute to socialization, to learning, to literacy, to symbolic competence or to family coherence. These rationalizing moves are consistent with the

215

treatment of the Imagination in the Western romantic tradition where from Kant to Dewey to Piaget play has been made a handmaiden to Reason. But they are also a part of civilizing play so that it can be accepted in proper society. Obviously, a lot of this domestication is essential because of the dangers and risks in play, but it should not blind us to the fact that the true energy of play often derives from its relatively unruly excitements.

Still, idealization is not the only motivating force when we are speaking about play interventions. Neither is control by adults. In most practical contributions to this volume, one is struck by the child-centeredness and the conscientious attention to the child's experiencing. Clearly, control is not what these authors, play counselors and play therapists are aiming at (although professional helpers need to always stay alert to this, perhaps unconscious danger). Instead, we encounter a definite tendency on their part not just to watch the children and to encourage them verbally, but to take an active part and to play along with their clients. Some sense of this promise of play as a function that beckons us all forward, can be found in the description by Bertha Mook of the players being played themselves by the autonomous phenomenon of play. In her terms, play provides the intrinsic medium for the player's own progress. The player becomes the plaything of the game, not of the therapist. The therapists themselves may even become such players. However, exciting as this sounds, no one suggests that play implies a complete surrender of control by the adult. The uncertainty and irrationality of the child's play may even necessitate some more explicit form of control, particularly with children who are so fully surrendering to what happens in their play that they definitely need some outside structuring. On the other hand, in some cases of nonplaying children, e.g., autistic children and other handicapped children, not even the children themselves are capable of that form of surrender.

What, then, is the motivating force for play interventions? Perhaps most probable: the idea that play is a part of "natural development"; that children often derive pleasure or zest for life from it. That children throughout all cultures and all ages have played. That they even continued playing in the most horrible circumstances (as documented by Eisen 1987). Does this not mean that play has a special meaning for children, perhaps even for all humans? Even though group play sometimes has its drawbacks for the underdog, there is always solitary play which can (and often does) take its place. In play, the child can relatively safely experiment with materials and with situations, physically, cognitively, as well as emotionally. Play seems for many children one of the easiest ways to assimilate experiences, to process information on their own level and in their own (play) language. It should be clear, however, that much of this experience or information may be confusing, uncomprehended or emotionally negative. Even then, play provides a relatively relaxed atmosphere, in which these facts of life, difficult though they are, can be assimilated and, hopefully, be coped with. Let it be clearly understood: this is not the child's own reason for play. Children play because of play itself, because of the pleasure, the excitement or the thrill they experience. And indeed, for the adults who develop therapies and training programs for different kinds of problems or for special children, this intrinsic motivation may be as strong an argument as the supposed external benefits of play. With these considerations in mind, let us review once again the different interventions discussed.

Play Therapy

As a serious scientific enterprise, play therapy is still in poor shape. In 1953, Lebo described the state of research as ". . . still meager, unsound, and frequently of a cheerful persuasive nature." Twenty-five years later, Barrett, Hampe and Miller (1978) contributed a modest paper to the authoritative handbook of Garfield and Bergin, in which they had to admit that this unsatisfactory situation was essentially unchanged. And in the third edition of that same handbook (Garfield & Bergin 1986), the editors decided there was insufficient new material in the field of psychotherapy with children to warrant a chapter of its own. And although recently some interesting work has been done in America and Europe, the emphasis in therapy literature is on theory.

But as we know, even without the stamp of scientific approval, play therapy has refused to go away. In fact, it can be reckoned as one of the major "growth industries" in the play field of this century. The recent founding of an Association for Play Therapy (A.P.T.) with a thousand members in its first three years is impressive and contrasts markedly with the more scholarly-oriented TASP (The Association for the Study of Play) and its European counterpart ICCP (International Council for Children's Play) that have been in existence for some fifteen and thirty years, respectively, but never had more than 200 and 400 members. Play therapy is clearly validated at the popular cultural level.

In this volume's section on play therapy, it becomes clear that the scientific foundations for the use of play in therapy mostly come from neighboring fields and not from therapy research itself. Process studies which might elucidate the process of change are still scarce, and therefore have little to offer as yet in terms of possibly active ingredients. And without these the informative value of effect studies remains limited (Kazdin 1988). Most therapists are practitioners and not all that much interested in research. Indeed, they often think that researchers are unable to grasp the essence of therapy. Some of this is undoubtedly true, but on the other hand, part of this view is almost certainly due to the idealization of play, mentioned before. Especially in our Western culture of personal pleasure and quest for self-actualization, "peak experiences" may be more popular than scientific quality control.

However, the theoretical foundation of therapy is much better documented than its empirical basis, and the major schools of therapy are well established in the Western world. The play therapy contributions to this book, although not in any way representative for all the work done in this field, all aim at clarifying the foundations for therapeutic work involving play, from different theoretic standpoints (hermeneutic, psychodynamic, client centered, behavioral). Play as a way of learning, as a learning experience in the broadest sense of the word, is one of the key words. As Jerome Singer points out, for children in trouble, with many kinds of deep-seated problems and often living in very difficult family conditions, play can be a way to explore their own ideas and feelings, can help them process negative and conflicting experiences so as to better cope with them, and provide an opportunity to search for and experiment with alternatives. From their different theoretical points of view, Schmidtchen, Goetze and Schäfer try to trace the ways in which such learning experiences might occur and function in therapy. In spite of the recognized complexity of the therapeutic experience, this process of clarification can also lead to a more systematic approach of therapeutic interaction. Just now, the search is on for more explicit criteria for the effective use of play and specific play interventions, as well as for the assessment of behavior and the changes caused by therapy. Some of this can be found in the practical contribution of Dorothy Singer with regard to therapeutic technique and in van Zanten's empirical study on indications and goals for therapy. Because the different therapy theories and "schools" remain the most important source of thinking, work in this field is largely deductive.

Play Programs for Special Children

In contrast to the deductive approach of most play therapists, very little theory is available in the field of special or handicapped children. Taking the children themselves as the starting point, including their specific possibilities and limitations, professional workers are looking for better ways to enable these children to grow up in a healthy way and to take their own place in society. Is it because handicaps are not really accepted in Western industrial society with its powerful work ethic, that relatively little work has been done here?

Regardless, in the last decade there is a growing interest in children with special needs. More and more, one is looking for the similarities between special and "normal" children instead of their differences. Consequently, developmental issues valid in normal development have acquired more importance when dealing with retarded children or children with physical or sensory handicaps, whereas formerly almost all efforts were directed towards compensating for their specific deficits. It seems to us that play is such a general developmental issue. It is remarkable how little attention is paid in handbooks on handicapped children to their play. But, to take just one example, it is a good sign that in a recent volume on *Children with Down Syndrome* (Cicchetti & Beeghly 1990) a whole chapter was devoted to play development. Interestingly, one of the main conclusions in that chapter (Beeghly, Weiss-Perry & Cicchetti 1990) is that most measures of play (including symbolic play) showed the Down syndrome children performing in about the same way as MA-matched normally developing children. Their pace of development, however, is much slower. Therefore, if play is seen as important for normally developing children, why should not the same be true for handicapped children? And if they do not discover play (or certain stages of play) on their own, would it not be worthwhile to help them?

A special problem perhaps is, that there are so many different kinds of handicaps or special needs. There are children who develop many play skills on their own, with no specific help needed (e.g., among mildly retarded children). Others may be less fortunate, for different reasons. There are people who are so convinced that handicapped children do not or cannot play, that it does not even cross their minds to provide them with playthings. Take, for instance, physically handicapped children with severely restricted mobility. Such children will be unable to explore play materials and their play possibilities, so long as nobody notices that they cannot reach the toys with their own hands and feet. For a blind child, every room, every object even, can be full of unseen dangers. Special children may feel so insecure that their ability for exploration and play is seriously impaired. Some of them have become demoralized and unable to take initiatives because they never felt they could succeed in whatever they undertook.

Caregivers, parents as well as professionals, also have a difficult task. If there is no discernible developmental progress, how does one continue to have hope? Normal children just play, but the more severe and the more encompassing a child's handicap, the more difficult it becomes to find alternative ways to catch the child's attention or to find out what it can or wants to do and what it cannot. Nakken et al., working with profoundly multiply handicapped children, draw special attention to the caregivers' plight and direct much of their intervention to them. For these children, as well as for autistic children, "play" sounds almost like a contradiction. Not surprisingly, in that context the word "play" is often replaced by "toy behavior" (cf. Van Berckelaer's chapter).

Therefore, special attention is needed to help caregivers help their children acquire the play skills that seem to come so naturally to others. It is the specific need of the child or group of children that decides what particular help is required. Physically handicapped children will need material help geared to their own specific inabilities, as is illustrated by de Moor et al.. Retarded children often need much repetition of games they are trying to master. However, as Hellendoorn discusses, in that case, special care is needed to preclude their newly found play skills becoming "tricks" to satisfy their caregivers. Mogford-Bevan describes how a communication-delayed child can be stimulated by devising appropriate interactive play activities. So it seems that the nature of the disability determines, at least to a large extent, the form of the play program to be devised.

This raises the question whether play programs for special children are geared to their handicap or, rather, to the children as individuals. And what are the programs' goals: play "skills" or play as a pleasurable way of being, doing, and coping? If the latter is important, "training programs" should take special care not to become a form of indoctrination (e.g., they must learn to play because that is good for all children) instead of a self-initiated and intrinsically motivated activity, containing at least some spark of "play pleasure."

In the contributions to this volume, the pioneering stages of play programs for special children become visible. Most of them are small-scale, starting almost from scratch, inductively trying out what works and what does not work. Much creativity is required from those who work with these children, but perhaps the ideas presented here can help them find more satisfying ways of interacting. McConkey gives some original suggestions as to how the children's family and cultural environment can be a valuable addition into play programs for special children.

Lastly, we would like to stress that these play programs are *not therapy*. Play therapy (better perhaps: play psychotherapy) aims at diminishing emotional problems and disturbances by means of play, whereas the play programs mentioned above aim at developing "normal" play skills and activities. Often, all kinds of play activities are called play therapy, but we feel that this too general use of the term leads to an unacceptable watering-down of the different goals of intervention and of the different professional competence involved.

Play Intervention in School

For this group of interventions, neither the emotional problems of individual children nor any specific disability determines the nature of what will be done, but rather the situation: the school or group in question and their teaching methods. It is the school that determines both the supply and the demand. It is a school's business that children acquire academic skills and they will use play if they think this can be helpful to that purpose. Thus, adventure play and rough-and-tumble will not often be seen in schools (if it is not actively banned). The emphasis is on the cognitive effects, whereas in play therapy it is on the emotional aspect, and in special play programs on the developmental possibilities.

Although this is a serious limitation of school play programs, this does not mean that they are without value. That would be far from the truth. A recent volume on play and early literacy development (Christie 1991) throws a critical but not unfavorable light on the effectiveness of play interventions. However, a crucial conclusion in that book is that teachers should not expect play to have a substantial impact on *every* child's literacy development, since young children have distinctly different play dispositions and do not respond alike to the same programs. The contributions in this volume (e.g., that of Smith) make clear that one should not attach too many expectations to play in learning, especially in hopes of promoting specific cognitive skills (symbol formation, language, literacy, arithmetic) by specific play interventions. This narrow kind of play intervention also runs a greater risk of being "just academic training" in a nice disguise, as Christie points out. However, it seems a reasonable assumption that play can increase intrinsic motivation in general and can promote interest in certain subjects which also have an academic aspect. A good example is the sociodramatic play described by Christie, in which children are encouraged to play all kinds of fantasy situations, in which arithmetic (making up the grocery bill in the play store), reading (as mother to the doll children, or when making a tasty dish out of a cookbook) or writing (a prescription in the play doctor's office) have a natural place.

As said before, perhaps even more important may be the general motivating force in play, which helps the children to feel good in school and thus to become more accessible to whatever the school wants them to learn (as Hartmann & Rollett suggest). Therefore, even more than in therapy and in work with special children, teachers have to beware of taking too much initiative, of controlling the play situation with their academic ends in view, instead of leaving the children to develop their own (even if sometimes unruly) play ideas.

The Case for Play Interventions

After overviewing the different interventions one point remains: Can play be a change agent, and should it be so? Although the somewhat contrasting problems posed by idealization of play on the one hand, and the danger of too much control by adults on the other should be clearly recognized, we feel there still is a case for play interventions.

Obviously, for children who develop well and along the expected pattern, in general no special attention to play is needed. They play on their own, so long as sufficient material as well as physical and psychological space is available. Even in more difficult circumstances, it may be enough to provide basic play conditions and simple support.

For instance, children in hospital or waiting for surgery are usually well able to use the offered play opportunities in preparing themselves for what is going to happen or in working through their experiences. If necessary, this can be enhanced by support from a play counselor. However, in practice this is not as easy as it sounds. In many hospitals, child care workers have a difficult position. Although they are often considered as the only persons able to help children individually with their emotional problems, at the same time they often meet with that well-known, somewhat derogatory attitude towards all nonmedical staff who usually have to yield priority to the medical and nursing professions. Consequently, in a hospital, a child's play will often be postponed or interrupted for a medical action, but never the other way round. Play conditions, although available, are therefore not always satisfactory. A closer working relationship between the medical and the child care staff, in which the child's well-being as a whole person becomes the central issue, may help to improve these basic conditions, thereby decreasing the demand for specialized interventions.

But there are also many children who need more. We have spoken of children with more or less severe and deep-seated emotional problems who are unable to cope with their daily life experiences. What they need is a temporary intensive individual contact in which the therapeutic properties of play can be used to the full. There are also many children who are less able to develop play because of mental or physical handicaps. For them, special conditions or extra stimuli may help them attain some of the play behavior that for other children seems so natural and normal. In schools, less spectacular perhaps, many children have difficulty adapting to the system or are poorly motivated for learning. In these cases, play interventions may be considered.

To sum up, there is a case for play interventions, given certain conditions. These conditions can be summarized as follows:

- Choose carefully what sort of intervention is necessary or desirable.

- Tune the intervention systematically to the specific goals, whether these are therapeutic, developmental or academic.

- Provide a suitable play environment and adequate feedback.

- Keep modest about the changing power of play, and keep in mind that this power may be dissimilar for different children.

- Be alert to the "playfulness" of the intervention and to the "play pleasure" it is supposed to evoke.

- Keep an eye to the individual children and their specific needs, especially in group play interventions.

- Use your results to help formulate more specific indication criteria for different interventions.

- Be open, creative and dynamic in your own ways of playing.

What all authors in this volume have in common, whether therapists, educators, or psychologists, is that they use play in their work with children needing some sort of help. Certainly, there are other forms of help than play, sometimes just as effective. Even then, play may be the first choice, because of its childlike quality, because of its nearness to the child's own way of feeling, doing, and thinking. Those who do use play, often testify to the gratifying feeling that not only has something happened to the child, but also to themselves and their relationship with the child. Not because they idealize play, but because childlike qualities may have their impact on all human beings.

NOTES

Play and Intervention

1. The First Amsterdam Play Symposium, titled "Play—Play Therapy—Play Research," was held in 1985. Its proceedings were published in Van der Kooij & Hellendoorn (1986).

Games of Complexity

1. This second thought was clearly worked out by Mannoni (1964, 1973) in therapy with seriously disturbed children.

Play: Positive Intervention in the Elementary School Curriculum

1. The play intervention program was sponsored by the Austrian Ministry of Education, by the Viennese School Authorities, by the "Toy-Association" (A G Spielzeug) at the Chamber of Commerce, by the National Bank of Austria and by the "Viennese Youth Circle" (Wiener Jugendkreis).

REFERENCES

Play and Intervention

Van der Kooij, R., & Hellendoorn, J. (1986). *Play—Play Therapy—Play Research*. Berwyn, PA: Swets North America Inc.

Paradigms of Intervention

Aries, P. (1962). *Centuries of childhood*. New York: Alfred A. Knopf.

Avedon, E., & Sutton-Smith, B. (1971). *The study of games*. New York: John Wiley.

Berger, P. L., & Luckmann, T. (1966). *The social construction of reality*. New York: Doubleday.

Berlyne, D. E. (1960). *Conflict, arousal and curiosity*. New York: McGraw-Hill.

Block, J. H., & King, N. R. (1987). *School play*. New York: Garland.

Carlsson-Paige, N., & Levin, D. E. (1987). *The war play dilemma*. New York: Teachers College, Columbia University.

Cavallo, P. (1981). *Muscles, morals and team sports*. Philadelphia: University of Pennsylvania.

Connor, K. (1991). *War toys, aggression and playfighting*. Doctoral dissertation, University of Pennsylvania.

Elkind, D. (1981). *The hurried child*. Reading, MA: Addison-Wesley.

Erikson, E. H. (1950). *Childhood and society*. New York: Norton.

Fantuzzo, J. W. (1990). *Play buddy project*: a preschool based intervention to improve the social effectiveness of disadvantaged high-risk children. Department of Health and Human Services, Head Start Bureau, Washington DC.

Foucault, M. (1973). *Madness and civilization*. New York: Vintage.

James, N. C., & McCain, T. A. (1982). Television games preschool children play; patterns, themes and usages. *Journal of Broadcasting* 26:783-800.

Kelly-Byrne, D. (1989). *A child's play life*. New York: Teachers College, Columbia University.

Kessen, W. (1981). The child and other cultural inventions. In F. S. Kessel & A. W. Sigel, Eds., *The child and other cultural inventions*, 26-39. New York: Praeger.

Kline, S. (1991). *Out of the garden: children's culture in the age of advertising*. Toronto: Garamond.

Liss, M. B. (1983). *Social and cognitive skills: sex roles and children's play*. New York: Academic Press.

Luke, C. (1989). *Pedagogy, printing and protestantism*. Albany: State University of New York Press.

Maccoby, E. (1990). Gender and relationships, a developmental account. *American Psychologist* 45:513-520.

Mangan, J. A. (1986). *The games ethic and imperialism*. New York: Viking.

Megill, A. (1985). *Prophets of extremity*. Berkeley: University of California.

Nilsson, N. (1990). Why are there international actions against toys of war and violence? *Playrights* 12(2):7-8.

Otto, K., & Riemann, S. (1990). Zur Spezifik der Beziehungen zwischen Kindern und Erwachsenen im Spiel. Paper presented at the 17th Conference of the ICCP, St. Andreasberg, Germany.

Pellegrini, A. D. (1988). Elementary school children's rough-and-tumble play and social competence. *Developmental Psychology* 24:802-806.

Piaget, J. (1951). *Play, dreams and imitation in childhood*. New York: Norton.

Postman, N. (1982). *The disappearance of childhood*. New York: Dell, Laurel.

Smilansky, S. (1968). *The effects of sociodramatic play on disadvantaged preschool children*. New York: John Wiley.

Snow, R. P. (1974). How children interpret television violence in play context. *Journalism Quarterly* 51:13-21.

Singer, D. G., & Singer, J. L. (1985). *Make believe: Games and activities to foster imaginative play in young children*. Glenview, IL: Scott, Foresman & Company.

————. (1990). *The house of make-believe*. Cambridge: Harvard University Press.

Sutton-Smith, B. (1954). *The unorganized games of New Zealand primary school children*. Doctoral dissertation, University of New Zealand.

————. (1981). *A history of children's play*. Philadelphia: University of Pennsylvania Press.

————. (1986). *Toys as culture*. New York: Gardner Press.

————. (1988a). War toys and childhood aggression. *Play and Culture* 1:57-69.

————. (1988b). Radicalizing childhood: the multivocal mind. In L. R. Williams & D. P. Fromberg, Eds., *Defining the field of early childhood education*. Charlottesville, VA: W. Alton Jones Foundation.

————. (1989). Play as performance, rhetoric and metaphor. *Play and Culture* 2:189-192.

————. (in press-a). A memory of games and some games of memory. In J. H. Lee, Ed., *Life before story: the autobiographies of psychologists from a narrative perspective*. New York: Praeger.

———. (in press-b). Dilemmas in adult play with children. In K. B. McDonald, Ed., *Parents and children playing*. Albany: State University of New York Press.

Sutton-Smith, B., & Sutton-Smith, S. (1974). *How to play with children*. New York: Hawthorne Press.

Sutton-Smith, B., Gerstmyer, J., & Mechley, A. (1988). Playfighting as folkplay amongst preschool children. *Western Folklore* 47:161-176.

Turner, E. S. (1948). *Boys will be boys*. London: Michael Joseph.

Vygotsky, L. (1978). *Mind in society*. Cambridge: Harvard University Press.

Wilcox, B. L., & Naimark, H. (1991). The rights of the child: progress towards human dignity. *American Psychologist* 46:49.

Zelizer, V. (1985). *Pricing the priceless child*. New York: Basic Books.

Zuckerman, M. (1976). Children's rights: the failure of reform. *Policy Analysis* 2:371-385.

Play Therapy

Harinck, F., & Hellendoorn, J. (1983). Procesresearch in de kinderpsychotherapie [Process research in child psychotherapy]. In C. A. M. De Wit, Ed., *Psychotherapie met kinderen en jeugdigen*, 503-523. Leuven/Amersfoort: Acco.

Harinck, F. J. H., & Hellendoorn, J. (1987). *Therapeutisch spel: proces en interactie* [Therapeutic play: process and interaction]. Lisse: Swets & Zeitlinger.

Schmidtchen, S. (1978). *Handeln in der Kinderpsychotherapie* [Therapeutic action in child psychotherapy]. Stuttgart: Kohlhammer.

———. (1986). Practice and research in play therapy. In R. van der Kooij & J. Hellendoorn, Eds., *Play, play therapy, play research*, 169-195. Berwyn, PA: Swets Publishing Company.

Smith-Acuna, S., Durlak, J. A., & Kasper, C. J. (1991). Development of child psychotherapy process measures. *Journal of Clinical Child Psychology* 20:126-131.

The Scientific Foundations of Play Therapy

Angyal, A. (1965). *Neurosis and treatment: A holistic theory*. New York: John Wiley.

Bakan, D. (1966). *The duality of human existence*. Chicago: Rand McNally.

Blatt, S. J. (1990). Interpersonal relatedness and self-definition: Two personality configurations and their implications for psychopathology and psychotherapy. In J. L. Singer, Ed., *Repression and dissociation*. Chicago: University of Chicago Press.

Bonanno, G., & Singer, J. L. (1990). Repressive personality style: Theoretical and methodological implications for health and pathology. In J. L. Singer, Ed., *Repression and dissociation*. Chicago: University of Chicago Press.

Bretherton, I. (1984). Representing the social world. In I. Bretherton, Ed., *Symbolic play reality and fantasy*, 3. New York: Academic Press.

Bruner, J. (1986). *Actual minds, possible worlds*. Cambridge: Harvard University Press.

Cantor, N., & Kihlstrom, J. (1987). *Personality and social intelligence*. Englewood Cliffs, NJ: Prentice Hall.

Ekman, P. (1973). *Darwin and facial expression: A century of research in review*. New York: Academic Press.

Ekman, P., Friesen, W. V., & Ellsworth, P. C. (1982). *Emotion in the human face: Guidelines for research and an integration of findings*, Revised Ed. Cambridge: Cambridge University Press.

Epstein, S. (1990). Cognitive-experiential self theory. In L. Pervin, Ed., *Handbook of Personality: Theory and Research*, 165-192. New York: Guilford Press.

Freud, S. (1962). Formulations regarding the two principles of mental functioning. In J. Strachey, Ed., *The Complete Psychological Works of Sigmund Freud*, Vol 12. London: Hogarth Press. (Originally published 1911).

Goldstein, K. (1940). *Human nature in the light of psychopathology*. Cambridge: Harvard University Press.

Izard, C. E. (1977). *Psychological types*. New York: Pantheon.

Kreitler, H., & Kreitler, S. (1976). *Cognitive orientation and behavior*. New York: Springer.

————. (1990). *The cognitive foundations of personality traits*. New York: Plenum.

Leslie, A. M. (1987). Pretense and representations: The origins of "theory of mind." *Psychological Review* 94:412-422.

Lewin, K. (1935). *A dynamic theory of personality*. New York: McGraw-Hill.

Mandler, G. (1984). *Mind and Body*. New York: Norton.

Mandler, J. M. (1983). Representation. In J. H. Flavell & E. M. Markman, Eds., *Cognitive development*, Vol. 3 of P. Mussen, Ed., *Handbook of child psychology*, 4th Edition. New York: Wiley.

————. *Stories, scripts and scenes: aspects of schema theory*. Hillsdale, NJ: Lawrence Erlbaum.

McAdams, D. P. (1985). *Power, intimacy, and the lifestory*. New York: Guilford Press.

————. (1989). *The person*. San Diego: Harcourt Brace Jovanovich.

Papousek, M., Papousek, H., & Harris, B. (1987). The emergence of play in parent-infant interactions. In D. Gorlitz, & J. Wohlwill, Eds., *Curiosity, imagination, and play*. Hillsdale, NJ: Erlbaum.

Piaget, J. (1962). *Play, dreams and imitation in childhood*. New York: Norton.

————. (1980). *Possibility and necessity*. Minneapolis: University of Minnesota Press.

Rank, O. (1945). *Will therapy and Truth and reality*. New York: Knopf.

Schachtel, E. G. (1959). *Metamorphosis*. New York: Basic Books.

Singer, D. G., & Singer, J. L. (1990). *The house of make-believe: Children's play and the developing imagination*. Cambridge: Harvard University Press.

Singer, J. L., Ed. (1973). *The child's world of make-believe*. New York: Academic Press.

——. (1974). *Imagery and daydreaming methods in psychotherapy and behavior modification*. New York: Academic Press.

——. (1985). Transference and the human condition: A cognitive-affective perspective. *Psychoanalytic Psychology* 2:189-219.

——. (1988). Psychoanalytic theory in the context of contemporary psychology. *Psychoanalytic Psychology* 5:2:95-125.

Singer, J. L., & Bonanno, G. A. (1990). Personality and private experience: Individual variations in consciousness and in attention to subjective phenomena. In L. Pervin, Ed., *Handbook of Personality*. New York: Guilford Press.

Singer, J. L., & Kolligian, J. (1987). Personality: Developments in the study of private experience. In M. Rosenzweig & L. Porter, Eds., *Annual Review of Psychology*, Vol. 38, 533-574. Palo Alto, CA: Annual Review, Inc.

Singer, J. L., & Salovey, P. (1991). Organized knowledge structures in personality: Schemas, self-schemas, prototypes and scripts. In M.J. Horowitz, Ed., *Person schemas and recurrent maladaptive interpersonal patterns*. Chicago: University of Chicago Press.

Singer, J. L., & Singer, D. G. (1976). Imaginative play and pretending in early childhood: Some experimental approaches. In A. David, Ed., *Child Personality and Psychopathology: Current Topics*, 69. New York: John Wiley and Sons.

Sutton-Smith, B. (1966). Piaget on play: A critique, *Psychological Review* 73:104-110.

Sutton-Smith, B., & Kelley-Byrne, D. (1984). The idealization of play. In P. K. Smith, Ed., *Play in Animals and Humans*, 305. London: Basil Blackwell.

Taylor, S. (1989). *Positive delusions: Creative self-deceptions and the healthy mind*. New York: Basic Books.

Tomkins, S. S. (1962, 1963). *Affect, Imagery and Consciousness*, Vols. 1 & 2. New York: Springer.

Van Hoorn, J. (1987). Games that babies and mothers play. In P. Monighan-Novrot, B. Scales, J. Van Hoorn, et al., Eds., *Looking at children's play*, 38. New York: Teachers College Press.

Vygotsky, L. (1962). *Thought and language*. Cambridge: Massachusetts Institute of Technology Press.

Therapeutic Play: From Interpretation to Intervention

Buytendijk, F. J. J. (1932). *Het spel van mens en dier* [The play of humans and animals]. Amsterdam: Kosmos.

Freud, A. (1928). *Introduction to the technique of child analysis*. New York: Nervous and Mental Disease.

Freud, S. (1937). *Construction in analysis* (Standard Edition 23). London: Hogarth Press.

Gadamer, H-G. (1982). *Truth and method*. New York: Crossroads.

Guerney, L. F. (1983). Client-centered play therapy. In C. E. Schaefer, & K. J. O'Connor, Eds., *Handbook of play therapy*, 21-64. New York: Wiley.

Hellendoorn, J. (1988). Imaginative play technique in psychotherapy with children. In C. E. Schaefer, Ed., *Innovative interventions in child and adolescent therapy*, 43-67. New York: Wiley.

Hirsch, E. D. (1967). *Validity in interpretation*. New Haven: Yale University Press.

Howard, R. J. (1982). *Three faces of hermeneutics*. Berkeley: University of California.

Huizinga, J. (1938). *Homo ludens*. Haarlem: Willink & Zoon.

Klein, M. (1932). *The psychoanalysis of children*. London: Hogarth Press.

Langeveld, M. J. (1955). Bevrijding door beeldcommunicatie [Liberation by image communication]. *Nederlands tijdschrift voor de psychologie* 2:443-455.

Lubbers, R. (1971). *Voortgang en nieuw begin in de opvoeding* [Progress and new beginning in child rearing]. Gent: Van Gorcum.

Meltzer, D. (1978). *The Kleinian Development, Part II*. Perthshire, Clunie Press.

Mook, B. (1988). Play in child psychotherapy. *The Social Work Practitioner-Researcher* 1(2):42-47.

———. (1989). Play and play therapy. *Journal of Learning about Learning* 1(2):5-20.

Ornstein, P. H. & Ornstein, A. (1980). Formulating interpretations in clinical psychoanalysis. *International Journal of Psychoanalysis* 61:203-211.

Ricoeur, P. (1974). *The conflict of interpretations*. Evanston, IL: Northwestern University Press.

———. (1976). *Interpretation theory*. Forth Worth: The Texas Christian University Press.

———. (1984). *Time and narrative*. Chicago: University of Chicago Press.

Schaefer, C. E., Ed. (1988). *Innovative interventions in child and adolescent therapy*. New York: Wiley.

Schaefer, C. E. & O'Connor, K. J., Eds. (1983). *Handbook of play therapy*. New York: Wiley.

Scheuerl, H. (1975). *Theorie des Spiels*. Beltz: Weinheim.

———. (1986). Some phenomenological aspects of play. In R. Van der Kooij, & J. Hellendoorn, Eds., *Play, play therapy, play research*. Berwyn, PA: Swets North America Inc.

Vermeer, E. (1955). *Spel en spelpaedagogische problemen* [Play and play-pedagogic problems]. Utrecht: Bijleveld.

Winnicott, D. W. (1974). *Playing and reality*. London: Pelican books.

Stimulating and Guiding Children's Spontaneous Learning in Play Therapy

Buck, H., Dinter, G., & Vogiatzi, L. (1989). *Analyse des Störungsverhaltens, des Störungsbewältigungsverhaltens und des motivationalen Verhaltens anhand von Fallbeispielen erfolgreicher Spieltherapien* [Analysis of disturbed behavior and of the ways to overcome disturbances, in successful play therapy cases]. Diplomarbeit. Universität Hamburg: Fachbereich Psychologie.

Heckhausen, H. (1969). Entwurf einer Psychologie des Spiels [Design of a play psychology]. *Psychologische Forschung* 27:225-293.

Hennies, S. (1989). *Analyse der Effekte des Therapeutenverhaltens im Rahmen der klientenzentrierten Spieltherapie* [Effects of therapeutic action in client-centered play therapy]. Diplomarbeit. Universität Hamburg: Fachbereich Psychologie.

Orlinsky, D. E. & Howard, K. J. (1978). The relation of process to outcome in psychotherapy. In S. C. Garfield & A. E. Bergin, Eds., *Handbook of psychotherapy and behavior change*, 283-329. New York: Wiley.

Piaget, J. (1969). *Nachahmung, Spiel und Traum* [Play, dreams and imitation]. Stuttgart: Klett-Cotta.

―――. (1972). *Theorien und Methoden der modernen Erziehung* [Theories and methods of modern child-rearing]. Wien: Molden.

Rogers, C. R. (1959). A theory of therapy, personality and interpersonal relationships, as developed in the client-centered framework. In S. Koch, Ed., *Psychology: a study of science*, 184-256. New York: McGraw Hill.

―――. (1974). *Lernen in Freiheit* [Freedom to learn]. München: Kosel.

Schmidtchen, S. (1986). Practice and research in play therapy. In R. van der Kooij & J. Hellendoorn, Eds., *Play, play therapy, play research*, 169-195. Berwyn, PA: Swets Publishing Company.

―――. (1989). *Kinderpsychotherapie* [Child Psychotherapy]. Stuttgart: Kohlhammer.

―――. (1991). *Klientenzentrierte Spiel- und Familientherapie* [Client-centered play and family therapy]. Weinheim: Psychologie Verlags Union.

Schmidtchen, S., Wörmann, D., & Hobrücker, B. (1977). Verlaufsanalyse des Spielverhaltens in der Kinderpsychotherapie [Process analysis of play behavior in child psychotherapy]. *Praxis der Kinderpsychologie und Kinderpsychiatrie* 6:208-217.

Schmidtchen, S., Hennies, S., & Acke, H. (1993). Bewirkt die klientenzentrierte Spieltherapie eine Persönlichkeitswachstum und einen Störungsabbau? [Does client-centered play therapy help in personality growth and problem decrease?] *Psychologie und Unterricht* 40:34-42.

Processes in Person-Centered Play Therapy

Axline, V. M. (1947). *Play therapy—The inner dynamics of childhood*. New York: Houghton Mifflin.

Borke, H. (1947). *Changes in the expression of emotionalized attitudes in sic cases of play therapy.* Master's thesis, University of Chicago.

Ehlers, B. (1981). Die personenzentrierte Gruppentherapie mit Kindern [Person- centered group therapy with children]. In H. Goetze, Ed., *Personenzentrierte Spieltherapie,* 44-63. Göttingen: Hogrefe.

Goetze, H., Ed. (1981). *Personenzentrierte Spieltherapie* [Person Centered Play Therapy]. Göttingen: Hogrefe.

Maslow, A. (1954). *Motivation and personality.* New York: Harper & Row.

Moustakas, C. E. (1953). *Children in play therapy.* New York: McGraw-Hill.

Oaklander, V. (1978). *Windows to our children.* Moab, UT: Real People Press.

Rogers, C. (1942). *Counseling and psychotherapy.* New York: Houghton Mifflin.

————. (1951). *Client-centered therapy.* New York: Houghton Mifflin.

Rogers, M. B. (1972). *The process of monitored play-therapy.* Doctoral dissertation, Georgia State University.

Wessels, C. (1982). *Prozesse in der personenzentrierten Kinderspieltherapie—dargestellt am Verlauf der Behandlung des Schülers S.* [Processes in person-centered play therapy]. Unpublished thesis, University of Hamburg.

Whitee, K. L. (1975). *A Descriptive Analysis of the Process of Play Therapy.* Doctoral dissertation, North Texas State University.

Games of Complexity

Bittner, G. (1976). Die "heilenden Kräfte" im kindlichen Spiel [The "healing power" of children's play]. In H. Halbfas, F. Maurer, & W. Popp, Eds., *Spielen, Handeln, Lernen.* Stuttgart: Klett.

Datler, W. (1985). Psychoanalytische Repräsentanzlehre und pädagogisches Handeln [Psychoanalytical representation theory and pedagogical action]. In G. Bittner & C. Ertle, Eds., *Pädagogik und Psychoanalyse,* 67-80. Würzburg: Königshausen und Neumann.

Fatke, R. (1980). Heilende und erziehende Kräfte in der kindlichen Phantasie [Healing and educational power of children's fantasy]. *Die Psychologie des 20. Jahrhunderts* 12:865-876.

Freud, A. (1965). *Normality and pathology in childhood.* New York: International University Press.

Mannoni, M. (1964). *L'enfant arriéré et sa mère.* Paris: Editions du Seuil.

————. (1973). *Éducation impossible.* Paris: Editions du Seuil.

Noy, P. (1969). A revision of the psychoanlytic theory of the primary process. *International Journal of Psychoanalysis* 50:155-178.

————. (1973). Symbolic and mental representation. *The annual of psychoanalysis,* 125-158. New York: International University Press.

————. (1978). Insight and creativity. *Journal of the American Psychoanalytical Association* 26:717-748.

————. (1979). The psychoanalytic theory of cognitive development. *Psychoanalytic study of the child* 34:169-216.

Pöldinger, W. (1985). Zur Ontogenese des symbolischen Denkens [On the ontogenesis of symbolic thinking]. In G. Benedetti & U. Rauchfleisch, Eds., *Die Welt der Symbole* [The world of symbols], 70-75. Göttingen: Vandenhoeck & Ruprecht.

Scarbath, H., Ed. (1991). *Pioniere psychoanalytisch orientierter Pädagogik* [Pioneers of psychoanalytical pedagogy]. Frankfurt: Lang.

Schäfer, G. E. (1979). Heilendes Spiel [Therapeutic play]. *Kindheit* 1:239-250.

———. (1980). Pädagogik oder Therapie? Psychoanalytisch orientierte Spielgruppenarbeit im Zwischenraum [Working with a psychoanalytic playgroup: between pedagogy and therapy]. In K. L. Holtz, Ed., *Sonderpädagogik und Therapie*, 213-222. Rheinstetten: Schindele.

———. (1986). *Spiel, Spielraum und Verständigung* [Play, play space and understanding]. Weinheim/München: Juventa.

———. (1989). *Spielphantasie und Spielumwelt* [Play fantasy and play context]. Weinheim/München: Juventa.

Schäfer, G. E. & Favier, A. (in press). Kontextorientierte Untersuchungen von Spielzeugwirkungen [Context-oriented research on toy influence].

Winnicott, D. W. (1965a). Ego distortion in terms of the true and false self. In *The maturational processes and the facilitating environment*. London: Hogarth Press.

———. (1965b). Ego integration in child development. In *The maturational processes and the facilitating environment*. London: Hogarth Press.

———. (1971). *Playing and reality*. London: Tavistock Publications.

Zulliger, H. (1965). Die deutungsfreie psychoanalytische Kinderpsychotherapie [Non-interpretive psychoanalytic child psychotherapy]. In G. Biermann, Ed., *Handbuch der Kinderpsychotherapie*, 192-198. München/Basel: Reinhardt.

———. (1966). *Bausteine zur Kinderpsychotherapie* [Elements of child psychotherapy]. Bern/Stuttgart: Huber.

———. (1970). *Heilende Kräfte im kindlichen Spiel* [The healing power of children's play]. Frankfurt/Main: Fischer.

Imagery Techniques in Psychotherapy with Children

Brandell, J. R. (1988). Narrative and historical truth in child psychotherapy. *Psychoanalytical Psychology*, 5(3): 241-257.

Bruner, J. S. (1964). The course of cognitive growth. *American Psychologist* 19:1-15.

de Mille, R. (1973). *Put your mother on the ceiling*. New York: Viking.

Gardner, R. A. (1983). Treating Oedipal problems with the mutual storytelling technique. In C. E. Schaefer & K. J. O'Connor, Eds., *Handbook of play therapy*, 355-368. New York: Wiley.

Goodnow, J. (1977). *Children drawing*. Cambridge: Harvard University Press.

Hellendoorn, J. (1988). Imaginative play technique in psychotherapy with children. In C. E. Schaefer, Ed., *Innovative interventions in child and adolescent therapy*, 43-67. New York: Wiley.

Horowitz, M. J. (1978). *Image formation and cognition*. 2nd Edition. New York: Appleton-Century-Crofts.

Kelly, E. (1973). *The magic if*. New York: Drama Book Specialists.

Koch, K. (1970). *Wishes, lies and dreams: Teaching children to write poetry*. New York: Vintage Books.

Lazarus, A. A., & Abramovitz, A. (1962). The use of "emotive imagery" in the treatment of children's phobias. *Journal of Mental Science* 108:192-195.

Leuner, H., Horn, G., & Klessman, E. (1983). *Guided affective imagery with children and adolescents*. New York: Plenum Press.

Martin, M., & Williams, R. (1990). Imagery and emotion: Clinical and experimental approaches. In P. J. Hampson, D. F. Marks, & J. T. E. Richardson, Eds., *Imagery: Current developments*, 268-306. London: Routledge.

Mowrer, O. H., & Mowrer, W. A. (1938). Enuresis: A method for its study and treatment. *American Journal of Orthopsychiatry* 8:436-47.

Piaget, J. (1962). *Play, dreams, and imitation in childhood*. New York: Norton.

Piaget, J., & Inhelder, B. (1971). *Mental imagery in the child*. New York: Basic Books.

Purkel, W., & Bornstein, M. H. (1980). Pictures and imagery both enhance children's short-term memory and long-term recall. *Developmental Psychology* 16:153-154.

Rosenstiel, A. K., & Scott, D. S. (1977). Four considerations in using imagery techniques with children. *Journal of Behavior Therapy and Experimental Psychiatry* 8:287-290.

Rubin, J. A. (1987). Freudian psychoanalytic theory: Emphasis on uncovering and insight. In J. A.Rubin, Ed., *Approaches to art therapy: Theory and technique*, 7-25. New York: Brunner/Mazel.

Singer, D. G., & Singer, J. L. (1990). *The house of make-believe: Play and the developing imagination*. Cambridge: Harvard University Press.

Singer, J. L., & Pope, K. S., Eds. (1978). *The power of human imagination: New methods in psychotherapy*. New York: Plenum Press.

Wolpe, J. (1958). *Psychotherapy by reciprocal inhibition*. Stanford, CA: Stanford University Press.

Wood, M. (1986). The circular floor painting game. In R. van der Kooij, & J. Hellendoorn, Eds., *Play, play therapy, play research*, 145-151). The Netherlands: Swets & Zeitlinger.

Indications and Goals in
Imagery Interaction Play Therapy

Adelman, H. S., Kaser-Boyd, N., & Taylor, L. (1984). Children's participation in consent for psychotherapy and their subsequent response to treatment. *Journal of clinical child psychology* 13:170-178.

Borke, H. (1947). *Changes in the expression of emotionalized attitudes in six cases of play therapy.* Master's thesis. Chicago: University of Chicago.

Day, L., & Reznikoff, M. (1980). Social class, the treatment process, and parents' and children's expectations about child psychotherapy. *Journal of clinical child psychology* 9:195-198.

Ginott, H., & Lebo, D. (1961). Play therapy limits and theoretical orientation. *Journal of consulting psychology* 25:337-340.

Harter, S. (1983). Cognitive-developmental considerations in the conduct of play therapy. In C. E. Schaefer & K. O'Connor, Eds., *Handbook of play therapy*, 95-127. New York: Wiley.

Hellendoorn, J., Groothoff, E., Mostert, P., & Harinck, F. (1981). *Beeldcommunicatie: een vorm van kinderpsychotherapie* [Imagery Interaction: a method of child psychotherapy]. Deventer: Van Loghum Slaterus.

Hellendoorn, J. (1985). *Therapie, kind en spel* [Therapy, children and play]. Deventer: Van Loghum Slaterus.

———. (1988). Imaginative play technique in psychotherapy with children. In C. E. Schaefer, Ed., *Innovative interventions in child and adolescent therapy*, 43-67. New York: Wiley.

———. (1992). Ambulante hulpverlening volgens plan [Planned outpatient treatment]. *Nederlands Tijdschrift voor Opvoeding, Vorming en Onderwijs* 8:124-134.

Hellendoorn, J., Riekert, E., & Zanten, B. van (1986). Evaluatie van beeldcommunicatie-therapie: analyse en eerste resultaten [Evaluation of imagery interaction play therapy: analysis and preliminary results]. *Kind en adolescent* 7:161-171.

Loeven, L., & Harinck, F. (1985). Praktijk in beeld: werkwijze en meningen van beeldcommunicatie-therapeuten [Methods and opinions of imagery interaction play therapists]. In J. Hellendoorn, Ed., *Therapie, kind en spel*, 257-273. Deventer: Van Loghum Slaterus.

Mook, B. (1982a). Analyses of therapist variables in a series of psychotherapy sessions with two child clients. *Journal of clinical psychology* 38:63-76.

———. (1982b). Analyses of client variables in a series of psychotherapy sessions with two child clients. *Journal of clinical psychology* 38:263-274.

Moustakas, C. E. & Schalock, H. D. (1955). An analysis of therapist-child interaction in play therapy. *Child development* 26:143-157.

Rhoden, B. L., Kranz, P. L. & Lund, N. L. (1981). Current trends in the use of limits in play therapy. *Journal of psychology* 107:191-198.

Rutter, M. (1982). Psychological theories in child psychiatry: issues and prospects. *Psychological Medicine* 12:723-740.

Schmidtchen, S. (1978b). *Handeln in der Kinderpsychotherapie* [Therapeutic action in child psychotherapy]. Stuttgart: Kohlhammer.

———. (1986). Practice and research in play therapy. In R. van der Kooij & J. Hellendoorn, Eds., *Play, play therapy, play research*. Berwyn, PA: Swets North America.

Soudijn, K. (1992). Doelstellingenanalyse: functies, vormen en valkuilen [Goal Analysis: functions, forms and pitfalls]. *Nederlands Tijdschrift voor Opvoeding, Vorming en Onderwijs* 8:81-90.

Zanten, B. L. van (1986). Evaluation of play therapy in clinical practice: how can researchers and practitioners work together? In R. van der Kooij & J. Hellendoorn, Eds., *Play, play therapy, play research*, 161-168. Berwyn, PA: Swets North America.

Play for Children with Special Needs

Casby, M. W., & McCormack, S. M. (1985). Symbolic play and early communication development in hearing impaired children. *Journal of Communication Disorders* 18:67-78.

Gregory, S., & Mogford, K. (1983). The development of symbolic play in young deaf children. in D. R. Rogers & J. A. Sloboda, *The acquisition of symbolic skills*, 221-231. New York/London: Plenum Press.

Hellendoorn, J., & Hoekman J. (1992). Imaginative play in mentally retarded children. *Mental Retardation* 30:255-263.

Hill, P. M., & McCune-Nicolich, L. (1981). Pretend play and patterns of cognition in Down's syndrome children. *Child Development* 52:611-617.

Hulme, I., & Lunzer, E. A. (1966). Play, language and reasoning in subnormal children. *Journal of Child Psychology and Psychiatry* 7:107-123.

Lyon, D. (1990). *The development of symbolic play in hearing impaired children*. Paper, presented at the 17th International Congress on Education of the Deaf, Rochester, NY, USA.

McConkey, R. (1986). Changing beliefs about play and handicapped children. In P. K. Smith, Ed., *Children's play: research developments and practical applications*, 91-106. New York/London: Gordon & Breach.

Morshuis, G., & Hellendoorn, J. (1992). Symbolisch spel en de expressieve communicatie vaardigheid van dove kleuters [Symbolic play and expressive communication ability of deaf nursery school children]. *Tijdschrift voor Orthopedagogiek* 31:209-217.

Imaginative Play Training for Severely Retarded Children

Beeghly, M., & Cicchetti, D. (1987). An organizational approach to symbolic development in children with Down Syndrome. In D. Cicchetti & M. Beeghly, Eds., *Symbolic development in atypical children*, 5-29. San Francisco: Jossey-Bass.

Cole, D., & Lavoie, J. C. (1985). Fantasy play and related cognitive development in 2- to 6-year-olds. *Developmental Psychology* 21:233-240.

Cunningham, C. C., Glenn, S. M., Wilkinson, P., & Sloper, P. (1985). Mental ablity, symbolic play and receptive and expressive language of young children with Down's syndrome. *Journal of Child Psychology and Psychiatry* 26:255-265.

Ehlers, W. H., Prothero, J. C., & Langone, J. (1982). *Mental retardation and other developmental disabilities: A programmed instruction.* Columbus, OH: Merril.

Fein, G. G. (1981). Pretend play: An integrative review. *Child Development* 52:1095-1118.

Hellendoorn, J. (1989). *Manual for the Play Observation Scale.* Leiden, Netherlands: State University, Department of Special Education.

Hellendoorn, J., & Hoekman, J. (1992). Imaginative play in mentally retarded children. *Mental Retardation* 30:255-263.

Hill, P. M., & McCune-Nicolich, L. (1981). Pretend play and patterns of cognition in Down's syndrome children. *Child Development* 52:611-617.

Hulme, I., & Lunzer, E. A. (1966). Play, language and reasoning in subnormal children. *Journal of Child Psychology and Psychiatry* 7:107-123.

Kim, Y. T., Lombardino, L. J., Rothman, H., & Vinson, B. (1989). Effects of symbolic play intervention with children who have mental retardation. *Mental Retardation* 27:159-165.

Ingalls, R. (1978). *Mental retardation: The changing outlook.* New York: Wiley.

Li, A. K. F. (1985). Play and the mentally retarded child. *Mental Retardation* 23:121-126.

McCune-Nicolich, L. (1980). *A manual for analyzing free play.* New Brunswick, NJ: Rutgers University, Department of Educational Psychology.

Morris, R. J., & Dolker, M. (1974). Developing cooperative play in socially withdrawn retarded children. *Mental Retardation* 12:24-27.

Motti, F., Cicchetti, D., & Sroufe, L. A. (1983). From infant affect expression to symbolic play: The coherence of development in Down's syndrome children. *Child Development* 54:1168-1175.

Murphy, G., Callias, M., & Carr, J. (1985). Increasing simple toy play in profoundly mentally handicapped children. *Journal of autism and developmental disorders* 15:375-388.

Odom, S. L. (1981). The relationship of play to developmental level in mentally retarded preschool children. *Education and Training of the Mentally Retarded* 16:136-141.

Payne, J. S., & Patton, J. R. (1981). *Mental retardation.* Columbus, OH: Merril.

Pellegrini, A. D. (1985). The narrative organisation of children's fantasy play: The effects of age and play context. *Educational Psychology* 5:17-25.

Piaget, J. (1962). *Play, dreams and imitation in childhood.* New York: Norton.

Rubin, K. H., Fein, G. G., & Vandenberg, B. (1983). Play. In P.H. Mussen, Ed., *Handbook of Child Psychology*, 693-774. New York: Wiley.

Singer, D. G., & Singer, J. L. (1985). *Make believe.* Glenview, IL: Scott, Foresman & Company.

———. (1991). *The house of make-believe: children's play and the developing imagination.* Cambridge: Harvard University Press.

Van der Kooij, R., & Groot, R. de (1977). *That's all in the game: Theory and research, practice and future of children's play*. Rheinstetten: Schindele Verlag.

Wehman, P. (1977). *Helping the mentally retarded acquire play skills*. Springfield, IL: C. C. Thomas.

Whittaker, C. A. (1980). A note on developmental trends in the symbolic play of hospitalized profoundly retarded children. *Journal of Child Psychology and Psychiatry* 21:253-261.

Zigler, E., & Hodapp, R. M. (1986). *Understanding mental retardation*. Cambridge: Cambridge University Press.

Families at Play: Interventions for Children with Developmental Handicaps

Baker, B. (1989). *Parent training and developmental disabilities*. Washington: American Association on Mental Retardation.

Bruner, J. (1975). The ontogenesis of speech acts. *Journal of Child Language* 2:1-19.

Chapman, R. S. (1981). Mother-infant interactions in the second year of life: its role in language acquisition. In R. L. Schiefelbusch & D. D. Bricker, Eds., *Early language: acquisition and intervention*. Baltimore: University Park Press.

Davie, R., Butler, N., & Goldstein, H. (1972). *From birth to seven*. London: Longman.

Donaldson, M. (1978). *Children's minds*. London: Fontana.

Gartner, A., Lipsky, D. K., & Turnbull, A. (1991). *Supporting families with a child with a disability: An international outlook*. Baltimore: Paul Brookes.

Goodnow, J. J., & Collins, W. A. (1990). *Development according to parents: The nature, sources and consequences of parents' ideas*. Hove, NJ: Lawrence Erlbaum.

Grunfield, F. V. (1982). *Games of the world*. Zurich: Swiss Committee for UNICEF.

Ivic, I. (1986). The play activities of children in different cultures: the universal aspects and the cultural peculiarities. In I. Ivic, & A. Marjanovic, Eds., *Traditional games and children of today*. Belgrade: OMEP (World Organization for Early Childhood Education).

MacDonald, J. D., & Gillette, Y. (1988). Communicating partners: A conversational model for building parent-child relationships with handicapped children. In K. Marfo, Ed., *Parent-child interaction and developmental disabilities: Theory, research and intervention*. New York: Praeger.

Marjanovic, A. (1986). The theoretical and methodological problems concerning the project on traditional games. In I. Ivic, & A. Marjanovic, Eds., *Traditional games and children of today*. Belgrade: OMEP (World Organization for Early Childhood Education).

Martin, H., McConkey, R., & Martin, S. (1984). From acquisition theories to intervention strategies: an experiment with mentally handicapped children. *British Journal of Disorders of Communication* 19:3-14.

McConachie, H. (1986). *Parents and young mentally handicapped children: A review of research issues*. London: Croom Helm.

McConkey, R. (1988). Educating all parents: An approach based on video. In K. Marfo, Ed., *Parent-child interaction and developmental disabilities: Theory, research and intervention*. New York: Praeger.

Mitchell, D., & Brown, R. (1990). *Early intervention studies for young children with special needs*. London: Chapman and Hall.

Moyles, J. R. (1989). *Just playing?—The role and status of play in early childhood education*. Milton Keynes, UK: Open University Press.

Nguyen, D. Q. (1989). An overview of Southeast Asian Culture. *Coalition Quarterly* 6:10-11.

Odom, S. L., & Karnes, M. B. (1988). *Early intervention for infants and children with handicaps: An empirical base*. Baltimore: Paul Brookes.

Opie, I., & Opie, P. (1969). *Children's games in street and playground*. Oxford: Claredon Press.

O'Toole, B. (1990). *Step-by-step: A community based rehabilitation project with disabled children in Guyana*. Paris: UNESCO-UNICEF-WFP Cooperative program.

Richardson, A., & Ritchie, J. (1989). *Developing friendships: Enabling people with learning difficulties to make and maintain friendships*. London: Policy Studies Institute.

Riddick, B. (1982). *Toys and play for the handicapped child*. London: Croom-Helm.

Sutton-Smith, B. (1972). *Folkgames of children*. Austin/London: University of Texas Press.

Tizard, B., & Hughes, M. (1984). *Young children learning: Talking and thinking at home*. London: Fontana.

Walker, S. (1986). Attitudes to the disabled as reflected in the social mores in Africa, In K. Marfo, S. Walker, and B. Charles, Eds., *Childhood disability in developing countries*. New York: Praeger.

Weikart, D. P., Epstein, A. S., Schweinhart, L., & Bond, J. T. (1978). *The Ypsilanti preschool curriculum demonstration project: Pre-school years and longitudinal results*. Ypsilanti, MI: High Scope Educational Research Foundation.

White, B. (1979). *The first three years of life*. London: W. H. Allen.

World Health Organization (1985). *Mental retardation: Meeting the challenge*. Geneva: W.H.O.

Play Within an Intervention for Multiply Handicapped Children

Bobath, B. (1967). The very early treatment of cerebral palsy. *Developmental Medicine and Child Neurology* 9:373-390.

Cook, T. D., & Campbell, D. T. (1979). *Quasi-experimentation design and analysis issues for field settings*. Chicago: Rand McNally.

Hallahan, D. P., & Kaufman, J. M. (1988). *Exceptional children*. Englewood Cliffs, NJ: Prentice Hall.

Hersen, M., & Barlow, D. W. (1986). *Single case experimental designs*. London: Pergamon Press.

Hogg, J., & Sebba, J. (1986). *Profound retardation and multiple impairment*. London: Croom Helm.

Kiernan, C. C. (1992). Development in the education and care of children and young people with special needs. In H. Nakken, G. H. van Gemert & T. Zandberg, Eds., *Research on intervention in Special Education*, 97-130. Lampeter, UK: The Edwin Mellen Press.

Kiresuk, T. J., & Lund, S. H. (1978). Goal Attainment Scaling. In C. C. Attkisson & W. A. Hargreaves, Eds., *Evaluation Human Services programs*. New York: Academic Press.

Le Gay Brereton, B. (1972). *Cerebral palsy, learning disabilities and behavior*. Mosman, N.S.W., Australia: The Spastic Centre of N.S.W.

Nakken, H., & Den Ouden, W. J. (1985). Research on a psychomotor program for children with severe motor or multiple disabilities. *International Journal of Rehabilitation Research* 8:47-60.

Nakken, H. (1990). Wonen op maat van ernstig meervoudig gehandicapten [Made-to-measure living for profoundly multiply handicapped persons]. In C. Hovenkamp, Ed., *Wonen, my home is my castle*, 53-61. Vierhouten: Stichting J.J. Dondorp fonds.

Nakken, H. (1992). Interventions in special education: definitions and positions. In H. Nakken, G. H. van Gemert & T. Zandberg, Eds., *Research on intervention in Special Education*, 15-21. Lampeter, UK: The Edwin Mellen Press.

Rossi, P. H., & Freeman, H. E. (1989). *Evaluation: a systematic approach*. Newbury Park CA: Sage.

Sameroff, A. J., & Chandler, M. J. (1975). Reproductive risk and the continuum of caretaking casualty. In F.D. Horowitz et al., Eds., *Review of child development research*, Volume 4. Chicago: University of Chicago Press.

Schneider, M. J. (1989). *Wennen aan plannen. Het invoeren van het werken met handelingsplannen* [Getting used to planning: implementation of treatment plans]. Amsterdam: VU Uitgeverij.

Sontag, E., Smith, J., & Sailor, W. (1977). The severely/profoundly handicapped: Who are they? Where are they? *Journal of Special Education* 11:5-11.

Vriesema, P., Miedema, S., & Van Blokland, R. (1992). Prevention of undue non-motor development delay with infants and toddlers with neuromotor disabilities by means of a home-based early intervention program. In H. Nakken, G. H. van Gemert & T. Zandberg, Eds., *Research on intervention in Special Education*, 299-324. Lampeter, UK: The Edwin Mellen Press.

Wolf, J. M., & Anderson, R. M., Eds. (1969). *The multiply handicapped child*. Springfield, IL: C. C. Thomas.

Wijck, R. van, Vlaskamp, C., Nakken, H., & Smrkovsky, M. (1991). *Verbeteren van de zorg voor meervoudig gehandicapten* [Better care for multiply handicapped persons]. Eindrapport deelonderzoek I en II. Groningen: Onderzoeksverslag Rijksuniversiteit.

Effectiveness of Play Training
with Handicapped Toddlers

Belsky, J., Goode, M. K., & Most, R. K. (1980). Maternal stimulation and infant exploratory competence: Cross-sectional, correlational, and experimental analyses. *Child Development* 51:1163-1178.

Belsky, J., & Most, R. K. (1981). From exploration to play: A cross-sectional study of infant free play behavior. *Developmental Psychology* 17:630-639.

de Moor, J. M. H., van Waesberghe, B. T. M., van der Burg, J. J. W., & van de Bercken, J. H. L. (1993). Het ontwikkelingsverloop van spel bij kinderen van 15.36 maanden [The development of play in 15- to 36-month-old children]. *Nederlands Tijdschrift voor de Psychologie* 48:183-188.

Filler, J. W. Jr., & Bricker, W. A. (1976). Teaching styles of mothers and the match-to-sample performance of their retarded preschool-age children. *American Journal of Mental Deficiency* 80:504-511.

Largo, R. H., & Howard, J. A. (1979). Developmental progression in play behavior of children between nine and thirty months. I: Spontaneous play and imitation. *Developmental Medicine and Child Neurology* 21:299-310.

Lowe, M., & Costello, A. J. (1976). *Manual for the Symbolic Play Test.* Experimental edition. Windsor: NFER-Nelson.

McConkey, R., & Jeffree, D. (1979). First steps in learning to pretend. *Journal of Special Education: Forward Trends* 6.

McConkey, R. (1986). Changing beliefs about play and handicapped children. In P. K. Smith, Ed., *Children's play: research developments and practical applications.* New York: Gordon & Breach.

Piaget, J. (1962). *Play, dreams, and imitation in childhood.* New York: Norton.

Riksen-Walraven, J. M. (1978). Effects of caregiver behavior on habituation rate and self-efficacy in infants. *International Journal of Behavioral Development* 1:105-130.

Smith, P. K. (1986). Play research and its applications: A current perspective. In P. K. Smith, Ed., *Children's play: research developments and practical applications.* New York: Gordon & Breach.

van der Burg, J. J. W., de Moor, J. M. H., & van Waesberghe, B. T. M. (1992). Speltraining bij gehandicapte peuters: Een interventie studie [Play training with handicapped toddlers: An intervention study]. *Tijdschrift voor Ontwikkelingspsychologie* 19:155-173.

Wehman, P. (1975). Establishing play behaviors in mentally retarded youth. *Rehabilitation Literature* 36:238-246.

Wehman, P. (1977). *Helping the mentally retarded acquire play skills: A behavioral approach*. Springfield, IL: Charles C. Thomas.

Play Assessment for Play-Based Intervention: A First Step with Young Children with Communication Difficulties

Hewitt, S. (1970). *The handicapped child*. London: Allen and Unwin.

Liddle, S. (1991). *Providing for the preschool child with speech and language disability: The parent's views*. Unpublished B.Phil. Thesis. University of Newcastle upon Tyne.

Lowe, M., & Costello, A. (1976). *The Symbolic Play Test*. Windsor, Berkshire: NFER-Nelson.

McEvoy, J., & McConkey, R. (1983). Play activities of mentally handicapped children at home and mother's perception of play. *International Journal of Rehabilitation Research* 6:142-151.

Mogford, K. P. (1979a). *Communication and interaction between handicapped children and their parents: a study of remedial play*. Unpublished doctoral dissertation. University of Nottingham.

———. (1979b). The observational play repertoires. In J. Newson & E. Newson with J. Head & K. Mogford, Eds., *Toys and playthings in development and remediation*. Harmondsworth, Middlesex, UK: Penguin Books.

Newson, E. (1979). Play-based observation for assessment of the whole child. In J. Newson & E. Newson with J. Head & K. Mogford, Eds., *Toys and playthings in development and remediation*. Harmondsworth, Middlesex, UK: Penguin Books.

Sylva, K., Roy, C., & Painter, M. (1980). *Childwatching at playgroup and nursery school*. London: Grant McIntyre.

Westby, C. E. (1980). Assessment of cognitive and language abilities through play. *Language Speech and Hearing Services in Schools* 11:154-168.

Wood, D. (1989). *How children think and learn*. Oxford: Blackwell.

Play Training for Autistic Children

American Psychiatric Association (1987). *Diagnostic and Statistical Manual of Mental Disorders*, 3rd Edition, revised. Washington DC: American Psychiatric Association.

Baron-Cohen, S. (1987). Autism and symbolic play. *British Journal of Developmental Psychology* 5:139-148.

———. (1989). The autistic child's theory of mind: a case of specific developmental delay. *Journal of Child Psychology and Psychiatry* 30:285-297.

Bender, L. (1956). Schizophrenia in childhood: Its recognition, description and treatment. *American Journal of Orthopsychiatry* 26:499.

Berckelaer, I. A. van, & Van Engeland, H. (1986). *Kinderen en autisme* [Children and autism]. Meppel NL: Boom.

DeMyer, M. K., Man, N. A., Tilton, J. R., & Loew, L. H. (1967). Toy play behavior and use of body by autistic and normal children as reported by mothers. *Psychological Reports* 21:973-981.

Frith, U. (1989a). *Autism: Explaining the enigma*. Oxford: Blackwell.

———. (1989b). Autism and "Theory of Mind". In C. Gilberg, Ed., *Diagnosis and Treatment of Autism*, 33-52. London: Plenum Press.

Leslie, A. M. & Frith, U. (1988). Autistic children's understanding of seeing, knowing and believing. *British Journal of Developmental Psychology* 4:315-324.

McCune-Nicholich, L. (1980). *Manual for analyzing free play*. New Brunswick, NJ: Rutgers University.

Rutter, M. (1974). The development of infantile autism. *Psychological Medicine* 4:147-163.

Rutter, M., & Schopler, E. (1982). Autism and pervasive developmental disorders: concepts and diagnostic issues. *Journal of Autism and Developmental Disorders* 17:159-186.

Schopler, E., & Reichler, R. (1979). *Individualized assessment and treatment for autistic and developmentally disabled children: Psycho-Educational Profile*, Volume I. Austin, TX: Pro-Ed.

Sigman, M., & Ungerer, J. (1984). Cognitive and language skills in autistic, mentally retarded and normal children. *Developmental Psychology* 20:293-302.

Sigman, P., & Mundy, M. (1987). Symbolic processes in young autistic children. In D. Cicchetti & M. Beeghly, Eds., *New directions in child development: Symbolic development in atypical children*, 31-46. San Francisco: Jossey Bass.

Tilton, J. R., & Ottinger, D. R. (1964). Comparison of toy play behavior of autistic, retarded and normal children. *Psychological Reports* 15:967-975.

Ungerer, J., & Sigman, M. (1981). Symbolic play and language comprehension in autistic children. *Journal of the American Academy of Child Psychiatry* 20:318-337.

Weiner, B. J., Ottinger, D. R., & Tilton, J. R. (1969). Comparison of the toy play behavior of autistic, retarded and normal children: A reanalysis. *Psychological Reports* 25:223-227.

Wing, L., Gould, J., Yeates, S. R., & Brierly, L. (1977). Symbolic play in severely mentally retarded and in autistic children. *Journal of Child Psychology and Psychiatry* 18:167-178.

Play Training: An Overview

Brainerd, C. J. (1982). Effects of group and individualized dramatic play training on cognitive development. In D. J. Pepler & K. H. Rubin, Eds., *The play of children: Current theory and research*, 114-129. Basel: S. Karger.

Brüggeman, J. A. (1978). The function of adult play in free-ranging macaca mulatta. In E. O. Smith, Ed., *Social play in primates*, 169-191. New York: Academic Press.

Bruner, J. S. (1972). The nature and uses of immaturity. *American Psychologist* 27:687-708.

Bruner, J. S. & Sherwood, V. (1976). Peek-a-boo and the learning of rule structures. In J. S. Bruner, A. Jolly, & K. Sylva, Eds., *Play: It's role in development and evolution*, 277-285. Harmondsworth, UK: Penguin.

Burns, S. M. & Brainerd, C. J. (1979). Effects of constructive and dramatic play on perspective taking in very young children. *Developmental Psychology* 15:512-521.

Carllson-Paige, N. & Levin, D. (1987). *The war play dilemma: Balancing needs and values in the early child classroom.* New York: Teachers College.

Christie, J. F. (1983). The effects of play tutoring on young children's cognitive performance. *Journal of Educational Research* 76:326-330.

————. (1986). Training of symbolic play. In P. K. Smith, Ed., *Children's play: Research developments and practical applications,* 57-66. London: Gordon & Breach.

Christie, J. F. & Johnsen, E. P. (1985). Questioning the results of play training research. *Educational Psychologist* 20:7-11.

Department of the Environment (1973). *Children at play: Design bulletin* 27. London: HMSO.

Fagen, R. M. (1981). *Animal play behavior.* New York: Oxford University Press.

Fink, R. T. (1976). Role of imaginative play in cognitive development. *Psychological Reports* 39:895-906.

Freyberg, J. F. (1973). Increasing the imaginative play of urban disadvantaged kindergarten children through systematic training. In J. L. Singer, *The child's world of make-believe.* New York: Academic Press.

Fry, D. P. (1987). Differences between playfighting and serious fights among Zapotec children. *Ethology and Sociobiology* 8:285-306.

Horn, H. (1978). Optimal tactics of reproduction and life history. In J. R. Krebs & N. B. Davies, Eds., *Behavioral ecology: An evolutionary approach*, 411-429. Oxford: Blackwell Scientific.

Hutt, C. (1979). *Play in the under-fives: Form, development and function.* New York: Brunner/Mazel.

Hutt, S. J., Tyler, S., Hutt, C. & Christopherson, H. (1989). *Play, exploration and learning: A natural history of the preschool.* London: Routledge.

Isaacs, S. (1929). *The nursery years.* London: Routledge and Kegan Paul.

Kramer, R. (1976). *Maria Montessori: A biography.* Oxford: Basil Blackwell.

Lawick-Goodall, J. van (1968). The behavior of free-living chimpanzees in the Gombe Stream Reserve. *Animal Behavior Monographs* 1:161-311.

Li, A. K. F. (1985). Correlates and effects of training in make-believe play in preschool children. *Alberta Journal of Educational Research* 31:70-79.

Lovinger, S. L. (1974). Sociodramatic play and language development in preschool disadvantaged children. *Psychology in the Schools* 11:313-320.

MacDonald, K. B. (1992). An evolutionary perspective on parent-child play. In K. B. MacDonald, Ed., *Parents and children playing*. Albany: State University of New York Press.

MacDonald, K. B. & Parke, R. D. (1984). Bridging the gap: Parent-child play interactions and peer interactive competence. *Child Development* 55:1265-1277.

Manning, K. & Sharp, A. (1977). *Structuring play in the early years at school*. London: Ward Lock Educational.

Newson, J. & Newson, E. (1970). *Four years old in an urban community*. Harmondsworth, UK: Penguin.

Parke, R. D., MacDonald, K. B., Beitel, A. & Bhavnagri, N. (1987). The role of the family in the development of peer relationships. In R. Peters, Ed., *Social learning and systems approaches to marriage and the family*, 17-44. New York: Brunner/Mazel.

Pellegrini, A. D. (1987). Rough-and-tumble play: developmental and educational significance. *Educational Psychologist* 22:23-43.

Rosen, C. E. (1974). The effects of sociodramatic play on problem-solving behavior among culturally disadvantaged preschool children. *Child Development* 45:920-927.

Rubin, K. H., Fein, G. G. & Vandenberg, B. (1983). Play. In P. H. Mussen & E. M. Hetherington, Eds., *Handbook of child psychology*, 4th Ed., Volume 4. Basel: S. Karger.

Saltz, E., Dixon, D. & Johnson, J. (1977). Training disadvantaged preschoolers on various fantasy activities: Effects on cognitive functioning and impulse control. *Child Development* 48:367-380.

Saltz, E. & Johnson, J. (1974). Training for thematic-fantasy play in culturally disadvantaged children: Preliminary results. *Journal of Educational Psychology* 66:623-630.

Simon, T. (1986). Play and learning with computers. In P. K. Smith, Ed., *Children's play: Research developments and practical applications*, 81-92. London: Gordon and Breach.

Smilansky, S. (1968). *The effects of sociodramatic play on disadvantaged preschool children*. New York: Wiley.

Smilansky, S. & Shefataya, L. (1990). *Facilitating play: A medium for promoting cognitive, socio-emotional and academic development in young children*. Gaithersburg, MD: Psychosocial & Educational Publications.

Smith, P. K. (1982). Does play matter? Functional and evolutionary aspects of animal and human play. *The Behavioral and Brain Sciences* 5:139-184.

———. (1988). Children's play and its role in early development: a re-evaluation of the "play ethos". In A. D. Pellegrini, Ed., *Psychological bases for early education*, 207-226. Chichester: John Wiley & Sons.

———. (1989). The role of rough-and-tumble play in the development of social competence: theoretical perspectives and empirical evidence.

In B. H. Schneider, G. Attili, J. Nadel & R. P. Weissberg, Eds., *Social competence in developmental perspective*, 239-255. Dordrecht: Kluwer.

———. (1990). The role of play in the nursery and primary school curriculum. In C. Rogers & P. Kutnick, Eds., *The social psychology of the primary school*, 144-168. London: Routledge.

Smith, P. K., Dalgleish, M., & Herzmark, G. (1981). A comparison of the effects of fantasy play tutoring and skills tutoring in nursery classes. *International Journal of Behavioral Development* 4:421-441.

Smith, P. K. & Syddall, S. (1978). Play and nonplay tutoring in preschool children: Is it play or tutoring which matters? *British Journal of Educational Psychology* 48:315-325.

Sutton-Smith, B. (1986). *Toys as culture*. New York: Gardner Press.

Sutton-Smith, B., & Kelly-Byrne, D. (1984). The idealization of play. In P. K. Smith, Ed., *Play in animals and humans*, 305-321. Oxford: Basil Blackwell.

Udwin, O. (1983). Imaginative play training as an intervention method with institutionalized preschool children. *British Journal of Educational Psychology* 53:32-39.

Vygotsky, L. S. (1978). *Mind in society*. Edited by M. Cole, V. John-Steiner, S. Scribner & E. Souberman. Cambridge: Harvard University Press.

Wood, D. J., Bruner, J. S. & Ross, G. (1976). The role of tutoring in problem-solving. *Journal of Child Psychology and Psychiatry* 17:89-100.

Play: Positive Intervention in the Elementary School Curriculum

Christie, J. F., Ed. (1991). *Play and early literacy development*. Albany: State University of New York Press.

Eichler, G. (1979). *Spiel und Arbeit* [Play and work]. Stuttgart: Fromann-Holboog.

Einsiedler, W., Ed. (1985). *Aspekte des Kinderspiels: Pädagogisch-psychologische Spielforschung* [Aspects of children's play]. Weinheim/Basel: Beltz.

———. (1990). *Das Spiel der Kinder: Zur Pädagogik und Psychologie des Kinderspiels* [The play of children]. Bad Heilbrunn/Obb.: Klinkhardt.

Erikson, E. H. (1963). *Childhood and society*. New York: Norton.

Fürnwein, L. (1992). *Förderung der Kreativität durch den Einsatz von Spiel und Spielmitteln*: Eine Untersuchung in 4 Grundschulklassen [Stimulating creativity by play and toys]. Master's thesis, University of Vienna, Austria.

Hanke, B., Lohmöller, J. B., & Mandl, H. (1980). *Schülerbeurteilungsbogen* [Student rating scale]. München: Oldenbourg.

Hartmann, W., Neugebauer, R., & Rieβ, A. (1988). *Spiel und elementares Lernen* [Play and elementary learning]. Vienna: Österreichische Bundesverlag.

Hartmann, W. (1989). *Advisory Assistance in the Production of Plastic Toys*. Report on social and educational Aspects. Study undertaken for the

Government of Egypt by the United Nations Industrial Development Organization (not formally published).

————. (1991). Current trends in the toy market in Europe and the impact of non-violent and safe toys on children. In UNICEF, United Nations Children's Fund, Ed., *Toys for child development*. Proceedings of the National Seminar on designing and producing toys and equipment. Seoul, Korea.

Hetzer, H. (1969). *Spielen lernen—Spielen lehren* [Learning to play—teaching to play]. München: Don Bosco.

Johnson, J. E., Christie, J. F., & Yawkey, T. D. (1987). *Play and early childhood development*. Glenview, IL: Harper Collins.

Knaak, R., & Rauer, W. (1979). Eine Schuleinstellungsskala für das zweite Schuljahr. Erste Ergebnisse einer empirischen Untersuchung [Attitude scale for the second grade]. *Zeitschrift für Entwicklungspsychologie und pädagogische Psychologie* 1:50-58.

Konvalina, G. (1992). *Spielmittel im Unterricht*: Sozial-, Arbeits- und Leistungsverhalten, Schulzufriedenheit und Lehrerbild in der 3. Klasse Grundschule [Play and toys in school education]. Doctoral dissertation, University of Vienna, Austria.

Kooij, R. van der (1983). Empirische Spielforschung [Empirical play research]. In K. J. Kreuzer, Ed., *Handbuch der Spielpädagogik*, Volume 1. Düsseldorf: Schwann.

Mainberger, U. (1976). *Test zum divergenten Denken (Kreativität) für 4-6 Klassen (TDK 4-6)* [Test for divergent thinking in grades 4-6]. Landauer Bildungsund Beratungssystem. Weinheim: Beltz.

Masendorf, R., Tücke, R., & Kretschmann, R. (1975). *Dortmunder Skala zum Lehrerverhalten ("DSL")* [Dortmund scale for teacher behavior]. Braunschweig: Westermann.

Rollett, B. (1989). Kinderspiel und seelische Gesundheit [Child play and mental health]. In W. Einsiedler & S. Martschinke, Eds., *Kinderspiel und seelische Gesundheit*. Bericht über das 4. Nürnberger Spielforschungssymposium. Nürnberg, FRG: Forschungsstelle "Spiel und Spielzeug" der Erziehungswissenschaftliche Fakultät der Universität Erlangen.

Rollett, B., & Bartram, M. (1977). *Anstrengungsvermeidungstest (AVT)* [Effort avoidance test]. Braunschweig: Westermann.

Schmidtchen, S. & Stüwe, A. (1989). Klientenzentrierte Spieltherapie [Client-centered play therapy]. In W. Einsiedler & S. Martschinke, Eds., *Kinderspiel und seelische Gesundheit*. Bericht über das 4. Nürnberger Spielforschungs-symposium. Nürnberg, FRG: Forschungsstelle "Spiel und Spielzeug" der Erziehungswissenschaftliche Fakultät der Universität Erlangen.

Sevcik, M. (1992). *Der Einfluß von Spiel und Spielmitteln auf Angst, Kontakt und Aggression der Schüler in der 1. Klasse Grundschule* [The influence of play and toys on anxiety, contact and aggression of first-grade students]. Doctoral dissertation, University of Vienna, Austria.

Seyfried, H., Ed. (1978). *AST 3: Allgemeiner Schulleistungstest für die 3. Schulstufe* [General school achievement test for the third grade]. Vienna: Ketterl.

Sutton-Smith, B. (1988). War toys and childhood aggression. *Play & Culture* 1:57-69.

———. (1990). *Dilemmas in adult play with children.* Paper presented to the biennial meeting of the International Council for Children's Play, Andreasberg, Germany.

Torrance, E. P. (1963). *Education and the creative potential.* Minneapolis: University of Minnesota Press.

UNICEF, Ed. (1990). *The state of the world's children 1990.* Oxford: Oxford University Press.

Weickl, E. (1988). *Die Bedeutung des Spiels für die soziale Interaktion und Schulzufriedenheit in der 2. Klasse Grundschule unter besonderer Berücksichtigung der Ausländerkinder* [Influence of play on sociale interaction and school satisfaction in second-grade students, particularly in foreign students]. Unpublished Doctoral Dissertation, University of Vienna, Austria.

Academic Play

Block, J. H. (1984). Making school learning activities more playlike: Flow and mastery learning. *Elementary School Journal* 85:65-75.

Christie, J. F. (1982). Sociodramatic play training. *Young Children* 37:4:25-32.

———. (1983). The effects of play tutoring on young children's cognitive performance. *Journal of Educational Research* 76:326-330.

———. (1991). *Play and early literacy development.* Albany: State University of New York Press.

Christie, J. F., & Enz, B. (1991). *The effects of literacy play interventions on preschoolers' play patterns and literacy development.* Paper presented at the meeting of the American Educational Research Association, Chicago.

Christie, J. F., & Johnsen, E. P. (1983). The role of play in social-intellectual development. *Review of Educational Research* 53:93-115.

Galda, L. (1982). Playing about a story: Its impact on comprehension. *The Reading Teacher* 36:52-55.

Garvey, C. (1977). *Play.* Cambridge: Harvard University Press.

Gehlbach, R. D. (1980). Instructional play: Some theoretical prerequisites to systematic research and development. *Educational Psychologist* 15:112-124.

Glickman, C. D. (1984). Play in public school settings: A philosophical question. In T. D. Yawkey & A. D. Pellegrini, Eds., *Child's play: Developmental and applied,* 255-271. Hillsdale, NJ: Erlbaum.

Götz, I. L. (1977). Play in the classroom: Blessing or curse? *Educational Forum* 41:329-334.

Hall, N., May, E., Moores, J., Shearer, J., & Williams, S. (1987). The literate home-corner. In P. K. Smith, Ed., *Parents and teachers together,* 134-144. London: Macmillan.

Hartmann, W., Neugebauer, R., & Reiss, A. (1988). *Spiel und elementares Lernen* [Play and elementary learning]. Vienna: Österreichischer Bundesverlag.

Johnson, J. E., Christie, J. F., & Yawkey, T. D. (1987). *Play and early childhood development*. Glenview, IL: Scott Foresman.

King, N. R. (1979). Play: The kindergartners' perspective. *Elementary School Journal* 80:81-87.

Manning, K., & Sharp, A. (1977). *Structuring play in the early years at school*. London: Ward Lock Educational.

Martin, P., & Caro, T. (1985). On the functions of play and its role in behavioral development. In J. Rosenblatt, C. Beer, M. Busnel, & P. Slater, Eds., *Advances in the study of behavior*, Volume 15, 59-103. New York: Academic Press.

Morrow, L. M., & Rand, M. K. (1991). Promoting literacy during play by designing early childhood classroom environments. *The Reading Teacher* 44:396-402.

Moyles, J. R. (1989). *Just playing? The role and status of play in early childhood education*. Milton Keynes, UK: Open University Press.

Neuman, S. B., & Roskos, K. (1990). Play, print, and purpose: Rethinking metaphors for early literacy development. *The Reading Teacher* 44:214-221.

Pellegrini, A. D. (1984). Identifying causal elements in the thematic-fantasy play paradigm. *American Educational Research Journal* 21:691-701.

Pellegrini, A. D., & Galda, L. (1982). The effects of thematic-fantasy play training on the development of children's story comprehension. *American Educational Research Journal* 19:443-452.

Piaget, J. (1973). *To understand is to invent*. New York: Viking Press.

Rubin, K. H., Fein, G. G., & Vandenberg, B. (1983). Play. In P. H. Mussen, Ed., *Handbook of child psychology: Volume 4. Socialization, personality, and social development*, 4th Ed., 693-774. New York: Wiley.

Saltz, E., & Johnson, J. (1974). Training for thematic-fantasy play in culturally disadvantaged children: Preliminary results. *Journal of Educational Psychology* 66:623-630.

Schrader, C. T. (1990). Symbolic play as a curricular tool for early literacy development. *Early Childhood Research Quarterly* 5:79-103.

Silvern, S. B., Taylor, J. B., Williamson, P. A., Surbeck, E., & Kelley, M. F. (1986). Young children's story recall as a product of play, story familiarity, and adult intervention. *Merrill-Palmer Quarterly* 32:73-86.

Smilansky, S. (1968). *The effects of sociodramatic play on disadvantaged preschool children*. New York: Wiley.

Smith, P. K. (1987). Children's play and its role in early development: A re-evaluation of the 'play ethos'. In A. D. Pellegrini, Ed., *Psychological bases for early education*, 207-226. New York: Wiley.

Smith, P. K., Dalgleish, M., & Herzmark, G. (1981). A comparison of the effects of fantasy play tutoring and skills tutoring in nursery classes. *International Journal of Behavioral Development* 4:421-441.

Smith, P. K., & Vollstedt, R. (1985). On defining play: An empirical study of the relationship between play and various play criteria. *Child Development* 56:1042-1050.

Sutton-Smith, B. (1987a). The domestication of early childhood play. *Education Week* (December 9), 28.

————. (1987b). School play: A commentary. In J. Block & N. King, Eds., *School play*, 277-289. New York: Garland.

————. (1990). Playfully yours. *TASP Newsletter* 16:2:2-5.

Vandenberg, B. (1982). Play: A concept in need of a definition? In D. J. Pepler & K. H. Rubin, Eds., *The play of children: Current theory and research*, 15-20. Basel, Switzerland: Karger.

Vygotsky, L. S. (1978). *Mind in society: The development of psychological processes*. Cambridge: Harvard University Press.

Wassermann, S. (1990). *Serious players in the primary classroom*. New York: Teachers College Press.

Wassermann, S., & Ivany, J. (1988). *Teaching elementary science: Who's afraid of spiders?* New York: Harper & Row.

Williamson, P. A., & Silvern, S. B. (1991). Thematic fantasy play and story comprehension. In J. F. Christie, Ed., *Play and early literacy development*, 69-90. Albany: State University of New York Press.

Epilogue

Barrett, C. L., Hampe, I. E., & Miller, L. C. (1978). Research on child psychotherapy. In S. L. Garfield & A.E. Bergin, Eds., *Handbook of psychotherapy and behavior change*, 2nd Edition. New York: Wiley.

Beeghly, M., Weiss-Perry, B., & Cicchetti (1990). Beyond sensorimotor functioning: early communicative development of children with Down syndrome. In D. Cicchetti & M. Beeghly, Eds., *Children with Down syndrome: a developmental perspective*, 329-368. Cambridge: Cambridge University Press.

Christie, J. F. (1991). *Play and early literacy development*. Albany: State University of New York Press.

Cicchetti, D., & Beeghly, M., Eds. (1990). *Children with Down syndrome: a developmental perspective*. Cambridge: Cambridge University Press.

Eisen, G. (1987). Coping in adversity: Children's play in the Holocaust. In G.A. Fine, Ed., *Meaningful play, playful meaning*, 129-141). Champaign, IL: Human Kinetics Publishers.

Garfield, S. L., & Bergin, A. E., Eds. (1986). *Handbook of psychotherapy and behavior change*, 3rd Edition. New York: Wiley.

Huizinga, J. (1955). *Homo Ludens: A study of the play element in culture*. Boston: The Beacon Press. (First published in Dutch, 1939).

Kazdin, A. E. (1988). *Child psychotherapy: developing and identifying effective treatments*. New York: Pergamon Press.

Lebo, D. (1952). The present status of research on nondirective play therapy. *Journal of Consulting Psychology* 17:177-183.

NOTES ON CONTRIBUTORS

INA A. VAN BERCKELAER-ONNES is Professor of Special Education and Child Care at the University of Leiden, the Netherlands. Her special expertise lies in the field of developmental disorders, in particular autism. On these topics she has widely published, for instance, *Early Childhood Autism: A Child-Rearing Problem* (1983) as well as papers in the *Journal of Autism and Developmental Disorders*, the *Journal of Communication and Cognition*, and *Link*. She coordinates the European Community Program (Erasmus Project) on Pervasive Developmental Disorders. She is a member of the editorial board of three Dutch professional journals.

JAMES F. CHRISTIE is Professor of Curriculum and Instruction at Arizona State University where he teaches courses in reading and early childhood education. He had previously taught at the preschool, kindergarten, and primary-grade levels. His research interests include children's play, early literacy development, and integrated language arts instruction. He is currently conducting a study of how teachers interact with children during play. He has published three books: *Play and Early Childhood Development* (1987), with James Johnson and Thomas Yawkey), *Integrated Reading and Writing Instruction in Grades K-8* (1989, with Ruth Noyce), and *Play and Early Literacy Development* (1991).

HERBERT GOETZE is Professor of Special Education, with a special interest in behavioral disordered children and youth. He is currently staying as a visiting professor at Purdue University, IN. He has been a faculty member at the University of Hamburg and the Teachers' Training College in Kiel, Germany, and is about to join the newly founded University of Potsdam in former Eastern Germany. Dr. Goetze has introduced Virginia Axline's approach to play therapy to the broader public in Germany, by co-authoring *Die Nicht-Direk-*

tive Spieltherapie (1974), followed by editing *Personenzentrierte Spieltherapie* (1980).

WALTRAUT HARTMANN is Lecturer on Children's play and literature at the Department of Developmental and Educational Psychology at the University of Vienna, Austria, and head of the Charlote Bühler Institute for Applied Child Research. As an expert on UNIDO and UNICEF toy projects she has worked in Egypt and South-Korea. She has developed educational play programs and was a founding member of the International Toy Research Association (1993). Her publications include *Play and Elementary Learning* (1988) and *Play: Cornerstone of Life* (1989).

JOOP HELLENDOORN is Associate Professor at the Center for Special Education and Child Care at the University of Leiden, the Netherlands, where she serves as director of a research program on play and play therapy. She published six books and many papers on these topics. For instance, she co-edited *Play, Play Therapy, Play Research* (1975), and contributed to edited books by C. E. Schaefer and others, such as *Innovative Interventions in Child and Adolescent Therapy* (1989), *Play Therapy in Action* (1993) and *Handbook of Play Therapy, Volume 2* (1994). She chairs the editorial board of the Dutch journal *Kind en Adolescent*.

ROY MC CONKEY is Director of Training and Research with the Brothers of Charity, an international organization providing services to people with intellectual disabilities in some 30 countries. He is author of many articles and several books on play for parents and front-line workers and has recently completed a consultancy for UNESCO on video-based training packages for use in parent education in African and Asian countries.

KAY P. MOGFORD-BEVAN is Senior Lecturer in Speech at the University of Newcastle upon Tyne, England, where she contributes to teaching programs for Speech and Language Therapists and teachers of children with language disabilities. In addition to research into the uses of play in assessment and intervention in children with communication disorders, she has published several books on language acquisition and language disabilities.

BERTHA MOOK is Professor in Clinical Child Psychology at the University of Ottawa, Canada. She is specialized in child and family therapy, and in phenomenological research. She published *Causal*

Thought in Schizophrenic Children (1972), *The Dutch Family in the 17th and 18th Century* (1977) and co-edited *Advances in Qualitative Research* (1987). She further published several book chapters and numerous articles which reflect a central interest in phenomenological and hermeneutic studies in child psychotherapy, family history, and family therapy.

JAN M. H. DE MOOR is Associate Professor of Special Education at the Catholic University of Nijmegen and clinical psychologist at the Rehabilitation Center for the physically disabled, Groot Klimmendaal in Arnhem, the Netherlands. He is (co-)author of several books and articles, particularly in the field of pre-school education for children with physical handicaps, rehabilitation psychology, and school psychology. He is a member of the European working party for early intervention with developmental disabilities, Earlyaid.

HAN NAKKEN is Professor of Education of Exceptional Children at the State University of Groningen, the Netherlands. He is author of several books on program development for the education of children with profound motor, mental, or multiple handicaps. He co-edited *Research on Intervention in Special Education* (1992).

HAN H. L. OUD is Associate Professor in Methodology and Statistics at the Catholic University of Nijmegen, the Netherlands. He has written a Ph.D. thesis titled *Systems Methodology in Social Science Research* and has published on a broad range of social research methods, especially longitudinal analysis methods, pupil monitoring systems, family assessment, and residential care.

BRIGITTE ROLLETT is Professor of Psychology and Head of the Department of Developmental and Educational Psychology at the University of Vienna, Austria. She is President of the Austrian Psychological Association and National Correspondent of EARLI (European Association of Research in Learning and Instruction), the European twin organization of AERA. She published over 120 articles and chapters in handbooks and is the author or editor of 11 books.

GERD E. SCHÄFER is Professor of Education at the University of Augsburg, Germany. He is specially concerned with pre-school and primary school education. In his work he endeavors to combine play theory and learning theory against a background of cognitive psychology, neuroscience, and psychoanalysis. After his recent books *Spiel, Spielraum und Verständigung* (1986) and *Spielphantasie und*

Spielumwelt (1989), he is now completing a book on early educational processes *Between Fantasy and Reality: About Learning and Education in Early Childhood*.

STEFAN SCHMIDTCHEN is Professor of Psychology at the University of Hamburg, Germany. He has published many papers and books, most of them in German, on practice and research in child psychotherapy, client-centered play therapy, and family therapy. Well known publications are *Handeln in der Kinderpsychotherapie* (1978). *Analyse des Kinderspiels* (1979), and *Klientenzentrierte Spiel- und Familientherapie* (1991). Currently, he is working on a project concerning play therapy with adults.

DOROTHY G. SINGER is Co-Director of the Yale University Family Television Research and Consultation Center. She is also a Research Scientist in the Department of Psychology at Yale and an affiliate of the Yale Child Study Center. She received her doctorate in Psychology from Columbia University. Her interests include research on social and emotional development. Her most recent book is *Playing for their Lives: Helping Troubled Children through Play* (1993).

JEROME L. SINGER is Professor of Psychology and Child Study at Yale University, and Co-Director of the Yale University Family Television Research and Consultation Center. He received his doctorate from the University of Pennsylvania. His interests span the areas of consciousness, imagination, and personality. Two recent books are *Repression and Dissociation* (1990) and (with Dorothy Singer) *The House of Make-Believe* (1990).

PETER K. SMITH is Professor of Psychology at the University of Sheffield, England. He is co-author of *Understanding Children's Development* (1988) and editor of *Play in Animals and Humans* (1984) and *Children's Play: Research Developments and Practical Applications* (1986). He is also co-editor of *Practical Approaches to Bullying* and of *Bullying in Schools, Insights and Perspectives*, and editor of *The Psychology of Grandparenthood, an International Perspective* (1991). A Fellow of the British Psychological Society, he is an Associate Editor of the *International Journal of Behavioral Development* and European Editor of *Ethology and Sociobiology*.

BRIAN SUTTON-SMITH is Emeritus Professor at the University of Pennsylvania, Philadelphia. He was formerly Head of the program of Interdisciplinary Studies of Human Development in the

Graduate School of Education. He is the author or editor of some 300 scholarly items including 30 books, mostly on play and games, including *The Folkgames of Children, The Study of Games, Child's Play, Die Dialektik des Spiels, Play and Learning, A History of Child's Play,* and *Toys as Culture.*

RIMMERT VAN DER KOOIJ is Associate Professor in Special Education at the State University of Groningen, the Netherlands, and Secretary of the International Council for Children's Play. His bibliography counts more than 60 publications in different languages, (edited) books, and papers in the field of play. He is chair of the editorial team of the *Dutch Journal for Education, Adult Education and Educational Psychology* and a member of the editorial board of the American journal *Play Theory and Research.*

RUUD VAN WIJCK is Assistant Professor at the University of Groningen, the Netherlands, in the Education of Exceptional Children as well as in the Human Movement Sciences. In collaboration with his colleagues, he published on program evaluation in the field of mental retardation and of children with physical impairments and movement disorders. He is preparing a Ph.D. thesis (to be published 1994) on the quality of care for children with profound mental and physical handicaps.

BERENDIEN VAN ZANTEN is a Clinical Psychologist and Psychotherapist, currently working in a private psychotherapeutic practice. She finished her contribution to this volume while participating in a research project on Imagery Interaction Play Therapy at the Center for Special Education and Child Care at the University of Leiden, the Netherlands.

CARLA VLASKAMP is Assistant Professor at the University of Groningen, the Netherlands. She (co-)authored several books and articles on the education of the profoundly multiply handicapped child. Recently, her Ph.D. thesis was published, titled *A Matter of Perspective: System Development in the Care for Profoundly Multiply Handicapped* (1993).

BETTY T. M. VAN WAESBERGHE is educational psychologist at the Rehabilitation Center for the physically disabled Groot Klimmendaal in Arnhem, the Netherlands. She is a member of the European working party for early intervention with developmental disabilities, Earlyaid. Her specialty is early diagnosis and early intervention with handicapped children.